ALASKA IS MY
Mistress
ALASKA'S ALLURE-BEAUTIFUL AND DANGEROUS

JERRE WILLS

PO Box 221974 Anchorage, Alaska 99522-1974
books@publicationconsultants.com—www.publicationconsultants.com

ISBN 978-1-59433-477-1
eBook ISBN 978-1-59433-478-8
Library of Congress Catalog Card Number: 2014947885

Manufactured in the United States of America.

Alaska is My Mistress

Jerre Wills

I'm on "mountain watch" this morning, meaning that I'm sitting in my favorite rawhide rocking chair in the front room of our snug, medium-sized log house and gazing at the mountains across Kachemak Bay. Christmas is over, so now the only thing that I really have to do is stir the raspberry wine that I'm brewing. Perhaps that doesn't sound like the most exciting event in our mid-winter world, but listen to this. The wine buckets are only a couple of feet from our pet chinchilla, Rambo. When I stir the wine, he begs for some of the fermenting berries. Being the good guy that I am, I of course give in to him, and after a couple of plump seedy morsels, he does the watusi. It's a highlight on a cold Alaskan day to watch this little gremlin "five sheets in the wind"!

Back at my mountain watch, I notice a sundog on the west edge of Doroshin Glacier, which tells me that the sun will soon be appearing. It's a late riser. It chooses not to make its daily arrival until almost 10:30 at this time of year. The days are short. There is less time to enjoy the outdoors, but more time to reflect. The mountains aren't going anywhere, and I've imagined all the animals and people that I can make with the configurations of the numerous peaks. One in particular between Doroshin and Grewingk Glacier looks like a woman lying down. She has Boone and Crockett boobs.

Our home sits on the north shore of Kachemak Bay, so the Kenai Mountain Range is our backyard. Actually the mountains are about five miles across the bay. The air is so clear in Alaska that everything looks closer and bigger than it really is. Even the stars at night are so bright that you'd swear you can see every star in the universe!

If you detect that I have a slight love affair with Alaska, you guessed it right. Why, Romeo himself would envy the smallest remnants of the love that I've lavished on Alaska. Even before I came here more than half a century ago, the affair was taking shape. Some people call it destiny. I like to think it was God's plan. I'll tell you about it, but first I've got to tell you where a "hybrid of a hybrid" like me comes from.

Contents

Introduction

Some people would consider my book as an autobiography or a memoir, but I'd like to refer to it as one of the most adventurous factual accounts of a lifetime love affair with Alaska. The great land and sea have occupied more than 55 years of non-stop excitement and adventure. I fished commercially for about 50 years. I guided for big game, and piloted bush planes most of my adult life. My family and I trapped during the winter and would go for months without seeing a soul. Too many near death experiences made me realize that surviving was not only something that I must have been born with, but was in my soul. As I reflect on those experiences, I now understand that they have been a great part of my romance with this super north land and sea. When pondering the meaning of the previous sentence, you might have a tough time interpreting such a statement unless you have had a brush with death while doing something that you enjoyed. Perhaps it is similar to someone that wants desperately to set a land speed record, or an Olympian that blasts down the great slalom course with no holds barred. These people know the dangers that could put them in the hospital or perhaps a morgue, but they are driven, as am I.

I am a simple man in many aspects of life, and writing the absolute truth about one's life is not an easy task. If I were a master of the use of adjectives like many natural writers I could possibly have given my readers a more vivid picture of the events that occurred in my "filled to capacity" life. But even though I lack in the field of adjectives, I do believe that it would be difficult to read my book without crying, laughing, and cheering.

I'm not terribly sentimental, but as I typed I found myself reliving all of the accounts like they were taking place as I wrote. Time wore on as I hammered on the keys of the computer. It wasn't because I lacked skills at typing or spelling, it was a matter of re-living the whole ball of wax. There were times that I found myself weeping, (more like sobbing violently), and I would have to put it aside. Then when describing a happy event, I enjoyed a good laugh.

I leave my readers with some well learned thoughts. Live life to the hilt! Think about others when you are making a decision that might affect them. If you screw up like I've done sometimes, you will never forget those times, so work hard at not making life miserable. Respect others like you would hope they do you. Be big and tell people you are sorry when you hurt them. If you were mistreated when you were young, don't dwell on it but move on. I don't think that any of us can forget the bad stuff, but don't occupy yourself with bad stuff on your shoulders. Don't hang out with perpetual snivelers because their sniveling might rub off on yours truly.

Be sure to watch for the wolves. Not just the furry ones, but those that are in sheep's clothing.

Share the good times with your kids and others. Teach your good values and skills to those that will appreciate them. Laugh a lot. Tell a joke to your friends or relatives even if you have to find one online. Treat the land and sea like you want your great grand children to see it.

Read a book, mine of course! I didn't have to look for adventure, it found me. You might not be so lucky, so go out and find some, but be prepared to survive.

Jerre Wills

Chapter 1

Blue Eyes Grows Up

My mom. I don't recall ever hearing such a name as was tacked on my mom: Glendower. I don't have the slightest idea where her parents dug it up, but that was her name, honest. Most people called her Glenny for short. If the name has a definition, it's probably something like "tough and dominant." Perhaps it was those two adjectives that made her a survivor. She went through a lot of bad stuff, and a few husbands, and lasted for about 85 years.

Her mom, Betty, was the same way. She was a tough, hard-working, resilient old gal. She too went through several husbands. The first one, the father of my mother, was a short termer. He was gored by a bull and died at a young age. Don't ask me how. What he was like and how he came to be killed by a bull have always seemed deeply mysterious to me.

"Mysterious" is definitely the word to describe the disappearing act that husband number two did. No one seemed to know Nana's real age until she was about 85. She always dyed her hair and lied about her age. There were two main reasons for this: so she could always get a job and so she could always get a man. Can't say that I blame her. She was good looking, and she stayed trim so she could lure the guys. She had an Irish temper— "hell on wheels" was how my mom put it—so the men in her life had to be submissive. But she was always nice to me.

One more generation back lie the seeds that were responsible for a line of surviving hybrids, the Crawfords. When I was very young, the traits that marked the Crawford clan were telltale in my makeup. I was a definite throwback. Even though there doesn't appear to be a lot of information as to what transpired during the early to mid 1800s, it is known that Great Grand-dad William Crawford was a Civil War veteran. He and his family were among the first white people to settle in Clare County, Michigan. At the time, it was occupied by Chippewa Indians and was called Kaykee, which was the name of the chief. But then, in 1843, an Irish surveyor decided to change the name to Clare, which was a county in Ireland. The Irish must have their way, right?

Anyhow, the area obviously had an abundance of timber, and was strategically located. A sawmill was set into operation and many millions of board feet of lumber were cut. The lumber was taken downstream via the Tobacco River and Muskegon River to Bay City and Saginaw.

I can pretty well imagine what it was like for William Crawford and his family homesteading and carving out a piece of wilderness with only Indians as neighbors. Although everyday tasks must have been paramount, they surely had unparalleled excitement. The only thing resembling a doctor in the area was the Indians who acted as midwives when there was a birthing. There were no stores. There was some trading, but most food was home-grown. The art of survival was an inbred gift. William enjoyed mingling with the Indians. Even as more white people moved into Clare County, William's best friends continued to be Indians. It was their help that kept his blunders to a minimum. They told him what kinds of seeds to plant to grow successful crops. In turn he showed the Indians how to build with logs and lumber. They shared. They loved each other as neighbors.

Before she died, my grandmother (Nana) told me that she was quite sure that we have Indian blood mixed with Irish and French. I have a book that has a picture of William and his wife. She looks much like the local Chippewa Indians. As I look back, I understand more and more why I became a homesteader and hunter. My brothers and sister were of the same womb, but have none of my characteristics. I've seen the same differentiation to be true with my own children, though, so it's not puzzling that each of us should take his own direction. I do know that I had a different father from the rest of the brood. Jack was supposedly the father of all four of us kids, but my blood type didn't match any that my mom and Jack could have produced. There had never been a blue eye in either family tree until I came along. It would have been cool to know who my biological dad was, but my mom would never tell. She said that she thought I was switched at the hospital. I checked that story out and found that there was only one other baby born that day, a girl. The last time I checked, I have no girl parts. I do believe that some of the terrible fights that Jack and my mom had were because of this little bastard, yours truly. I don't ever expect to know who my dad was, but it doesn't matter; it's ancient history.

Although Jack wasn't my biological father, it's necessary to know a bit about the man in order to appreciate my childhood. His ancestry is of little significance, but I'll give a brief description of him so you might comprehend the effect he had on me.

My mom was quite young when she met Jack. He impressed her from the get-go. Good looking, intelligent, and a party animal, Jack swept my naive mom off her feet. She was ga-ga head over heels in short order. After a brief romance he proposed to her in their favorite hangout, the local pub. She didn't hesitate, and their marriage was immediate.

Although Jack had many good qualities, they were overshadowed by his love for alcohol. Even before he and my mom married, the alcohol was eroding his grey matter, but as a businessman, he had an uncanny ability to make money. He was in the tool and die business, and would buy low and sell high. Harder than it sounds, I bet, but nevertheless, he always made enough during the 30s and 40s to raise a family and support his bad habits. Habits that got worse by the day. Habits that destroyed him and his family.

Sometime around the age of twenty, Jack thought it would be cool to hop a railway car and go afar. The train was moving faster than he anticipated and he didn't quite make it. He lost his grip, and the next thing he knew, he was in the hospital. When he woke from the anesthesia, it was the sober look on the nurse's face that made him realize that there was something drastically wrong.

"You lost your left leg," the nurse told him.

It wasn't long after his mishap that he got outfitted with a wooden leg. He named it Rosie, and it was held on the stump by a two-inch-wide leather strap that crossed over his right shoulder. He never quite got the swing of things though. When walking, most people step with one foot and swing the opposite arm. Not Jack. He swung the right arm with the right foot, and vice-versa.

His alcohol use accelerated full speed ahead after the loss of his leg, and along with the alcohol came mean, nasty, angry, et cetera. As so often happens in cases such as this, he vented his feelings through family abuse.

In my younger years, I had no way of knowing that either I was a bastard or the hospital screwed up and gave my parents the wrong kid, but the older I got, the more I realized that I was the only blue-eyed left-hander on either side of the family. I really don't care so much, but I think Jack didn't feel too kindly about the matter, and my very presence gave him more reason to hit the bottle and take it out on our mom and us kids. It's not for me to say whether he was justified in the fights with Mom, but it seemed as if the strap that held Rosie on was getting more use whopping the asses of us kids than it was for keeping Rosie on the stump.

Many times we kids would have to wait in the car while our parents partied in the pub. If we weren't total angels while they were in there sucking the suds, we would get a strapping when we got home. Mickey and I were responsible for the behavior of all four kids, so the two of us got the whippings. If Jack was too drunk to get the job done, our mom didn't mind at all spanking our bodies with her iron hand until we ran out of tears. Mickey was the oldest, so he got it first. He was as brave as he could be, but the spankings were so lengthy and severe that even he couldn't hold back the tears. When it was my turn, Mickey would tell me, "Don't cry, Jerre; it'll be all right."

I have grown grandchildren now, but the memory of the numerous times that we were beaten to the point that we couldn't sit for hours afterward still brings tears to my eyes. It's a wonder that I have an ass at all.

I'm sure that many times Mickey and I deserved some discipline, and I realize that in those days it was more commonplace to spank kids than it is in this generation, but I really can't believe that two little boys did so many things that were so wrong that they justified such brutal beatings.

Through the years, though, we kids began to realize that these trouncings were not nearly as bad as having to watch our folks fighting. We eventually got hardened to the iron hand of our mom and the strap of Jack, but the anything-goes bloody battles that our parents so frequently got into left lifelong scars on all four of us kids. Perhaps these scars were partially or totally responsible for my two brothers becoming alcoholics. Too many times we would be awakened by loud arguments with profanity to the max, usually followed by hand-to-hand combat. There were no rules. Fists, kicking, hair pulling, biting, scratching—you name it; it all happened. There we were: four kids huddled together on the balcony of the staircase, all of us terrified and crying our eyes out, too young to do anything about it, and knowing that when the current episode ended, many more would follow. There were so many bouts that it would be hard to recall any particular battle—except one.

Both parents drank, but our mom didn't get sloppy, nasty drunk like Jack. If things went well, Jack would get slopped out of his mind and just pass out. He might piss on himself and the carpet, but no big deal. We would just hold our noses and step over him while getting ready for school the next morning. But one particular night things got a little uglier than usual. It all started pretty much the same way as all the other fights: drinking followed by name-calling, each of them trying to outdo the other with four-letter-word abuse. But that night things suddenly took a different twist. Jack staggered to the gun closet. Even in his drunken stupor, he was able to load his 16-gauge pump shotgun to the hilt. At the time my mom had no idea what Jack was up to. She was sitting on the ottoman of Jack's favorite stuffed chair with her back to the dining room from whence Jack was staggering in her direction with gun in hand.

Jack slammed the barrel of the shotgun against the back of my mom's head and announced that he was going to blow her head off. When Mickey and I heard the commotion, we sneaked over to the top of the balcony. We were so horrified by the scene that we didn't dare move or make any noise for fear of our lives too. Mickey was about nine, and I was a year and a half younger, so we were helpless. As for me, I remember thinking that Jack was going to kill all of us. Our mom was going to be first, but I was so scared that I couldn't think of how to save her.

Jack kept swearing, calling her every name in the book, and threatening to blow her brains out. After all the fights they had had, Mom had grown stronger both physically and mentally, but now with a shotgun at the back of her head, she had zero control of the situation and she knew it. She pleaded with him, knowing full well that he had racked a round of #6 shot in the chamber, had the safety off, and his finger on the trigger. The scene was so intense that I peed on the stairs, which frightened me even more because it would give Jack more reason to kill me too. An eternity of screaming, cussing, and pleading finally screeched to a halt with the bloodcurdling sound of the shotgun blast. BLAM!

Mickey and I held each other, imagining our mom's body bloody and headless—and that we were next. I'll never know whether Mom ducked or Jack pulled up intentionally, but he missed her head. The shot blew some ceramic figurines and the top of the TV to bits. Mom didn't hang around long enough for him to rack another round in. She ran out the front door as fast as her feet would move and didn't stop till she reached a neighbor's house. They had had to call the cops for her before, so they responded to her cries for help immediately. Meanwhile Mickey and I got the little kids and we all hid in the upstairs bathtub. The cops were able to subdue and disarm Jack, and they hauled him off to jail. Mom came upstairs and found us huddled together in the tub. We all cried for hours until, totally exhausted, we went to sleep.

As I've grown older, I've realized that when a couple is having marital problems, the only people on earth that know exactly what is going on between the two is the couple themselves. People often speculate as to who is to blame, but more goes on behind closed doors than we can imagine. In the case of Jack and my mom, perhaps they were each guilty of antagonizing the other, perhaps not. I will never condone the overuse of alcohol or guns, but I won't attempt to judge either Jack or my mom other than to say that permanent scars were left on the whole family. The good news is that my ass is still intact.

I was told that before I learned to walk I got deathly sick with pneumonia, whooping cough, and measles all at once. So, for the first few years of life, I was a skinny little runt. I was probably three or four years old when we moved to Bowles Harbor, a small community on the shore of Lake Erie, about six miles from Monroe, Michigan. Our parents rented a small brick house at the end of the road, right on the beach. There could not have been a more adventurous place for a kid. Adventure is not something a person necessarily looks for, but look or not, it had a way of finding Mickey and me.

When Mickey was five or six years old, he got typhoid fever. He was so sickly that nobody thought he would make it. I can't forget how he appeared to be nothing but skin and bones, a skeleton with skin on it. He would lie motionless, both night and day, and he had the pale white skin of a dead person. Once, when I was passing by his bed, I noticed his fingers moving. I reached in through the rails of the crib that my mom had put him in, and he gave my hand a light squeeze. I was too young to realize it, but this was one of the first signs that he was on the mend. I was so happy when he started talking again. It had been so boring for me with Mickey in bed all the time, because I didn't have anybody to get into trouble with.

The nature of two boys is trouble, and we were the living proof of it. Real soon after Mickey was once more able to get around, he and I ventured to the storm drain by the gravel road that led to Monroe. We had done this plenty of times before, so we had no reason to believe that there was any danger. Mickey had taken his shoes off so that he could wade in the bottom of the drain. We were gathering crawdads, (sort of like fresh water shrimp) when he stepped where he shouldn't have. Bent over in the bottom of the drain, he let out a yelp. He scurried up the ladder and sat on the top of the cylindrical storm drain. He had no way of knowing, but a broken beer bottle lay in the murky water, and it almost cut his foot in half. Blood was running all over the place, and I could see his little toe just dangling by a thin piece of skin. Boy, were we scared! Neither of us knew what to do, and to make matters worse, Mickey said that we were really going to get spanked when we got home. Finally we decided that I would have to go home and tell our mom. I ran as fast as I could and covered the three hundred yards or so in short order. I was frightened at the thought of telling my mom, but Mickey was bleeding like the proverbial stuck pig. I burst into the house and screamed, "Mommy, come quick; Mickey cut his foot bad. Blood is all over the place!"

I didn't realize how fast my mom could move. She grabbed a rag, and out the door we went lickety-split! When we were almost to Mickey, I could tell by the look on his face that he was more concerned with the ramifications of screwing up than he was about his foot. My mom gasped when she saw the cut, which extended up both sides of the arch and across the bottom of his foot. The little toe was barely hanging by a thread. Mom quickly wrapped the wound with the rag she'd brought, and we helped him hobble back home. By the time the doctor arrived, Mickey had lost lots of blood, and we thought he was doomed again. The doctor sewed up the entire cut, including the reattachment of his little toe, and being the resilient little bugger that he was, Mickey made a full recovery and regained total use of foot and toe. Despite the seriousness of Mickey's injury, my mom spanked me for being a part of such a "dumb-assed thing," as she put it.

Lake Erie was a favorite locale for winter fishing. Perch and pike were abundant, and anglers from near and far would bring their homemade "shanties" when the ice was thick enough and vie for their favorite spot. Shanty Town was as bustling as any city, especially on weekends. How a shanty was built didn't vary much except for its size. Usually they were built on skids, framed, and covered with boards and tarpaper. The reason for the tarpaper covering on the outside was not just to help keep the shanty warm, but also to block the glare of the sunlight and thus make it easier to see the fish as they approached. A shanty had a floor that covered about three fourths of the space inside it. The part opposite the door was left open so that a hole could be spudded through the ice. Jigs were used to attract the fish, and then a spear was thrust to harvest them. Some shanties were barely the size of a two-hole outhouse, while others were big enough for six or eight guys to party in comfort while fishing.

We kids couldn't get enough of this winter activity, and most of the adults loved the camaraderie, the beer, the jokes, and the fishing. Laughter could be heard ringing out non-stop from all the shanties. The sight of a big pike sneaking up on a jig was enough to make you pee your pants. Even a school of perch darting around would have us kids rigid with excitement. Besides, perch were so delectable. None of us had to be called twice when the cast iron skillet was filled with luscious fried perch.

As a matter of pride, people would share their catch, which was a way of bragging, but nonetheless, sharing. So, even if Jack had too many beers and made "otter tracks," he still brought somebody's fish home.

For the most part, these were good times. But as the winter season ended, the lake would show its ugliness. There were always those that were so intent on fishing just one more weekend that they would not heed the warnings of others. The ice would melt from underneath as well as on top, and would not only thin, but would also get rubbery. Twice I remember hearing cries for help in the night. Our whole family went outside with flashlights, but neither time could we see anyone, let alone help them. Their cars would be their final resting place in Davy Jones's locker.

It would be late spring before the frigid waters of Lake Erie were warm enough to swim in, so we kids, who so dearly loved the water, would have to be content with wading in the shallows. Of course there were plenty of other ways to use up our excess energy, but the lake was so inviting, especially on those hot, still days around the first of May. Once the water had exerted its magnetism on us and drawn us into the shallows, we were often lured to total submersion.

The beach in front of our house was windrowed with zillions of tiny, bleached, spiral shells, which made for a ton of fun. If our sister Gwenlaurie, whom we loved to tease, was playing with us, Mickey and I would scurry up the beach a hundred yards or so, bury ourselves with shells, then call to her. Of course she never could find us. Usually we would jump out of the pile of shells and scare her so badly that she would scream bloody murder, or we would wait till she passed us, and then make weird ghost-like sounds. The results were the same either way. She would go running back home, crying as loudly as she could bellow it out. Sometimes we could bribe her with the promise of candy if she would stop crying and not tell our mom. The ploy worked some of the time, but often she just ramped up the show and cried louder and louder the closer she got to the house.

You would have thought she'd just battled with the devil if you'd heard that awful cry. It sure was effective at getting Mom's attention, and before Gwenlaurie could tell the hideous story of how terrible we were, Mom would storm up the beach, screaming our names at the top of her lungs. Even though we hadn't done anything seriously wrong, we knew without a doubt she had one thing on her mind: SPANK our little white asses! To make matters worse, we usually hid in the weeds adjacent to the beach, which of course drove her into a rage. As you might guess, we could only hide for so long, but at the time it seemed the wisest thing to do. Being the eldest, Mickey would make up a lie that we would stick with no matter what. But parents are so intelligent! Mom knew how devious and mean we two boys were, so our side of the story went unheeded, and the inevitable was at hand. Blister-butt time! Sometimes Mom was too bushed from a long day of housework, so she would let us sweat it out until Jack got home from work, whereupon we would get lashed with his strap. He had gotten a new wooden leg, which he called Esmeralda, and it was held on with a wider belt than Rosie's. Once in a while he would come home so drunk that not only was he unable to whoop us, but the problems he created dwarfed our escapade. Not very often were we so lucky.

One fine spring day when our uncle Bill was visiting, Mickey, Gwenlaurie, and I were playing on the lawn, when all of a sudden we were startled by a bloodcurdling scream coming from the weeds just a short distance away. It sounded a lot like Gwenlaurie when she was putting on her famous crying act, but she was standing beside us and was as terrified as we were by the persistent scream. The noise was so loud that at first none of us could move, but then curiosity took over. Sneaking as quietly as six- and eight-year-olds could, Mickey and I inched our way through the head-high weeds. The screaming was getting weaker as we parted the last weeds and got our first peek at a sight that I will never forget and that gave me nightmares long afterward. A giant bull snake was swallowing a live, half-grown cottontail rabbit! The shock sent a gasp through both of us, and we bolted out of there like someone had stuck a hot poker up our backsides.

"Uncle Bill," we yelled as we neared the house, "come quick!"

Bill was hoeing a flower garden in front of the house, and he recognized the urgency in our voices. It was good fortune for us that he was there because our mom and dad would have thought we were making up another one of our farfetched stories. We stealthily led Uncle Bill to the scene, and when he saw the size of the snake, he made the same gasping sound that Mickey and I had made just a minute before. The next few minutes turned out to be a real lesson in what it means to be brave. Although he was obviously shocked at the sight of this "double celestial hercomite" snake devouring a rabbit, Uncle Bill raised the hoe that he clutched with both hands and slammed it into the snake's neck over and over until he had almost severed its head. By then, our mom had heard all the commotion, and she came running out. The moment was intense, and the scene so awesome that it made the short hairs on my body come to full attention. It took all of us to drag the snake out to the lawn, and we did so with the pride of a hunting party coming home with the kill. I have no idea how many years it took to create a creepy crawler of such goliath proportions, but this monster was almost as long as our garage was wide, and as big around as a quart Mason jar. Unfortunately, the cottontail didn't survive. Bull snakes don't normally get to such a horrendous size, but my childhood belief that the snake was fifteen feet or more was confirmed later in my adult life by a photograph of the snake laid out next to the garage.

The country was in the clutches of World War Two during the years that we called Bowles Harbor our home. It was impossible for me, at such a young age, to realize the complexities of such an event, but no matter where on this planet a person called home, there were reminders that we were at war. One of them was the picture of Uncle Louie in full dress uniform that sat on a shelf in the living room. Our family was pretty much unscathed by the ravages of the war. Jack didn't have to go because of his wooden leg, and his brother Louie made his tour with not so much as a scratch. Yes, we were the lucky ones. So often while visiting friends or neighbors, we would learn of someone's father or son that was killed.

We were also reminded on our mile and a half walk to school that the war was in full swing. In the fields not far from our little white one-room schoolhouse were Japanese prisoners guarded by American soldiers. These were American Japanese that someone thought might be a threat to our country at the time.

There were times in the early fall that we kids had to go to the weed fields and gather milkweed pods, which we were told were used to make parachutes. It was not a glamorous job, to say the least. It was hot and sweaty, and our clothes were cluttered with sand burrs before we'd filled an onion bag with the silky pods.

Even though Mickey and I had been deathly sick during the first few years of our existence, he with typhoid fever, and I with pneumonia, whooping cough, and measles all at one time, we toughened quickly. The work in the fields and the mile-and-a-half walk to and from school turned out to be just what the doctor ordered. But, it was on one of those lengthy walks home from school that I would have an encounter with a nasty dog that would prove almost fatal. I was six years old at the time. It was a hot September day, and it was dryer than a popcorn fart. My school buddies had just left me to go their separate ways when I heard a car coming behind me. I glanced around to see an old Model A Ford approaching, kicking up a terrible cloud of dust. I scurried to the side of the road, grabbed my shirt, and pulled it up to cover my mouth and nose to keep out the dust. The old rattle-trap Model A had no more than gone by when something hit me in the back and knocked me sprawling. Fear shot through me. With the suddenness of it all, and with the blinding cloud of dust, I had no idea what had taken me to the ground. Whatever it was, it was losing no time biting every part of my body, all the while growling and snarling.

Finally, as the dust cleared, I could see that my enemy was a red Irish Setter. Something had sent him into such a rage that he was apparently intent on killing anything in his path, and I happened to be in that path. Talk about being in the wrong place at the wrong time! The ravaging dog, unsatisfied at having thoroughly bitten my arms and ribcage, sank his fangs in my cheek. As ferocious as a lion making a kill, he had me pinned to the ground and his teeth planted so deep in my face that I was unable to scream. I was completely at the mercy of this killer. I knew I would soon die, but all of a sudden the dog let out a yelp, jumped off of me, and went off running like he was on fire. Somehow or other, the driver of the car had caught a glimpse of the attack through the cloud of dust. He screeched to a halt, grabbed a tire iron, and ran back to the scene. One blow from the iron was all it took to make Ol' Red exit, pronto. Talk about a hero in white clothing! I was one lucky kid. If he hadn't seen that dog on me, I would surely have bought the farm at only six years young. I barely remember him picking me up, but I do remember that as he was carrying me to his car, he said, "You poor little shit!"

Mickey, who had been walking quite a way ahead of me, wasn't aware of the traumatic experience I had just suffered. We pulled into the driveway simultaneously with Mickey's arrival on foot. When the man picked me up from the seat to carry me to the house, Mickey couldn't believe his eyes. I looked like a sieve that had had berries squished through it. Not only did I have zillions of new bloody orifices from head to toe, but mingled in the mess were gobs of frothy saliva. With one glance, Mickey started screaming for Mom. Before we reached the house, she came bolting out the front door. As strong minded as she was, she couldn't hold back a horrified "Oh, no!"

It took the doctor some time to get to our place from Monroe, but when he finally arrived, you could readily see the concern in his eyes. Most of my wounds were punctures, which didn't require sutures. That was the good news. The bad news was that it was unanimous that the dog was probably RABID. Guess what! You're right if you guessed that it would be mandatory for me to have the series of fourteen shots… in the STOMACH! Did they ever hurt! The dog bites were bad, but they took place in a flash.

For fourteen days I got a big-assed needle, which seemed as big as a full-length pencil, stabbed into my stomach. Yeouch! It was confirmed that the dog had rabies, and it was put to sleep permanently.

Recovery took a long time, and I got skinny again. I loved all the attention I got when I was well enough to go back to school, though. My bandages and battle scars were the topic of the week, and I felt like a puppy getting his head scratched. The kids wanted all the gory details of the attack and the shots, and I took full advantage by playing it up to be every bit as awful as it was and then some. More important, though, was to make it very clear that I was brave through it all.

I was about to write, "As I reflect on my childhood," but some happenings in life are tattooed on my brain so strongly that I don't need to reflect or reminisce. Lots of the stuff that I experienced is deep in my soul. It never goes away. I've survived plane crashes, forty-foot seas, rogue waves, the 1964 earthquake, bear attacks, hyperthermia, and heartaches, but none of the above is more vivid than my childhood.

There was the time when Mickey and I screwed up the shingles on the roof by dancing naked up there when we thought no one was watching. Our parents took turns beating our butts for that one. Another time the two of us decided to ride our big tricycle to Monroe to see our Aunt Sadie. She wasn't really our aunt, but we called her that. Mickey did most of the pedaling while I rode on the back. It was a long six miles. I guess we were expecting a nice visit, with milk and cookies. Instead, she promptly called one of our parents, and yes, it resulted in one of the worst beatings we ever got with Jack's two-inch strap.

I peed the bed. Damn, I hated it, and tried my hardest to quit because every time I did, I'd have to pull my pajamas down and get a spanking from my mom. Damn the bees too. Honeybees would nest in our attic and come through the ceiling cracks and sting Mickey and me while we were trying to sleep. Most summer mornings would reveal several welts on both of us and lots of dead bees in our bed. After a while it didn't hurt so much. You can get used to most anything, I guess.

One of the last memories I have of that place on the shore of Lake Erie is when Mickey was at the age when it wasn't cool anymore to have a little brother hanging around. We were on the beach one summer day when, out of the blue and without cause, he grabbed me by the ankles and dragged me, belly up, into the lake. There was a surf, so I immediately began swallowing water. The more I fought, the more water I swallowed. As death was closing in on me, my last attempt to kick free was successful. It must have tired Mickey out too because he didn't have the strength to chase me back to the beach. I puked a ton of water once I'd crawled to safety. Prior to that day we had seemed inseparable. After that day it was rare that we spoke, and when we spoke it was not nice. Older brothers have the advantage. They have more experience. They learn how to swear first, and they quickly learn how to verbally abuse little brothers like it's a natural thing to do. We've all heard the phrase "there is always some good that comes from the bad." I didn't throw in the towel. I became strong. I was a fighter.

I learned quickly that you must be very selective when choosing friends. My best friend when I was in school was Bill Long. His parents took me under their wings and made me realize that parents can be loving and understanding. In return I respected and loved them dearly. These people were a genuine gift to me. They were extremely hard workers and, even with seven kids, were always loving. If their kids did something wrong, they showed their disapproval by scowling or with a slight tongue lashing, never by beating. Later in life I was able to put to use the lessons that I learned from them when I raised my own children.

Mickey and I worked, both around the house and at paying jobs, from an early age. We cooked a lot of the meals, and we learned how to can veggies and fruit in the fall. When I was eleven and twelve, I caddied. I carried two herky-sized bags for golfers so I could make more money, and I got there in the morning before they opened so that I could do two rounds. Yes, 36 holes, seven days a week. Jack was a bad boy and eventually went to prison. After that, it was imperative that Mom and we two boys have jobs. Among the three of us, we were able to feed four kids and pay the bills.

When I was fourteen, Bill and I hauled coal during the winter months. He had an old half-ton pick-up truck, and we would shovel it full with all the coal it would carry, and then deliver it to customers in the area. Because of school, we were only able to do this on weekends, but it made muscles on our muscles. At lunchtime we would buy a loaf of bread, ten slices of bologna, and two quarts of milk. Yep, five sandwiches each. We couldn't afford catsup or mustard, but it didn't seem to matter. It was just something to fill our gut. By the day's end, we were totally black.

Toward the end of the winter, a bunch of us kids had a snowball fight. All was fun until an older kid came over and, for some unknown reason, hit me in the stomach as hard as he could. It seemed like five minutes passed before I could breathe again. He just walked off laughing. Someone told me that his name was Charlie, and that he just liked beating kids up. Billy Welland, who often joined Bill Long and me when we were having fun, had a weightlifting set. All winter long I went to Billy's place as often as I could and lifted weights. At first I thought that it wasn't doing anything for me, but after a few weeks, I looked in the mirror and noticed the beginning of some muscle tone. The next spring I saw Charlie at school and told him to meet me outside after the last bell. Obliging me turned out to be a big mistake because I beat him so fiercely that it took several kids to pull me off his bloody, sorry carcass. Whenever I saw him in school after that, he gave me a wide berth. Sometimes there is justice in life.

Summers in Michigan can get pretty hot, so it was great when we could take some time to go to one of the nearby lakes and go swimming. One time in particular it was boat safety weekend on Lake Chemung. My grandfather had a cottage on the lake, so that made it doubly great. One of the neighbors had bought a navy surplus twenty-man inflatable raft and anchored it upside down for us kids to play on. Ten or twelve of us kids were playing "king of the castle" on the raft. I was in the water next to my friend Mike. A rich guy with a speedboat was towing his two beautiful daughters on skis. I heard the roar of the speedboat and turned just as he slammed into the raft. Bodies flew everywhere! I got knocked under the boat, but was able to make it to the surface. I was shaken up, but okay. I couldn't see Mike anywhere, so we all started diving for him. Nobody seemed to know how deep the water was there, but I couldn't see bottom while diving. The guy that was driving the boat just sat in his captain's chair—drunk. A couple hours later somebody called in a scuba diver, and he found Mike's body, decapitated from the prop. I was unscathed; Mike was dead. This was my second brush with death after Mickey nearly did me in seven years earlier.

Mike's death left a terrible scar in my heart that never went away. So much for boat safety.

Sitting here at my computer in my peaceful house, with the sun glinting off the bay and magpies hopping on the deck rail, I ponder that dreadful day, and time passes unnoticed as my mind takes me to other times during my years as a commercial fisherman when I barely escaped the jaws of death. Those stories will find their way into this narrative too, but all in due time. First there are my teen years to put on paper.

Bill's parents got jobs at the new golf course in Livonia. His dad was the head greens keeper, and his mom was the cook at the country club. Bill and I got hired as greens keepers and, at $1.25 an hour each, we were in the tallest of cotton. The benefits were as good as it gets too. Bill's mom made us the best burgers in the world, and we got to play golf every night. We got so good at the game that in two seasons we could beat the pro. Don Patterson was the owner and the pro of Idle Wild, and was the nicest, most smiley guy I'd ever met. He often told Bill and me that we worked too hard. That just made us work harder.

I played football in high school, and Coach Richard Hudnut worked us till we dropped and then worked us some more. They said that he used to play pro ball, so had no use for twinkles and wimps. Many nights after practice I would get the nastiest cramps in my legs. Yikes! it hurts just thinking about it. Anyhow, I loved it. I was a natural Attila the Hun. A 5' 6", 155-pound warrior! Football was so compatible with the golf club work, and vice-versa.

My hormones were in overdrive, but I was too darn shy to say diddly-squat to a girl. My time would come (no pun intended), but for now I'd just have to keep bouncing off the walls.

Life was wonderful. Bill and I did a lot of hunting. Included in our quest were pheasants, rabbits, squirrels, and raccoons at night. Bill's mom loved it when we came home with a coon or two. She knew how to roast them to perfection. The fur was a bonus, and would fetch $1.50 or so. One time we met two older black guys who said that they had some good coon dogs and asked us if we knew where to go coon hunting. We were glad to take them because our dogs were only good for pheasants. The four of us headed out on a dark, moonless, night. We had to go through a cemetery to get to the woods. When those two guys realized that we were in a cemetery, they screamed like girls and took off running. We never saw them again.

When deer season rolled around each November, everything else came to a screeching halt. Stealthy as Indians, we managed to harvest deer when no one else had any luck. It was a passion for me.

The first time I went deer hunting, it sucked big-time, but was a memorable experience worth mentioning. I wanted desperately to go when I was twelve and again at thirteen, but Michigan law didn't allow deer hunting until age fourteen. Mickey had gone with Jack and his three booze buddies the year before. There was no meat brought home, and because Mickey and I didn't talk much, I didn't hear any details. The year of my first hunt Jack and a few of his hunting buddies drove us to a small cabin in northern Michigan the day before the season opened. While settling in, I couldn't help noticing that there was much more booze and beer than food. Liquid diet, I guess. Jack's buddies were all bigger than he was, so when Jack got drunk and nasty, they just laughed it off. During the night, I had to go out to take a leak. It was dark, so I didn't see Jack passed out on the floor. He must have thought I was a whore or something, because he grabbed my leg and was talking like I was a woman, wanting me to give him oral sex. He tried his damndest to get me on the floor, but I was able to pull free and get out the door. Nobody said squat about it in the morning.

Mickey and I were equipped with 16-gauge shotguns with slugs. Jack had a 35 Remington. Mickey took a stand about fifty yards away from Jack and me. I was not about to get too close to Jack, so stayed fifteen or twenty feet away from him. We hadn't been there more than half an hour when two does and a buck came running by. Jack shot first, but the buck didn't flinch. I took aim and shot it through the heart. It ran another twenty yards and dropped.

When we got to the deer, Jack yelled out, "Yes, I got him!" He was claiming the kill!

I was dumbfounded, but said nothing. Later, the taxidermist told me that the bullet hole was without a doubt from a shotgun slug. It was big. I had to gut the deer while Mickey looked on and Jack puked several times.

The next day it was Mickey's turn. A big buck walked out in the clearing in front of us, and Mickey pulled his gun to his shoulder, pumped all three rounds on the ground, and never squeezed the trigger. The buck looked at us and trotted off. The so-called hunt, my first deer hunt, got worse as it progressed, but I don't dare to write anymore about it. I never hunted with them again.

Jack, as I said before, ended up in prison. Gambling seemed to go so well with alcohol, and betting on horses was his forte. It all led to cheating, stealing, and writing bad checks. As with most bad things, some good came from Jack going to the big house. My mom divorced the man that she used to be madly in love with.

Soon afterword she married Herman. He was a good guy and treated her and us kids well. I even had a good deer hunt with him and his brothers and nephews. When Herman came into the picture, I was old enough to shovel coal and play football.

Because of my involvement with my job, golfing, hunting, and football, I was able to avoid Mickey. My little sister Gwenlaurie and little brother Joel were several years younger, so we didn't really do much together.

Some of the hardest things in life are to reflect on the past. For sure I don't want people to think that I'm a sniveler, and yet that is what it is. Lots of us had some crappy times when we were in our childhood, but for me, writing about it was like rolling a log uphill in deep sticky snow. I wish I could remember more of the good that happened during my childhood but I am convinced that kids are prone to have strong thoughts of the bad stuff and not much of the good. There is an unknown in the brain that blocks good memories but allows us to dwell on the dismal crap. I'm sorry but for the life of me I can't think of a time when either of my parents told me that they loved me, or that they were proud of me. It could have been because I wasn't very lovable and hadn't done much to be proud of, but I'm guessing that my blue eyes were to blame.

Winter months were tough. Most of the things in life that were worthwhile ceased temporarily. I don't remember exactly how I started trapping, but when I was old enough to set a size $1\frac{1}{2}$ trap, I trapped muskrats, mink, and raccoon. I would get up during the night and go down to the creek and run my trap line. My family thought I was wacko, but I made a few bucks and it was so exciting.

Several of the classes in high school seemed mind-numbing and a waste of time, and my grades reflected it. In particular and topping my list were poetry and Shakespeare--ugh. Also history became a hated class because of the terrible so-called teacher. His mission was to find a student that didn't appear to be paying attention and then thump him on the head or slap his fingers with a ruler. It's too bad that he was such a jerk, because history is really interesting. On the other hand, the teachers that knew how to relate to their students, who showed some kindness and understanding, not only taught successfully, but also were special people in my life that I will always remember. Topping my list were Mr. Ort, shop teacher and "one of the guys"; my typing teacher; and my math teacher. They knew how to make learning fun. Then there was Coach Hudnut who disciplined boys into men and taught us to give our all to whatever we set out to do, RESPECT others, including our opposition, and to know the feeling of winning.

A new kid moved to our area in Livonia, and at the time I had no idea of the major part in my life that he and his family would play. Forrest was quite shy, but because our lockers were next to each other, we became buddies. Good timing, I'd say, because Bill Long had quit school, so I appreciated making another close school friend. Near the same time that I met Forrest, I bought my first car, a '46 Merc that was pretty sharp-looking. It gave me more independence and allowed me to visit Forrest's house as often as I chose. Six of the seven kids in Forrest's family were living at their home, which, as I would soon learn, was ruled by a strict, put-you-down stepfather. BUT, on my first visit to their home, something sweet caught my eye.

Margie was a year younger than I. Whenever her stepdad wasn't watching, she would melt me with her sweet smile. Nobody on planet Earth had more racing hormones than the two of us. Her parents were very religious, and I thanked God for that because it was when the parents went to prayer meetings that Margie and I became amorous. Whatever you might call it, we definitely took advantage of every opportunity we could find. It was more than problematic, though, because the stepfather was no dummy, and most parents have no problem detecting a teenage boy's lust for their daughter. I can make this statement with authority, having later had five girls of my own. When you are that age, though, you think that you can deceive the wisest of parents. Forrest was my cover-up, I thought, but of course they saw through my fake innocent look. Anyhow, rabbits don't use condoms, so at age seventeen, I married my pregnant sixteen-year-old bride.

Chapter 2

Knock, Knock, Who's Calling?

It seemed like hardly any time at all before we were sitting at the dinner table admiring our three beautiful daughters. During that time I had worked at a number of jobs, including apartment maintenance, grave digging, and on the assembly line at G.M. Diesel, to name a few. There were times when I worked two jobs, which made for a higher-quality lifestyle. The grave-digging job was actually fun and rewarding. There were several young bucks like myself that enjoyed competing to see who could dig a grave the fastest. Also, there was Bud Lutz. Most people would think of a cemetery as a place for solemn faces. Not Bud. He was continually doing stuff that made the rest of us laugh. One day he came over to my section and told me to follow him back to his section because he had something to show me. When we got close, he motioned for me to crawl and be quiet. We sneaked up behind a monument and peeked at an old lady kneeling by a gravesite. She was talking and singing to her dead husband. Bud chimed in with a deep voice, as if it were her husband replying. She started answering him. I couldn't believe it! She actually thought her husband was talking to her. After several minutes of the hysteria, I had to crawl back out of there so I could laugh out loud. Later that day, Bud came over and we laughed some more. He said that the old lady came every week at the same time, and he went through the act each week.

The wife and I and our three girls were renting a nice old farmhouse in the country near Southfield when God tapped me on the shoulder in a most peculiar way. The first time I didn't seem to get the picture, but the second time was more like he grabbed me by the collar and gave me a shake. Both times I was reading the newspaper at lunchtime at G.M. The first time it was an article about a world record brown bear that had been killed in ALASKA. I believed that was the greatest event I had ever heard of, and I must admit that at that very instant it stirred my wanderlust genes.

A couple of months later I happened on the article that determined my destiny. It was my instructions from The Man. The article was about two families who were going to Alaska to homestead. Oh, yes! They said that they would love it if others wanted to join them. I was one of the first to meet with them and to be dubbed a "59er." When I told my wife that we were going to Alaska to homestead, she looked at me like I had really lost my mind. Her response was quick and absolute: "No!"

Within about a month there were lots more people wanting to join us 59ers. Considering such a move in those days, not to mention committing to it, was thought to be totally insane. Nobody would travel nearly five thousand miles to a harsh, desolate, cold place like Alaska, especially with three little kids. The only person that thought it would be a fantastic venture was my grandmother. She knew from the time I was ten or eleven years old that I had her Grandfather Crawford's genes. He too had homesteaded, but in Michigan.

I carefully made a plan and presented it to my wary wife. We would sell everything that we owned and buy a small house trailer to tow up there. I had learned that a car rental agency would actually pay $150 to some of us to drive new Ford station wagons to Anchorage. We would buy a year's supply of food to take, mostly dry goods of course. The wifie could see that I was serious as a rock.

A few days passed and she came to me and said that I could go alone, and that after I got a homestead and a good job, she and the girls would follow. She didn't know it at the time, but she had more homesteading spirit in her than she realized. She went with me to the next meeting with the other 59ers. The excitement that sparkled in everybody's eyes and voices was contagious. She was hooked. She was going with me. Ha!

It wasn't easy, but everything went as planned. I put a tow-hitch on one of those new station wagons and hooked up to the used 28-foot house trailer that I bought cheap. The guy that sold it to me gave me a super deal because he loved the thought of the adventure that we were embarking on. Quite a few stores gave us dry food to take. People took to us because we were the youngest of the group and had the most kids. Actually most of the people were older and had no kids. We were interviewed by newspapers from Detroit, and one of them asked me if I would be a correspondent. They would pay me. Oh, yes, I would do that!

Preparing for the trip was like getting ready to move to Antarctica. So much to do, so many crucial details to ensure a safe trip. One cold but sunny Saturday a few weeks before our departure, the stress was starting to get to me. I felt a strong urge to spend a couple of hours alone. I ambled over to the backside of the barn and sat with my back resting against the grey, weathered boards. The sun felt yummy; it had a pure relaxing effect.

Had the huge decision that I made for my family been selfish and without merit? Most decisions are made by weighing the pros and the cons, but in this case, the pros were pretty much guesswork. I needed confirmation from God.

What were we leaving behind? Neither my wife nor I had strong ties with relatives. Her parents never visited, and mine were good for three or four visits a year. The congregation at the Lutheran church was cordial, but we didn't socialize with them except on Sundays. Schoolmates had scattered in the wind. I didn't have to speculate on the hunting in Alaska. It would undoubtedly be fantastic. The most important consideration by far was my three little daughters. The big question in my mind was whether I was doing the right thing for them.

There would be a few skeptics that doubted whether a young Michigander barely 22 years old could possibly be making the right decision for his family. What they didn't know was that God was not only the captain at the helm, but also the driving force. I sat there mulling over "leaving everything behind" versus "having the Alaskan adventure" so long that the shadows lengthened and the strength of the sun waned to the point that it provided little warmth, but when I got up and headed for the house, I knew I had made the right decision. Now there were no negatives; I had complete peace of mind.

If God had given me a clue as to what my Alaska lifestyle would consist of, I might have questioned who it was that was talking to me. Little did I know.

As I sit here in our marvelous Alaskan, warm log home, I glance out the front window and see that Little Girl, a yearling moose, is here again. She's having a tough winter without her mom. It's not easy for yearling moose, even those that have a mom. Little Girl's mother was killed by a car less than a quarter of a mile from here. Mama moose teach their young so much in their first year. There is so much to contend with. Predators, mostly bears and wolves, hunters, cars, and starvation are more than happy to bring about the death of a young moose.

It's April and winter doesn't want to let go. This is a good place for a moose to hang out. It's warmer here by the shore of Kachemak Bay, but there are limited amounts of good browse for these huge herbivores. If she is to survive, I know that I have to help. She is grazing too much on last year's grass in our yard and in the field, so I try to provide her with some willow and birch branches. There will soon be new growth, so when that time comes I will send her on her way. She is so beautiful. Without touching her grey-brown face, I know it is as soft as the most expensive velvet. Her mane is dark chocolate, and each side is as blond as my daughter Laurie's hair. Actually her back and sides look like the fur of a wolverine. We keep each other company. I keep her alive, and she shows her trust in me by allowing me to approach within a few feet of her.

Chapter 3

Here We Come, Alaska

There were nearly forty of us ready to go on departure day, and still others rendezvoused with us up the trail, so eventually, as we progressed, there were 49. We were "the 59ers." Our mission was simple: stake out a homestead and farm it. But it would take considerable time to cover the 4500-mile trek over some of the toughest roads in North America. As one might expect, plenty of mishaps occurred on our 21-day journey. Yes, that's a terrible long time to be on the road, but traveling as a group meant that we would all help each other so that we would reach our destination together.

One of the first outstanding memories I have of the trip was how cold it was in North Dakota. Yikes, it was 40° below zero at Minot! We prayed to God that we wouldn't have any car problems. Our car and travel trailer made it through this coldest part of the trek, but we had to stop and help others with flat tires and overheated engines because of inadequate amounts of anti-freeze. Once we got a ways into Canada, the temperature and the roads got better, at least until we got to the infamous Al-Can highway. It was a gravel road, but it had an ice pack built up on it, so most of the time no gravel could be seen. It was a wicked highway. Frost heaves, potholes, and slick ice all lent to potential danger. Oh, yes, did I mention how narrow the Al-Can was, and how we would barely squeak by oncoming trucks, some of which were loaded with explosives that were used for oil exploration? We saw lots of little red signs along the road that marked the places where people had died, constant reminders of how important it was to use our best driving skills. When we were driving through the States, people greeted us wherever we made stops, but once we got on the narrow Al-Can, the people generally weren't so friendly. I guess it was because the Canadians had had more than their share of arrogant American tourists that thought everyone should bow to their wants and desires. Actually, we did meet plenty of very friendly Canadians that realized we were just common folks headed to Alaska to homestead. Other than having to stop for gas, we were pretty self-sufficient. When we started on the trip, I had only $250. When we got to Alaska, my total wealth had been whittled down to $80. Eating at restaurants was not an option.

As we got up into the mountains, we found ourselves awed by their majestic beauty. Often beauty is accompanied by danger, and this time was no exception. I spun out two or three times and had to have someone with four-wheel drive help us to the summit. One time on Steamboat Mountain we spun out and started sliding back down. I was helpless to control my car as the trailer jackknifed. Luck was on our side, because the trailer wheels caught one small spot of gravel and we stopped safely. The kids were really scared, but they didn't let out a peep. Going down the other side of some of these herky-sized hills became as hairy as going up. It seemed like the trailer was in a race to pass us.

The frost heaves took their toll. The big 1934 Rio van that was donated to us 59ers, which had a bunch of farm equipment in it, broke in half. The Alcan Highway was brutal. Another truck was donated to us, but we had to wait for it to get through a snowstorm. When it finally arrived, we transferred the farm equipment and got under way. Three miles down the road it broke too. We had to abandon the truck and most of the equipment. When we stopped for the night, I would write notes as to the happenings of the day and then try to find a phone so I could call the *Detroit Times* and report to them. If I had time, I would also call two radio stations, WWJ and WXYZ. They were all excited to hear from me, so I tried to do as good a job as I could as a correspondent.

I've always been an early riser, so each morning we were the first of the convoy ready to rumble. With all of our food supplies, sleeping quarters were on the tight side. If it wasn't too cold, my wife and I would try to sleep in the car and give the kids more room in the trailer. Before we went to bed, we would mix some millet with hot water for our breakfast. I'd never had millet before we headed to Alaska. People told us that it kept well and that it would be a staple that should definitely be taken along. I've got to tell you, I have never looked at another grain of the stuff since that trip. It did keep well though.

All of Canada was beautiful. It seemed a shame to blast through a place of such diverse scenic beauty, but we were headed to our new home and wanted to make good time. Despite our haste, though, we made progress at a turtle's pace. The van breaking in half was just one incident of many that made the journey so long. Vehicle repairs, car accidents, asthma attacks, and waiting for stragglers to catch up all made for an extremely slow trip. It would have been easy for some to go on ahead, but we all stuck together and helped each other when help was needed. I nearly cried happy tears when we crossed the border from Canada into Alaska. It was the first day of officially being an ALASKAN.

Unbeknownst to me, a hazard lurked ahead: ah, yes, frost heaves. The road in Alaska was paved with asphalt, and it wasn't holding up with all the freezing and thawing of early spring. It was like three- to five-foot ocean waves, hundreds of them. I drove as slowly as possible, but still it took a toll on our trailer tongue. Once it started bending, there was no stopping it. Luckily I found a small repair shop, and the owner knew just how to solve the problem. He welded a bunch of angle iron to the tongue after he straightened it. He did a great job, and he only charged us a few bucks. He didn't want any of our leftover Canadian money though. Soon after that, the roller coaster road ironed out and was in pretty good shape for the next 250 miles to Anchorage.

None of us could have imagined the reception in store for us when we got there. We were met by a contingency led by the renowned Mukluk Marston and a band. We were like our own parade. It was as though we were some kind of celebrities, but we had done nothing to deserve such a lavish welcoming. I felt embarrassed, but smiled as congenially as I could. My kids were shy, but you could tell by their eyes that they were enjoying the attention. So many people wanted to shake our hands or give us a hug. Many of these people had made the same trek at one time or another. Quite a few of the onlookers that lined the street were Eskimos and Indians. Dressed in parkas and mukluks, they were an awesome sight. Some of the early settlers from the Matanuska Valley greeted us and gave us produce and homemade jellies and jams. The mayor gave a speech and there was more band music. People danced in the street. I can't begin to remember all the good that happened that day, because it came as such a surprise that anyone would be there or that anyone cared at all about a small group of people from Michigan, the 59ers. I think it was an excuse to celebrate the coming of spring after a long cold and dark winter.

Soon after our arrival, I found myself suddenly without a car because I had to give the station wagon that we drove up for Hertz back to them. Even though I got it there without a scratch, Hertz reneged and never paid us the $150 that they promised. I was really counting on the money, but I had to be consoled by the fact that the car had provided us with good transportation while we had it. The *Detroit Times* was really great about paying me for my correspondence, and when we got down to the Kenai Peninsula, there were checks waiting for me. It was a good thing too because I was nearly broke. One of the other group members towed our trailer down to Cooper Landing where we met Fred Henton. He owned Henton's Lodge, and was glad to let all of us park at his charming, rustic place next to the Kenai River. Its location is at the confluence of the Russian and the Kenai rivers where the famed red salmon fishery still exists. Fred taught us some of our first Alaskan lessons, and we worked for him in return. I knew of him before leaving Michigan because he held the record for the second-largest brown bear ever killed, a feat that was of course one of the reasons that Alaska was so magnetic for me.

We were referred to as the "FIFTY-NINERS" as we headed up the Al-Can Hwy.

My family and I are below the white circle on the van that was donated to us.

As I write, the snow is falling. It is April 15 and my taxes were filed last week, so it's good to sit in front of the computer and pound away at the keys. I was hoping that winter was done. Except for diehard skiers, most Alaskans share those sentiments, as do the moose. Yesterday there was no snow to be found down here by the shore of Kachemak Bay. For the past several weeks I've had four-legged furry lawn mowers here. The moose love our lawn, raspberry bushes, lilacs, and flowers. They are great company, and they know my voice so well that they sometimes don't bother looking up when I'm outside working. I can be within ten feet of them and they show no concern.

Fred Henton took to me and my family and we took to him in return. One evening he served us clam nectar from some clams he had recently harvested at Clam Gulch. When I asked him about his brown bear, his eyes lit up and he proceeded to tell us in detail how the hunt went. If he were still alive, he would love hearing the numerous bear stories that I now have to share. More later on that subject, but for now I know that clam nectar is a yummy treat.

Even though it was easy to get sidetracked with things like digging up frozen water pipes or painting or whatever, the time came when we had to go look for a homestead. I was still without a car, but most of the time it was easy to get a ride hitchhiking. The Sterling Highway, which ended in Homer, was gravel, narrow, and rough. Someone had generously given me an old pair of Tubbs snowshoes, and I put mucho miles on them. Most of the available homestead land was between Soldotna and Homer. After the second trip to Homer, I was beginning to see potential there for our group. When I returned to Henton's after that trip, I found the group inside the lodge, and they were all excited about a new area up by Talkeetna that they heard about. "The soil is rich for farming" was the first thing I heard when I entered the room. The next comment was "We will have to leave right away because we have to get across the big Susitna River before breakup."

When I spoke up and told them that I had a good report about the Homer and Anchor Point area, they said that they had already decided on Susitna. I was so happy about what I was learning about homesteading on the Kenai Peninsula, and now someone let all the air out of my balloon. I questioned these decision-makers about crossing the Susitna River, and how we would get back to civilization if we needed medical attention or supplies.

"Oh, we'll set off some dynamite and someone will come and get us." Sounds simple right? NOT! The Kenai Peninsula was our plan right from the start. Besides, I had three little kids to care for, and one more little item that definitely entered the picture. When we got to Anchorage the week

before, we found out that we were going to have another child in September!
Yes, I know what you're thinking. This guy is a baby-making machine.

It kind of reminds me of Sven and Oly. They were having lunch at their
job site when Sven says, "Hey, Oly, didn't you yust have your ninth kid?"

"Ya, that I did," said Oly.

"Don't you know vhat's causing your vife to get pregnant so often?" asked
Sven with a smile on his face.

"All I know," replied Oly in his Swedish accent, "is that one night I voke
up and there she vas, yust helping herself."

I never once regretted having my kids. I'm proud of them all, and love
them dearly. It was because of my love for my family that I had to part ways
with most of the 59ers. One other family, the Bennetts, and a single young
farmer guy named Hugh decided to stay on the Kenai Peninsula. The others
went to Susitna. As the days and weeks went by, I made several more trips,
looking for the ideal spot to squat. Now I saw things differently. I only had
to find enough land for one homestead instead of thirty or more. I had it
on my mind that I wanted to be on a lake. Topo maps were with me wherever I went, and I learned how to use them well. Whenever I found a place
that seemed to fit the bill, I would hitchhike to Anchorage and go to BLM
(Bureau of Land Management) and check to see if that tract was open. I
had several disappointments, but I never lost faith.

One day when I was hitchhiking, a fellow named Woody picked me
up. Clam Gulch was his home. He invited me to his cabin to spend the
night because I had been snowshoeing all day and it was getting dark.
He had a sawmill that he and his buddy, Jay Cook, were running. After
having a bowl of beans with moose meat, I watched the two of them play
cribbage. Their cabin was only 8X10 and had two bunks. I was glad to
have a place to stay for the night and didn't mind sleeping on the floor.
The next morning when I woke up, there was an eyeball staring at me! I
jumped up, startled, and those two jokesters laughed and laughed. Woody
had a glass eye, and he had put it on the floor close to my face before I
woke. I think those two were starving for company, because they wanted
me to stay for a few hours and have a little competition. I was pretty
strong, so I went along with it. They had an axle with wheels that we
used to see who could "press" it the most times. At first sight, Woody
appeared to be on the scrawny side. Ha, he was all sinew. Jay was tough

too, but Woody was a smidgen tougher. I could beat Jay, but Woody and I tied. We tied in arm wrestling and everything else that they came up with. Woody was an ex-marine, but I had too much Irish blood to allow him to beat me.

We became lifelong friends. Woody towed our travel trailer down to Clam Gulch, and Per Osmar told us that we could park it by his grocery store. Per and his family had come to Alaska in the late 40s from Holland, Michigan. Per enjoyed a prank now and then. I was considered a Cheechako, which meant a newcomer, so I was the natural target for a prank. All of the local people dug razor clams at this time of the year. Per and Ray Lafrenere told me to go to the beach and find the clam's "trail," and when it ended, to take the biggest shovel I could find, and dig like crazy. Of course I fell for it and spent some time playing the fool, inspecting the beach for trails, which I thought must take some kind of x-ray vision to spot since I wasn't seeing any. I didn't want to look like I didn't know what I was doing and everyone else was busy digging up clams, so, trail or no trail, I dug several monster holes and never saw hide nor hair of a clam. Finally after watching some locals, I figured how to determine the right place to dig for those delectable morsels: a telltale dimple in the sand. I've never missed a clam season since. I even dug clams commercially the second year that I was in Alaska. There is a super beach across Cook Inlet called Polly Creek. Alaska Packers hired me to dig razors, and that, ladies and gents, is one of the toughest ways to make a living, except maybe fishing for crab in the Bering Sea. I'd rather dig graves any day!

One day I met a fellow at the Kasilof Post Office, and I mentioned that I was looking for a homestead, preferably on a lake. Carl Swanson was the fellow's name, and he said that his homestead was on a lake between Kasilof and Soldotna. He was sure that the next lake to the north was available. He showed me the spot on the topo map that I always carried with me. I promptly hiked over there and knew instantly, without any doubt, that this was to be mine. I sat down on the north end of the lake, and the sun warmed my whole body. The lake was still frozen over, and there was scattered snow, but on the very spot where I sat, the sun had bared it completely. There were lots of birch trees around, and I knew that was a sign of good growing conditions. There were also plenty of tall straight spruce trees, which would be ideal for building a house. What more could I ask for!

The next morning found me hitchhiking to Anchorage. I could file on 160 acres, but elected to start with 80 because I didn't know how difficult it might be to "prove up" on it. Under the federal Homestead Act, you had to build a habitable house, live on it for three years, and put ⅛ of the land under cultivation and plant a crop. I did lots of yahoos when my application was approved.

When the ground thawed in the spring, I hired a "cat" to doze a trail the six-tenths of a mile from the Sterling highway to our homestead. Then I had him tow our trailer through the muddy quagmire. The kids loved it. My wife loved it. We all loved, loved, loved it! We were doing what we had set out to do.

Now the work began. I chopped a hole in the ice for water for drinking, bathing, and washing clothes. I cut firewood with a Swede saw for heating water. The first project at hand was to build an addition to the trailer so we wouldn't be too awfully cramped. I bought some rough lumber from Woody, and with some instructions from him and Frank Char, built a nice 10X28 lean-to. Frank was one of many great neighbors that were genuinely nice and made us feel accepted and loved. The first time he visited, he brought two dozen eggs from the chickens he raised, and a chocolate cake. We were in Fat City. He was also a carpenter by trade, and soon afterward he hired me to help him build a house for a neighbor. After that learning experience, I could build anything from the cement foundation up.

During the daytime, we were constantly improving our home and the surroundings. At dusk we would pump up the Coleman lanterns, make supper, and then read stories to the kids. Then we would turn the battery radio on and listen to "Mukluk Telegraph." The program was for "bush Alaskans" to send messages to each other. Quite often the 59ers that were homesteading on the west side of the Susitna River would send messages to each other, and we would learn how they were doing. There were no telephones, so the service was thoroughly appreciated.

We gradually learned that we were blessed with great neighbors in every direction. Arne Murto from the next lake to the south asked us if we would like to join him and Don Madden in planting a potato patch. Arne and his wife, Thelma, and their eight daughters were of Finnish descent and were hard workers. Yes, you heard it right, eight kids, and all girls. They had a spot that had been tilled the year before, so it was fairly easy to spade it up again. We planted a humongous garden of spuds. When we dug those nuggets in the fall, our share was 1,200 pounds!

In the meantime, a forest fire had started at Kenai Lake. I had learned well the use of a chain saw and an axe, so off I went with my sleeping bag on my back. I worked 18 to 24 hours every day for a month. The last two weeks, I sharpened the saws and axes. I was treated well when I got home because I had more money than we had ever seen at one time. The lion's share of it would be used in the fall when we would have our fourth child.

I needed a car. Don Madden had a 49 Olds that he said he would sell pretty cheap, so I bought it. We were in hog heaven.

Speaking of Don Madden, once when he and his sweet wife Marge came over to visit, Don took a quick glance at my meager woodpile and boldly told me, "You can judge a man by the size of his woodpile."

Don was a sourdough, so I didn't reply, but quickly remedied the situation by spending the next three days cutting wood and stacking it neatly. Ever since, I made sure that my woodpile was as big as anybody's.

A year or two later an old-timer asked me if I qualified as a sourdough. I had no idea what the qualifications were that he was referring to, so I just told him that I doubted it. He couldn't wait to tell me. "There are three things that are mandatory," he quipped, grinning from ear to ear. "You have to pee in the Yukon River, fight a bear, and have sex with a native woman." Then he went on to add, "Be sure not to mix up the last two requirements!"

My wife and I were always working hard. Day after day, month after month, and year after year we toiled, but it didn't seem like it was that tough at the time. I don't remember thinking about it, but years afterward I realized how privileged I was to take part in the U.S. Homestead Act.

Quite often people that we had never met would come to our homestead and introduce themselves. Cecil and Helen Rhodes, along with their little son David, braved the muddy road to pay a visit. They were renowned photographers and were so genuinely nice. Cecil had packed their camera gear in and wondered if it would be all right if they took some movies of us. I didn't know what we could do of interest, but we agreed to it. The kids were super shy, but the Helen insisted that it was fine for the kids to just go about their daily chores and routine. Cecil and his family lived on the shore of Kenai Lake at Cooper Landing. In the years that followed, we would drive to their place and play penny ante poker in the warmth of their spectacular log home where laughter was the theme. How thoroughly we enjoyed these wonderful Alaskan friends!

On one of my first trips to Soldotna, which was six miles to the north, I got a job. An exploration company, United Geophysical, was just getting ready to do some seismic work. Ed Back was the senior observer, and after a short conversation, he hired me. I started out "setting jugs" (it had nothing to do with women), then became a driller's helper, and then the fun stuff began. I got the position of "shooter" or powder monkey.Oh, yes, I love dynamite! Actually it was referred to as a blasting agent and it came in one-pound cans. I could screw cans together and use as many as necessary. Most of the time I would load ten or more cans in each hole that the driller had augered. Each site had three to six holes to fill with the blasting agent. I would set them off when Ed was ready to record the sounding.

Several of the guys that I worked with were Kenaitze Indians. The Showalter brothers— Emery, Jay, and Ward, and Georgie Peterson, Emil Dolchok, Alfred Ivanoff, and Harold Wik—were always fun to be around. They were hunters, so I was drawn to them. Every day we would fly to the jobsite and return in an S-55 Sikorsky helicopter flown by ace pilot Glen Wheeler. What a thrill to fly in a helicopter every day! During one of our hunting talks, Emil looked at me so as to direct his message to me in particular and said, "When a brown bear charges you, he is always smiling."

I still laugh at Emil's Indian wisdom every time I think of that. Since then I've had several bears charge me, but I'll save that for later. One day I was working with Georgie Peterson. He was a driller. The day was bad for Georgie. Every time he drilled a hole, he hit a rock and wasn't able to finish it. He cursed that one and the next one and each one after that. Finally, he looked up to the sky and cried out, "Give me a break!" Pretty funny after all of the swearing he had done. Actually he usually was a really nice guy, and a good friend. I learned so much from these Indian friends. I admired and loved them as brothers.

Two other guys that I was drawn to were John Richards, who hailed from Nebraska, and Dino Anderson. They were gun nuts. Between the two of them, they had more guns than Winchester and Remington together. John talked a lot, so I learned plenty about various calibers and makes of rifles and handguns. Both were bachelors and lived in small cabins. Dino was a quiet loner, but when I showed interest in guns, he opened up to me. I was to learn later that this was not all good.

The following spring I went on my first Alaska bear hunt with John. I was by then officially an Alaskan, as I had been there more than a year, so I could get a resident hunting license. We lined his canoe up the Kasilof River to Tustumena Lake. Once on the lake, we hugged the shoreline because the water was rough. John didn't like the looks of the situation. He asked me if I wanted to take the tiller of the two-horse motor. I had no problem with that, so John lay down in the bottom of the canoe with his eyes closed. With John lying down, the canoe had more stability. The waves were only two feet or so, but John never looked up until we had gone the full length of the lake. Several of my friends and neighbors have died on Tustumena through the years. It can get as rough as the sea. We only saw one bear on that trip. John shot at it from the canoe, but missed. I acquired great respect for the 28-mile-long lake and any open water that I encountered after that. A few years later, three of my neighbors were making the same crossing, but perished in the attempt. It's not a good idea to get out in the middle of the lake, because it can change from flat calm to sea-like conditions in a half hour or less. The glacier at the head of the lake seems to make its own weather and cause the sudden changes.

While I'm on the subject of Tustumena Lake, I must tell you about Joe Secora. Joe lived in a small cabin at Indian Creek near the eastern end of the lake. He had a one-man placer gold operation that didn't produce much, but it was tailor-made for him. I gathered that Joe didn't care to be around other people, because he only came out of there a couple of times each year. His vision must have been close to nil. His glasses were a half-inch thick. I had crossed his path a couple of times at the Kasilof Post Office, and he seemed to enjoy talking with me, but the conversations were short when I asked anything about his lifestyle. Bud Tri, who was a friend of mine that knew Joe quite well, flew his plane up the lake to give Joe a "buzz." There was no place to land his wheel plane up there, but he thought it would be a nice gesture to make a fly-by. Just as Bud was about to fly over Joe's place, Joe came running out of his cabin with his rifle. Bud saw the smoke burst from the gun, and it was pointed at him. He made a quick right-hand bank and got out of there as quick as he could. He glanced back and saw another puff of smoke come from the gun, so he gave the plane full throttle.

I heard that another plane got shot at during the same year. Joe was not shy about letting people know that they weren't welcome. Talk was that Joe got to thinking that people were trying to steal his gold.

A couple of years later, Wayne Bishop learned to fly and decided to visit Joe in the winter when he could land on the frozen lake. He knew Joe and, as conjecture had it, landed and talked Joe into going for a flight with him. They hadn't gone more than a short distance when something happened to the plane. When Wayne didn't return, the search party found the wreckage with two dead men. Tommy Corr, Jr., who has become a master log home builder, acquired Joe's place at Tustumena Lake. He worked on the cabin for several years and then sold it.

One day, after working for United for a year, Dino, the gun nut whom I mentioned before, asked me if I wanted to go elk hunting on Afognak Island with him. I quickly said, "Yes!" so that following fall we took a commercial flight to Kodiak and from there chartered a bush pilot to take us to Afognak. I believe it was Harvey Air, and I think that the pilot was Harvey himself, who crashed later that year and died. We barely got into Waterfall Lake because of the scuddy weather. Typical weather for rain forests like Afognak is rain, wind, and fog, and that is what we were to live with for the duration of the hunt. Perhaps I shouldn't even refer to it as a hunt, because for the fourteen days we were there, the weather never changed. Never could we see more than fifty to a hundred yards. Our hunt was supposed to last seven days. Dino supplied the tent, and it was not waterproof. Within 48 hours, everything was soaked. We couldn't leave the shoreline for fear of getting lost in the thick spruce forest and fog. It was difficult to keep the fire going that I started when we set up camp, but I knew that we depended on it for our very survival.

About the third day Dino started getting different. By day five he was getting weird. I probably wasn't being the best companion either. The weather was relentless. Judging by the appearance of the elk sign, there hadn't been any in the area for a couple of weeks. On day six I shot a beaver because we were already getting low on food. I guess Dino thought I was bringing all the food for the trip, so he hadn't brought much. Beaver meat, especially without salt, tastes like wood. It's edible, but I'd prefer lynx, muskrat, or even porcupine. Day six was when Dino stopped talking to me. He acted like I wasn't there. He raged on about the weather, the island, and

It's easy to see why I named our homestead lake Reflection Lake.

then cussed out the pilot. He smoked nonstop until he ran out of cigarettes. Then he really gritted his yellow teeth. Had it not been for the constant howling wind, every critter within a mile would have heard Dino screaming obscenities and gnashing his teeth. I kept busy cutting firewood and occasionally walking some of the nearby shoreline, which gave me a bit of a feeling that I was hunting and got me away from the dark side of Dino. He had a good side, but the weather was getting the best of him. It definitely was taking its toll on both of us. Each day after day seven, we listened for the drone of the plane, but we knew that it was impossible to fly in weather like that. I shot another beaver because we had nothing left to eat except for a couple of pieces of pilot bread. I honestly thought that Dino might not make it. He was scary to look at, and he wouldn't eat any beaver. Finally, on the fourteenth day, there appeared a very slight opening in the sky to the north, and just as quick as it opened, there came our ride. Dino never spoke a word all the way back home. Sadly, later that year he used one of his big handguns to end his life.

Chapter 4

New Life—An Alaskan Is Born

Meanwhile, on September 12, 1959, the first 59er was born in Alaska: Cindy Lynn Wills, our daughter. Doc brought our new little Alaskan daughter into the world with all her parts, and she was healthy. We had to go to Seward, which is about 105 miles from our homestead. Dr. Isaac, the attending doctor, later became a good friend and hunting buddy. Cindy was as beautiful as her three older sisters. It sure was easy making girls! I was beginning to get some teasing about it, but I was too proud of my family to care. Besides, I was just being consistent with my surrounding neighbors. Zeke had one, Tom had two, and Arne had eight, all girls. Occasionally someone would tease me about having four little step-stone daughters. I was quick to tell them that I only had half as many as Arne!

We had no electricity, so we used oil lamps and Coleman lanterns for light. Our most luxurious item was a battery-operated radio, which kept us somewhat in touch with the world. There was no refrigeration, so we couldn't stock certain items until freeze-up.

I had dug a hole in the ground to serve as a makeshift root cellar. This was where we kept our 1,200 pounds of taters. For the most part the cellar worked, but during the coldest part of winter some of the taters froze. We found that the frozen ones were deliciously sweet. When we lived in Michigan, we canned fruits, vegetables, and sometimes meat. Things were different in Alaska. With no electricity and no set-up for canning, improvising was important. One of my first lessons, taught to me by Jack Edelman, one of the first Alaskans I met, was how to salt salmon in a barrel. It was an art that had to be done to perfection; otherwise you could end up with a barrel of rotten fish.

Not too long after moving to Alaska, I received a telegram. My dad, Jack, had died. Although he wasn't my biological father, he was my dad. Perhaps he had more reasons to be the way he was than I would ever know. A couple of years after Jack's death, I heard that my brother Mickey had died too. They both died from alcohol-related stuff.

Winter was approaching. The leaves had turned yellow and there was an occasional frost. It was our first Alaskan winter, and I sure didn't like the idea of going through it without some red meat to nibble on. Potatoes and millet wouldn't cut it. This was before I qualified for a resident hunting license. I couldn't afford a non-resident license, so I was starting to consider "homesteader season," a unique way of providing for your family that several of my most resourceful neighbors had informed me about. We had frequently seen moose around, so I knew that it probably wouldn't be too hard to get one. Just how to do it without getting caught was the question. It had to be done with one shot, I was told.

I was out picking low bush cranberries and was less than 50 yards from home when a young bull sauntered by. I carried my gun for protection, and I protected myself by shooting him in the brain. When I walked over to the downed critter, my heart started thumping like a drum. Even a young bull is big. I pretty well knew how to skin it and cut it up. My wife helped, and by nightfall we had it hanging and covered. The next day I buried the guts and head. Oh my, was the meat yummy and tender! We had moose meat and taters almost every night, and the kids always cleaned the platter. Sometimes we ground the meat with a hand grinder and made hamburgers or spaghetti. We were simple, poor homesteaders, but we were eating high on the hog. We had obtained a dog that fall. Her name was Timber, and she loved the bones and scraps. Not one morsel was wasted.

All was cool until late winter when Abe Thayer, Fish and Wildlife officer, paid us a visit. He said that someone had been in the bars boasting about killing a moose out of season. Abe asked if I knew anything about it. Well, I didn't, because I hadn't been in a bar. I'm sure to this day that he knew I had taken a moose. Timber had scattered bones all over the place. I believe that the officer also knew I had four little kids. Abe was a genuinely caring person who might turn a blind eye when feeding kids was at stake.

One day Woody trudged through our muddy homestead road in terrible pain from an abscessed tooth. Doc Pollard was the only dentist in the area, but he had gone on a trip. Woody said that he wanted me to pull his tooth. He only had two, and they were long, yellow, and ugly! He didn't have to tell me which one was the troublemaker, because the abscessed one had a huge black cavity. I had never pulled a tooth before, but it didn't look like it would be too hard to get that miserable-looking thing out. Woody suggested that I use a good pair of pliers, but I was the doctor, so I got a three-foot piece of strong nylon twine to do the job. Woody didn't care; he just wanted that pain-causing fang gone. He sat down on a chair and opened wide. I carefully tied a clove hitch on that gem and then made another single hitch to be sure it didn't come off. Woody was still muttering instructions when I yanked as hard as I could. It sounded like a gun going off. The noise was awesome! Woody looked shocked, because he was supposed to say, "Go!" My wife and kids were all in shock too. When they saw the long, ugly tooth dangling on the twine, they cheered. Woody didn't cheer though. He just put his coat on and trudged back out our road and went home. A week later he came by and thanked me.

I spent most of my spare time cutting tall, straight spruce trees for house logs. I had no machinery to get the logs out of the woods and to the building site, so I decided to build a stockade style log house, i.e., using eight-foot logs and standing them vertically instead of horizontally. By doing it that way, I could carry the logs on my shoulder. My, they were heavy! I love log houses. There is so much warmth, strength, and character to them. I first built the floor on pilings, then, after peeling the logs, stood them up and ran my chainsaw between them until there was no gap. The logs glistened inside and out from all the coats of varnish that we put on. When we moved in that fall, it was as though we were in a mansion. It only had two bedrooms, but was bigger than the travel trailer, and it was our home. What's more, we didn't owe a penny for our first house. The wood stove, which I made from a 55-gallon barrel, and the Coleman lanterns kept the place cozy and bright during the short, cold days of winter. The Coleman lanterns used white gas called Blazo. They sold it in wood cases that held two 5-gallon metal containers. All the homesteaders used the cases to make cupboards and shelves, and the square metal containers for hauling water. I made a yoke that let me carry two of them to bring water from the lake to the house. Galvanized tubs were a necessity for bathing and washing clothes.

Thank God for chainsaws. I used mine so much that I got accurate enough to fall a tree exactly where I wanted it to land. Several years later I made good money clearing right-of-ways for the power company. Of course the chainsaw was mandatory for clearing land on our homestead. As a matter of fact, the land clearing was coming along so well that I filed on an additional forty acres. That meant I would have to "prove up" on 120 acres.

My job with United Geophysical was coming to an end when Ed Mallette, Frank Char's son-in-law, came to our house and asked me if I'd like to become a lineman. There was a company in Kenai that was going to start a telephone service. At the time there were no phones in the area except in the town of Kenai where they had magneto-operated phones. I readily accepted the offer. Ed was the foreman and was always fun to be around. The superintendent was from Oregon and was one of the best pole climbers in the country. He taught a few of us how to climb and to be comfortable doing it. Norm McGahan and I were the main climbers. We soon found ourselves competing to see who could get up and down a pole the quickest. When we were putting up cross-arms and wire, we would scale 50 to 75 poles a day for each of us. Open wire gathers lots of conductivity, and until it's "tramped," it builds up lots of voltage. One of the climbers got knocked off the pole he was on and got burned pretty badly on his arms.

One evening after climbing a zillion poles, I sat by the beach of our homestead lake, watching the loons with their young chick. The sun was setting and the lake was glassy calm. The golden leaves on the birch trees reflected a double image on the lake. Oh, yes, I thought, I will name this Reflection Lake. My family loved the name, and to this day the lake retains it.

It was obvious that, without giving it any thought, I was ever so naturally doing all the things that Alaskans do. I considered myself Alaskan. Michigan was only a place where I grew up, a place of the past. My lifelong love affair with everything Alaskan was now well underway. The homestead was as dear to my heart as anything could be. I enjoyed everything about it. Nothing seemed to be a chore. The kids were all strong and healthy. They were blessed with the perfect place to grow up. The lake offered swimming in the summer and skating in the winter. They sometimes grumbled a bit about having to walk more than half a mile to the school bus, but it was good exercise for them.

Completing the construction of the new telephone system took just a little more than a year. When that was done, it was time to check out commercial fishing. Salmon were harvested in Cook Inlet by drift gill-netters or by set net beach fishermen. The fish "traps" that had been used for many years had been outlawed since statehood. Zeke Shadura, whose homestead adjoined mine, was a set-netter. Zeke is a strong man of Russian descent, who was pleasant and easy going. He offered to take me out with his picking-skiff and show me how it was done. It was so exciting to see all the red salmon in the net, but I couldn't figure out how to get the fish out of the tangled mess. Zeke made it look easy with his huge, strong hands.

Jack Edelman had set net beach sites across Cook Inlet on the north end of Chisik Island in Tuxedni Bay. He told me that there was nobody fishing within miles of him, and that anyone could stake out sites and fish there. You guessed it: Jerre was soon to become a fisherman.

Actually, my first commercial fishing venture happened in a totally different form: clamming. Cook Inlet is renowned for its larapin huge tides. During the spring months, it's common to have 22-foot high tides. Approximately six hours after high tide, comes low tide, which can be as low as minus five feet. It's on these minus tides that the clams show on the sand flats. Polly Creek, which is across the Inlet, is one of the better razor clam digging places in the world. This is where I learned that there has to be a better way to make a living. Yikes! Each digger had Blazo boxes to put the clams in, and they held about eighty pounds. We were paid $5 for each box. Alaska Packers provided wall tents for us, and we had to purchase food from them, and coal for the small stoves that kept us from dying from hypothermia. Then at the end of the season, they deducted these items from our net profits. I got to where I could dig seven boxes on a tide, but the work made for a voracious appetite, so my food bill was eating up the profits! Oh, well, it was a good experience, and I met lots of wonderful local people, but I'm obliged to advise you that if you ever contemplate digging clams for a living, you should forget it!

After digging clams that spring, I borrowed a skiff and loaded it with lumber for a cabin and everything else that I thought would be necessary for commercial fishing. Snug Harbor cannery was the only cannery on the west side of Cook Inlet, and the owner/operator was the nicest guy imaginable. Tall and slender, Joe Fribrock took me under his wing. He let me charge nets, lines, buoys, and any other supplies that I needed. At the end of the season he would deduct my expenses from payment for the fish I had caught.

I built a small cabin above the tide line. Pitching a tent would have been easier and cheaper, but the brown bear outnumbered fishermen there at Tuxedni. I started my operation on the south side of Tuxedni at Fossil Point. Like I mentioned earlier, the tides rise and fall as much as 28 feet every six hours, so allowing for the effects of the tides was crucial. Jack came by one day and gave me an on-the-spot lesson in how to make a wooden sledge hammer that he called a beetle. He also taught me how to make a running line by making a long splice and how to drive the stakes for my buoys. Most old-time fishermen wouldn't give a newcomer the time of day, but Jack was an exception.

When the season opened, I had a terrible time setting my first net. The 20-horsepower Merc that I was using kept quitting, and the swift tide would cause me to miss the buoy at the outer end, so I'd have to pick up the net and try again. After the fourth or fifth try, I sat in the skiff, crying like a baby. I wasn't a fisherman; I was a whimpering, snot-nosed baby. I thought for a while and then said out loud, "Get a hold of yourself and stop sniveling!" After lengthening my lines and then making a bigger arch, I got the net set, but I wasn't seeing any fish hit the net. I guess I thought the net would be full of fish in a short while, but not so. During the course of the first 24-hour opening I managed to set another net, but only caught about 25 red salmon. At the closure, I pulled my nets in and skiffed my fish to the cannery ten miles away. It was embarrassing to deliver such a meager amount of fish. Some of the fishermen had 400 to 500 reds. The good news was that I received my first pink delivery slip. When I got back to my fish camp, the tide was already out, so I was unable to get to my mooring. I had to leave the skiff in the flats and trudge through the mud to the beach.

After a couple of frustrating fishing periods, I knew that I needed another site. I went across the bay and staked a spot on Chisik Island. There were no mud flats on that side, but I would have to commute back and forth no matter what the weather was. I came very close to going to Davy Jones's locker one night. I had some soggy nets and some other fishing equipment in the skiff and was attempting to get to the island. The wind was out of the southeast at 25 knots or so. This put the sea on my quarter stern. My 20 Merc labored as I chugged through the breaking rollers. With one hand on the tiller, I used the other hand to bail with my homemade "scoop," trying to keep up with the deluge of water coming in. It was so dark I could barely make out the sloped top of the island. The closer I got to the island, the bigger the waves. I was soaking wet even with my rain gear on. I bailed faster, but one monster wave swamped the skiff, and she went out from under me. I was less than 100 yards from shore, so rather than chancing getting tangled in my nets, I swam towards shore. Every big wave caused me to swallow gulps of salt water. My legs weren't helping much because of the bulky rain pants and heavy boots. As strong as my arms were, they were giving out. I'm a good swimmer, but with the freezing water, it was only through the help of God that I made it to the beach. I had a cache of supplies at my site, so I was able to get a fire going. I was barely able to strike a match because I was shaking violently, and my hands were totally numb. While snuggling up to the fire, I realized how lucky I was to be alive. I was physically and mentally exhausted, and I dozed off near the comfort of the fire. I think I had been lying there for only a few minutes when I sprang up, thinking that I heard someone calling my name. I peered into the dark sea and saw a mermaid. I really wasn't sure that she was a mermaid because I couldn't see her bottom half. She kept repeating my name in a sweet, soft tone. I couldn't believe how beautiful she was. Her long, flowing blond hair blew freely and revealed her perfectly shaped upper body. Before I thought to talk to her, she faded into the darkness. I realized that I must have been dreaming, but it seemed so real.

At dawn I awoke to a flat calm, sunny morn, and lo and behold, there was my skiff less than fifty yards away! The tide delivered her like a good neighbor. I worked on the motor all day and got it going. The nets were scattered a bit, but I didn't lose any.

Ever since I had that real life experience with the mermaid, I have had a whimsical belief in them, but we all know that there is no such thing, right? My wife has bought me several castings of mermaids. Some are cast of bronze and others of stone and clay. There are no ugly mermaids, only innocent beauty.

As strange and irrational as it may sound, it was events like the skiff going down that lured me to a life at sea. The more I endured, the more I craved. No, I'm not a masochist; it just grew on me. The "law of averages" did pass through my mind shortly after this incident. The various life-threatening experiences that I endured made me realize that I was participating in a somewhat dangerous occupation. I always had the utmost respect for the sea, but like most captains throughout history, never gave much thought to dying. Never have I felt more comfortable and capable than when I was at sea. Being blessed with a cast iron stomach helped me realize that I was born to be a mariner. Little did I know at the time, but the fact that I was so drawn to the sea, that it would steal more of my life than I care to admit. I guess that I justified it by believing that I was making a living for my family, but the truth was that I was in the clutches of the sea's excitement. She was definitely becoming my mistress!

I wasn't the only Cheechako in those parts. Mert Osmore from Clam Gulch was a good artist, and he had a nice wife and two kids. He had staked some sites way up the bay, far from any of the other set netters. The brown bears were thick up there. Imagine how tense it would be trying to sleep in a tent with bears prowling close by or pulling up a net full of fish onto a beach where bears frequently wander. Mert battled with them daily to keep his equipment and himself intact and out of their claws. I saw at least three dead bears float by that season, and for some reason, they had no paws. Mert was isolated and alone at his camp, and he caught fewer fish than most of the other set netters. He seemed quite depressed at the end of the season. Less than a year later, his car went out of control and hit a power pole. It was a sad ending indeed to a fellow who was always pleasant to me.

Toward the end of the sockeye (red) salmon season, a man named Frenchy told Joe Fribrock that he was quitting early and that, if I wanted, I could fish his sites across from the cannery for the remainder of the season.

The Coho (silvers) were the later-returning salmon, and it looked like the run would be good. I accepted his offer and moved into his luxurious cabin, which, compared to my tiny cabin, was more like a mansion. Frenchy obviously had his priorities in alignment, because he had a real bed with a mattress, and a nice full-length couch. Even among all this unaccustomed luxury, the silvers did come, and I made a season.

Whenever I made a delivery, I was so envious of the drift fleet. They always had larger numbers of fish than I did. I wanted a boat! I wanted to chase the fish, not set net on the beach, hoping that the fish would find my stationary net. When the season ended, I approached Joe Fribrock and asked him if there was one of the Snug boats available. I promised that I would take good care of the boat and that I would be a good fisherman. I don't imagine that was much of a sales pitch coming from a 23-year-old greenhorn. Most of Joe's fishermen were well-experienced high-liners (top fishermen) from "Outside," the term that Alaskans always use when referring to the rest of the United States… or the world, for that matter. Joe thought for a bit, and then with a slight grin he turned and pointed to an old, smaller boat that was high and dry. "You can fish the *Not So Snug*."

It hadn't been in the water for several years, and it had no hydraulic system, so I would have to pull the net by hand. It didn't matter. I was going to fish a Snug boat the next year! I was so thrilled that I wanted to give Joe a hug. He reminded me that it would be extremely tough pulling the net by hand, and that I would pay 22½% of my catch for the use of the boat. I was so excited. I couldn't wait to share the news with my family and the world. Next year I would be a captain of a boat! I felt like I'd won the lottery. I sauntered over to the boat and stroked the cedar hull as if it were a sleek cat. I could see daylight between the planks, and the engine was quite rusty, but it didn't matter. I was now the master of a commercial fishing vessel. I was officially a drift fisherman!

I had met Joe and Sally Munger that summer. They had beach sites on Chisik Island. Joe was tall, slender, and muscular, and you could tell by his face that he spent most of his time out in the fresh, crisp air of Alaska. Sally had big boobs. According to her, she'd met and fell in love with Joe while working as a "professional" lady in Anchorage. She wasn't at all bashful about telling me that bit of news. I think she enjoyed seeing me blush. They were two of the finest people that I've ever met.

One early morning I was on the beach near their cabin waiting for the tide to go out so I could walk to the cannery. They didn't know that I was out there, and Joe came out his front door stark naked and took a leak. Wow! I realized what Sally's attraction to Joe was.

An hour or so later, Sally came out and called to me. When I went over there, she invited me in for breakfast. Then she said, "You saw Joe come out and take a leak didn't you?"

"Yes," I answered shyly.

"He sure is hung like a horse, isn't he?" she coyly replied with a twinkling smile.

Yikes, I had never heard a woman talk like that before, but I couldn't help but laugh.

Joe was a big game guide, and we had some super talks about hunting. I think he was in his mid-fifties when I met him. His hair was turning silver and he was as handsome as the Marlboro man. After I had been guiding for a few years, Joe told me about the biggest bear that he had ever encountered. Having seen the tracks up Silver Salmon Creek, Joe knew that the bear was more than ten feet. He had booked a bear hunter for the following fall, so he was anxious to wrap up the fishing season. He was disappointed when the hunter arrived, because he had brought a 7mm Mauser, which was not adequate for bear unless it was a well-placed shot. During the evening of the hunter's arrival, Joe could tell that the hunter had never seen a brown bear. Joe was suspicious as to the hunter's experience because his stories seemed a bit stretched.

After breakfast the next morning, Joe informed the hunter that he would take the lead and that the hunter needed to do exactly as Joe instructed him. The creek was cluttered with alders on both sides, so the only way up it was to follow the bear trails. For the first mile or so, visibility was very limited. The creek was only twenty feet wide, and silver salmon were constantly splashing, startling both hunter and guide. Suddenly, Joe stopped in his tracks and stood looking across the creek. There, all too close was the monster bear that he had dreamed of seeing. The gargantuan bruin was standing upright and had his eyes fixed on the two intruders. The hunter pulled his small-caliber rifle to his shoulder, but Joe grabbed the barrel and

Part of the Snug fleet waits for the next salmon opening.

The sun is nearly obliterated from the haze that Iliamna volcano has produced. Commercial fishermen always stand up when rowing.

My daughter Suzie counts while I send the fish flying with the use of a Pugh.
Photo courtesy of Tor Holmboe.

pushed it toward the ground. Joe knew that the bear could be on top of them in a split second, so he didn't want the hunter to agitate him with his peashooter. The bear just stared at them for what seemed like an eternity. When it was convinced that they were harmless, it went down on all fours and, with a woofing noise, ran off into the thick alders. While Joe was telling me the story, I could see that it made him nervous talking about it. He said that he was afraid that the hunter would wound the bear and then the bear would munch their skulls.

Several times when I was making a fish delivery at the cannery, I talked with Hank Kroll and his two sons Hank Junior and Herbie. You couldn't help but notice that Hank was the best beach fisherman around. Many times he would come to Snug with his scow named Shrimp loaded to the gills. The boys would use a sort of one-pronged pitchfork called a Pugh, to throw the fish from their scow to the brail while Hank impressed anyone within hearing distance with his b.s. Joe told me that Hank only had a third-grade education, but when you listened to him talk, you'd have guessed that he was a college scholar. He learned how to fly small planes and helicopters by himself. He spoke four languages fluently and could play just about any instrument. He would sit on the counter in the cannery store and play the guitar or banjo and sing in different languages for hours. I went into the store one day after delivering my fish in a heavy rain. Hank was singing at the top of his lungs and seemed as happy as he could be. There were about a dozen fishermen in the store being entertained by his stories and music. He glanced up at his two boys, who were soaking wet and looking quite forlorn. While looking soberly at the boys, Hank quipped, "Would you look at those two soaking wet little bastards?"

Chapter 5

Bush Planes, Hunting, and Fishing

After the fishing season, I honed my hunting skills. I worked hard at stalking, shooting, skinning, and cutting up meat. I shot respectable moose, Dall sheep, mountain goat, and a seven-foot black bear. I learned how to judge the size of big game and became very quiet when stalking. I knew that I wanted to be a big game guide, so the skills I was learning would help me not only to provide meat for my family but also to be a first-class guide. I passed my guide's exam that winter, so I was primed. I began reloading ammo and turned out some "to the hilt" 220-grain loads for my 30.06. I couldn't afford a bear gun, so the 220's would do for close encounters if need be.

Early in the winter Dr. Isaac and I flew his Cessna 180 to Montague Island to hunt black-tail deer. There were lots of deer, and we came back that evening with two deer each. They tasted as good as Dall sheep. Num, num, as the natives say.

Hunting with "Doc" was never your run-of-the-mill hunt. The following year we hunted moose with the aid of his Super Cub on floats. We landed on a small lake and after taxiing to shore, we turned the plane around and pulled the back of the floats up on land. We stalked a really big bull. Doc popped it, and we gutted it and started loading meat in the Cub. When it looked to me that the floats were about to sink, I mentioned to Doc that maybe he should take that load home, then come back for me and the remainder of the meat. He said, "I think we can get it in one load."

I'm thinking, NO WAY. Well, guess what. All the meat did go in. Then he said for me to get in. There was about ten inches between the meat and the ceiling. I was only 150 pounds, but not a contortionist. He helped me lie down backwards and crammed my feet against the bags of meat. When he shut the door, I thought we would surely sink and I would have a terrible time trying to open that door. The throttle on a Super Cub has two positions, one in front and one next to the passenger's seat in back, and because of the immense load one of the rifles was too close to the rear throttle. The first time Doc tried to give it full throttle, it jammed up against the rifle. The second effort got us moving, but the floats were barely visible. There was no way the plane was going to get on step, so he made a big circle to make some waves. The next time he came around, the Cub actually got enough "umph" to break one float off the water. He pulled full flaps and leaned forward and we were airborne. He could have made some money if he had made a bet with me.

The following fall I took Doc to a place where I had seen some rams earlier. He had always wanted a sheep, but hadn't had the right opportunity. These rams stayed down in the glacier during the day and only came up out of there in the early morning. After positioning Doc, I peered over the ledge and watched six rams working their way up towards us. I told Doc to doodledash (kill) a particular one, and I would get one of the others. He made a nice kill, but when I shot mine, it started rolling down toward the glacier. It didn't stop until it hit the ice. He always told people that he never would have gotten a ram if it hadn't been for me. He was that kind of greatness.

The next hunt we went on turned out to be more of a "hairy" adventure. Again, it was to Montague in early winter for deer. It's a fairly long flight from Soldotna where Doc kept his 180 Cessna. He said that we didn't have to refuel at Seward because he had some gas stashed at LaBountys' place on the island. The weather was okay when we left, but as we crossed the Gulf of Alaska, it started snowing. We had to get lower and lower to have any visibility at all. The snow got worse, and soon we were only ten feet off the water. I wished we'd turned around while we had the chance, but it was too late to attempt it. Doc said that we should see land at any time, but all we could see was snowflakes. All of a sudden the darkness of the beach was just feet from our wheel-skis. Neither of us had a clue where we were, only that we were somewhere on Montague. He plopped her down immediately, and fortune was with us, because we didn't hit any driftwood or rocks. The snow was soft, so we stopped abruptly.

As soon as the motor shut down, we heard someone hollering. The island is eighty miles long, and as far as we knew, LaBountys were the only occupants, but we figured that we were at least twenty or thirty miles from their place. An old bearded face pushed against the plane window on my side. "Boy, am I glad to see you," hollered the old but happy guy.

Doc and I looked at each other, wondering if we should open the door.

"Come on in and have some tea," he yelled.

I cautiously opened the door, and the weathered face smiled from ear to ear. From that moment on, he never stopped talking. As he was preparing tea for us, I couldn't help notice that the mugs hadn't been washed for some time. He took a used teabag and dipped it in each mug for a short time. Obviously he was totally out of tea and coffee. The poor old guy (John was his name) had been dropped off five months earlier by a charter operator, who forgot to come back to pick up the old trapper. The pilot was six weeks overdue!

John invited us to spend the night, and we gladly accepted. By ten or eleven o'clock that night, he was still wound up and yakking just as much as when we arrived. I sneaked off to a corner and went to sleep. Doc was more gracious than I. He listened to John most of the night.

In the morning the snow had stopped, so after promising John that we would have his pilot pick him up, we cranked up the 180 and headed out. We started to go around the island where we had hunted before, but encountered another snow squall coming our way. Doc decided to head home and come back another time. I asked if he was going to stop and get the gas that he had at LaBountys'. He glanced at the fuel gauge and said that he was pretty sure he had enough to get to Seward. With no load, we easily climbed to 10,000 feet. There were whitecaps on the sea below, which indicated a headwind. It seemed like it was taking forever to get to the headwaters of Resurrection Bay. I kept glancing over at the fuel gauge. It was bouncing on empty. We were on fumes. When the engine quit, it quit right now. No sputtering, just silence! I don't know if Doc had ever been in a plane that had the engine quit, but I never had. I want you to know that I'm not scared of anything, but I was puckering. The airstrip at Seward was still miles away.

We agreed on the best descending speed and attitude. Again, it seemed like time ticked on forever. I really didn't think we had much of a chance to make the strip. As we were descending, the snow began, but we could see the town, so the airport was just another mile. Talk about holding your breath. Wow! we just barely made it onto the approach and hit land with a big bounce. A sigh of relief would be a super understatement.

Just a short ways in front of us was a grader plowing snow off the runway. The operator leaned out and hollered, "Hey, Doc, you got problems?"

"No, I just heard a slight sputter, so I thought I'd check it out."

With that, the operator offered to tow us to the place that sold fuel.

Both of us knew that only a few feet separated us from life or death.

I truly believe that Doc and God had an agreement. Doc would save people's lives and bring new ones into the world, and God would keep Doc alive.

Dr. Isaac and I had so much in common. Both of us enjoyed adventure, hunting, and laughter. He delivered our daughter Cindy and our son, Eric. While my wife was in the last couple of hours of labor with Eric, Doc and I sat by her side joking and talking about hunting. The baby arrived a few minutes after the new year rang in. When Doc lifted it up, he smiled and said "It's a boy."

I thought for sure that he was kidding because my wife and I were quite certain that we would have another girl. I remember asking if it really had a penis.

Ray and Ruth Sandstrom introduced us to a fun and interesting bachelor, Art Frisbee, and his dog, Tippy. Neither was your average critter. Art had retired from being sheriff of Seward and had built a cabin in Soldotna. The first time we visited him, Tippy opened the door with his two paws. He was a Heinz 57 and just barely big enough to reach the door handle. When we went in, he pushed the door closed.

Art also had a prime piece of property on an island on Skilak Lake. Some folks from Anchorage saw Art's cabin while boating, so stopped and visited a while. Art didn't take to the city folks, so the next time they came by, acting like they were old friends, Art invited them for supper. They seemed delighted until Art had Tippy lick the dirty plates clean and then set them on the table. The visitors immediately remembered that they had to be somewhere else. They left and never returned.

One time while I was visiting Woody, a friend of his landed his Piper PA-12 on the highway and came in to visit. I thought, Wow, landing your own plane on the road! How cool was that? Cal was a good pilot. He made it look easy, as if it was just an everyday occurrence. The first time I flew in a small bush plane, I knew that I wanted to own one, but I was just a poor homesteading fisherman. I quizzed Cal as to the cost of a plane, and he immediately told me about an Aeronca Champ that was on Merrill Field in Anchorage. He said that it hadn't been flown for a couple of years and the guy would sell it cheap. Even though I didn't have high expectations of being able to afford it, I went up to look at the bird. The fabric was a little faded, but she had an 85 Continental engine and 850 tires, which would allow a person to land on the beaches and tundra. The owner asked me if $1,200 was too much. I couldn't write the check quickly enough! I was the owner of a plane and I didn't even know how to fly.

I signed up for ground school at Kenai, and passed it with one of the highest scores. I'm not all that smart, but I did well because I wanted it so much. Then I began flying lessons with my Champ. A total of three and a half hours of flying time later, the instructor jumped out and told me I could solo. Holy mokus, that was quick! From that moment on, I flew everywhere. I soon was landing on the shortest beaches and places that didn't even resemble a strip. I became as proficient as any Alaska bush pilot. My Champ couldn't get airborne as quickly as a Super Cub, but it was close. The plane allowed me to hunt and trap in places where there was nobody else around. I could leave the house in the morning and be back in the evening with a load of caribou or moose meat. In two hours flying time I could be at Snug Harbor; three hours and I could be on the west side of the Alaska Range to build cabins, go trapping, or hunt. Sometimes I would put two kids in the back seat and fly around buzzing friends. The kids enjoyed flying, but didn't like it when I pulled it up quickly and did a "power head stall." They would scream like the little girls they were, but their eyes twinkled when they told their mother about it later.

Apparently the little Aeronca Champ had a cracked landing gear because it gave me a bit of a problem coming back from Snug Harbor after working on the fishing boat. When I took off to go back home, everything seemed normal, but while cruising along I glanced down at the flat, calm, azure-colored water of Cook Inlet. Uh-oh! I was shocked to see my right landing gear dangling like a duck with a broken leg. I had time to think about it, but thinking was futile because there was little I could do other than make as nice and slow a landing as I possibly could. When I neared the Soldotna airport, I buzzed the manager's little office, and Red Grange came out. When he saw my predicament, he got in his pickup and headed out the taxiway. I made a soft landing and held the right side up until it fell to the ground. By then, my ground speed was so slow that it turned only about 45 degrees; it didn't even rub the fabric off the wingtip. We lifted the wing up and put it on the bed of Red's pickup, and he drove alongside as I taxied to my tie down. I had the landing gear welded and never had any more problems with it.

During the course of the next forty-some years, I bent a prop slightly, but nothing else. I'm sure that there was a certain amount of luck involved, but I became quite good at short take-offs and landings. Perhaps Lady Luck smiled on me, but most of the time I felt comfortable and relaxed when I was piloting my own plane. White-knuckle pucker times were infrequent. I know that I was a good bush pilot because I'm still alive.

There were a couple of times when I was a passenger in some of my flying buddies' planes that weren't so fortunate though. There was an incident in the mid-60s that nearly ended it all. A friend of mine, who hadn't been in Alaska long, desperately wanted to kill a bear. Because he knew that I had been successful at harvesting bears, he asked me if I would help him get one, so one sunny spring morning we took off with both of our planes, Herman in his Super Cub, and me in my Champ. We flew across Cook Inlet, and south along the Alaska Range. I knew a couple of places that hosted plenty of bears. It was a balmy, crisp spring day, so the bruins would be basking in the sun. We decided that we would park my plane on a nice beach and both go in his plane when we got close to bear country. In a short time we were spotting bears. Each time we saw one, Herman wanted to land and shoot it. I had enough experience to know how to judge a bear's size, so I told him that those bears were either too small or sows with cubs. It was a matter of finding a big boar that was not too hard to get to.

After looking over a dozen or so, I located one that was plenty big. One nice thing about the small bush planes is that you can put them into slow flight, which enables you to see lots of critters. When I pointed out the bear to Herman, he made an abrupt turn to head back to the beach to land. Oops, too abrupt! The Cub stalled out so quickly that we were in the water faster than you could snap your finger. Suddenly we were up to our necks in the cold waters of Chinitna Bay. Immediately upon impact the plane was full of water. I hollered to Herman to open the door. We didn't even know if either of us was hurt. The water was so cold when we bailed out and started swimming toward shore that our bodies were stiffening, which made it difficult to swim. Thankfully it wasn't too far before we touched bottom. The tidal flats go out a long way in that part of the Alaska Peninsula. When we reached the beach, we were both shivering uncontrollably. Once we knew that we were safe, Herman looked at me and asked what had happened. I told him that he stalled it out. He just stared at me in disbelief.

Herman had a big gash above his eye, and our legs and bodies hurt in several places, but neither of us thought that we had any broken bones or internal injuries. If either of us had gotten knocked out or suffered a broken leg or back, the situation could very well have been grave. I don't know if I would have been able to get Herman to the beach if he hadn't been in good enough condition to help himself or vice-versa. Even though it took a long time to walk and jog to my plane, our teeth were still chattering. The water temperature was probably 34 degrees or thereabout. It was a good thing that we didn't have any farther to swim, or we wouldn't have made it.

No bears would be killed on that day—at least not by Herman or me. I flew us back home. Herman was white as an unused piece of toilet paper when he told his wife of our near death experience. Both of us realized how fortunate we were to have survived.

Everyone that learns how to fly, especially in Alaska, is taught how to recover from a stall. A stall is when the plane is going too slowly and there is not enough air flowing across the wing to produce the lift necessary to keep it in the sky. If there is enough distance between the plane and the ground when the craft stalls, the procedure is to push the stick forward so that the plane is in a nose down position, thus increasing air speed, and then it will recover. In this instance we were too low.

When I bought that little Aeronca Champ, I thought of it as a means to get anyplace I wanted in Alaska. I didn't give a thought to the word "adventure." Now, as I sit in my rawhide chair, more than fifty years later, I know that the "bush" planes that I've owned produced more adventure than Lewis or Clark could have imagined. I only wish that I had the ability to describe those adventures like someone as proficient with the pen as "old Ernie," as in Hemingway. My memories still serve me well though, so I'll pass them along Jerre style.

I flew the dickens out of my first bare bones Champ. Even though she only had 85 horses under the cowling, she was so light that, with my small carcass, she would leap off the ground. In a short time I realized that the biggest drawback to the two-seat bush planes was that there was never enough room to carry all the stuff or people that I wanted to take along. I modified the rear seat area by taking the stick out and covering the stub with a customized box. That way, I could pack more five-gallon cans of "av" gas. I could also take two kids along and not worry about them pushing against the stick when they got excited about seeing a bear or when they were squirming because they had to pee really badly. I had scratched a mark on the throttle panel so that I would know where to set it when I hand-propped it. That way, it wouldn't take off and leave me.

Being in the pilot world, I soon became acutely aware that other pilots were either dying or losing their planes, and more often than not it was because they flew in bad weather. Other than one time, I made sure NOT to make the same mistake. The day that I pushed the weather, I was working on a pipeline job across Cook Inlet. I always flew across to the job site, which was more than fifty miles away. We worked long hours seven days a week. One day the bending machine broke down, so the boss asked me if I wanted to go home for the day. Because he offered to pay me, I knew that he had run out of booze. No doubt, I wanted to see my family as badly as he wanted a drink. I never was good at staying away from my wife and kids more than a couple of weeks at a time. So, off I went.

I had the Champ on skis, so I could land almost anyplace. Anyplace except on water! I gained as much altitude as I could until I was almost into the scuddy winter clouds. Those clouds kept getting closer to the deck the farther I went. It wasn't long before I couldn't see anything but pan ice beneath me. There was no land to be seen. Darn. I realized too late that there would be no turning around, because I couldn't see anything behind me either. All I had for instruments was a small compass and a "turn and bank." I knew I had screwed up, but all I could do was try to keep my cool and fly due east, and not touch the ice with the skis.

It seemed to be taking too long to reach the other side, and I was beginning to squirm. The scud was so thick I couldn't see squat. All of a sudden the east foreland bluff loomed up in front of me. I made a ninety-degree turn on the proverbial dime! Yikes! I now had to follow the beach and hope that the fog would thin. Finally it did thin and I saw the town of Kenai. From there it cleared, and I landed on our homestead lake. I didn't mention my blunder to anyone. I remember thinking to myself, Self, you were kind of scared, and you aren't scared of nothing. Don't do it again.

When I went back the next day, the boss was so glad to see the bottle that I presented him with that he paid me for the day before. That day Mount Redoubt blew its top. The job went on even though we were just a few miles from it and we wondered if rocks would start raining down on us. She belched big plumes of smoke and grumbled daily, but never heaved a rock our way.

Spring is always a wonderful time. Authors have spent as much time writing about spring as they have love. After a long winter in a cold clime, it's such a vibrant time. Happiness floods my body when the first geese fly over with their constant honking. Returning sand hill cranes harmonize as they rejoice about their return to their summer home. I realize that it's a special time for them too.

The ice was not all melted in Reflection Lake when the pair of loons took possession of their territory again. I was their welcoming host. I called back to them when they made their melodious sounds like a saddened child. Often the sound was followed by a short happy note. The moose were scarfing up every new green morsel. The kids frolicked outside without heavy coats. The car started and I didn't have to jump it with a spare battery!

Breakup is in the spring when winter is melting away. On our homestead it could last from six weeks to eight weeks or so. We had learned the importance of stocking up with everything that we would need until its effects had subsided. The mud could get deep during breakup. It was time to park the car at the end of our homestead road, time to shed the heavy winter boots in exchange for knee boots.

It was also time to think about commercial fishing, which meant boat work, and hanging new nets. I had to fly to the airport in Soldotna to take the skis off the plane and put the big wheels on. After planting the garden, it was time to go to Snug Harbor cannery and go up to the web loft where fishermen went to join with the other fishermen every spring to hang nets. The cannery was located about sixty miles to the southwest, which meant that I would have to fly across Cook Inlet (with plenty of altitude), and follow the beach at low tide. Alaska has way more than its share of magical places, but none more spellbinding than Snug Harbor. The setting is special in its own right. Located on the south shore of Chisik Island, in Tuxedni Bay, it has to be one of the most scenic places in the world. The cannery and a few fishermen's cabins are the only signs of civilization. This is rustic wilderness. It sits in a snow belt, so there were still several feet of snow lingering in the spring. After enjoying the awesome beauty, I began to notice the sounds, unheard in most parts. The very first to capture my attention was the screaming of the big birds. The southeast end of the island, which is next door to the cannery, is sanctuary to hordes of seagulls, kittiwakes, and a variety of ducks. Eiders, scoters, puffins, cormorants, old squaw, and others spend their spring squabbling over nesting rights, and mates. The noise was deafening! The roof of the cannery seemed to be the meeting place of the seagulls. There was always standing room only on the peak. It was "bird-poop white."

When the cannery was in full swing, the sounds inside were from a wonderful surreal dream. All of the machines were run by monstrous leather belts that were connected to the main steam engine. The belts made a musical slapping noise. The "iron chink" chimed in with a *ka-chunk*, the torts puffed steam, lines of cans tinkled as they went down the conveyor, and the processed cans made a *plink* as they sealed. I could barely hear the many Filipinos yakking because of all the great sounds. So, so memorable!

Above the cannery was the web loft. It was there that I spent many days each spring, hanging nets. Hanging nets is as much a part of fishing as actually casting the net. The procedure is basic, but doing the rudimentary process correctly is extremely important. A newcomer to the event is at great disadvantage because there are no courses in net hanging. Fortunately, a few kind, experienced fishermen took me under their wings. For several reasons, it wasn't easy blending in. I was (as I was to find out later) "a young punk Alaskan kid." Keith Ball was close to my age, so that was a common denominator. He and his dad, Vern, both fished for Snug Harbor, and were referred to as highliners, or top fishermen. There were a half dozen other high-liners, and several of them were Alaskans. Karlo Kokko, Brad Temple, and Morry Porter were as good as they get. Later, Brad's boy, Tom, and Morry's boy, Willie, followed in their fathers' footsteps and became high-liners. Tom worked too hard at being the best and had to exchange his heart for a slightly used one, but he still high-lined! About five years ago he decided to let his wife and daughters do the fish picking while he ran the controls. Late last fall the used heart decided that it was too tired to keep up with Tom's ambitiousness. He had a way of making the worst days seem humorous.

Between Keith, Vern, and Stoney (Russ Stone), they took precious time to teach me the art of hanging a net. First I had to go to Joe Fribrock and buy lines, web, corks, and hanging twine. It was staggering when I found how much it cost. A shackle of gear is fifty fathoms long. We fished three shackles, which came to 150 fathoms, or 900 feet of net. To attach a cork line and a lead line to the web was a lengthy project for a greenhorn, especially an ambidextrous beginner. Even though I use my left hand for most meticulous stuff, my two-handedness made it tougher for my mentors to instruct. I would begin by filling a couple of fids with hanging twine and then start tying knots. It was emphasized that the knots must be tight and that the spacing be exact! I would learn why they were so emphatic about those two issues.

By the next year I could hang nets as fast as any of the guys. Spending time out in the web loft was so pleasant. I didn't have to speak a word. It was all about fish stories. There were definitely tons more fish caught in the web loft than at sea.

Mug up. Between breakfast and lunch, and between lunch and supper, the canneries had "mug up." Everybody quit what they were doing and went to the mess hall and had coffee and some goodies. Linda, the head cook, would always make sure I had some extra goodies to put in my pocket when I was leaving because she knew I was a poor young soul with a family. I had to chuckle whenever she flirted with the two Danes and they jauntily sneaked off to her room.

By the time I finished hanging my nets, most of the snow was gone, so I began the task of making the boat seaworthy. The Snug boats were made of yellow cedar planking, and because they were high and dry most of the year, the seams would open, and there was always some corking to be done each spring. Einer, a stout Norwegian, was the cannery carpenter and boat repairman. At first I thought he didn't want anything to do with me, but he warmed up to me when he saw that I was willing to do my own work. He patiently showed me how to put the oakum into the seams. Too much or too little was not good. It had to be done just right or the seams would leak or make the planks swell out of place.

All of the cannery crew were old-timers, each one with his own title. They all had Snug boats and fished salmon. I learned so much from them just by watching. For the most part, they liked it when I asked them questions as long as I didn't make a pest of myself. I tried to make them feel important, because they were. To work effectively with boats you have to have an understanding about them. If you were to set out to build a boat, you'd start by throwing most of what you know about building a house out the window. Nothing is square. Lines are not straight. When you get the gist of it, it's an extremely satisfying feeling to have learned such priceless knowledge.

There were a number of essential items that each skipper kept on board at all times. Top priority was a full set of rain gear (slickers). Hot on the list were pilot bread and Bag Balm. Pilot bread could be found on every boat. You could snatch up one of the bland round wafers without removing your nylon picking gloves. They helped keep hunger pangs at bay when you were too busy to fix something to eat. Bag Balm is a strong but pleasant-smelling hand lotion. It resembles Vick's VapoRub with a yellow tint, and it helps keep hands from drying and chapping from the constant wetness. Salt water can take its toll if you don't take preventative measures.

All of the Snug fishermen fished their boats by themselves. No deckhands! I was no exception. It was a test of strength, because the *Not So Snug* had no hydraulics. All of the other Snug boats had hydraulic-powered reels to pull their nets. For the most part, I could do the job, but when the wind was up, or if I had gobs of fish, the chore was more than any man should have to do by himself.

Cook Inlet tides rip! Every six hours the tide rises or lowers twenty feet or so. When the high tides are at their biggest, they float logs and other goodies off the beaches. All this stuff ends up in the rips. Because we fished night and day, we had to stay alert. A rip tide could suck you into its trap in a matter of minutes if you dozed off. I've watched many fishermen lose their whole net to the "net-gobblers," logs or full-fledged trees that would get into their nets, and there would be no getting the net back. I had some close calls during my first couple of years, but always managed to get the net in before it was gobbled.

For the most part, we fished three 24-hour days each week: Monday, Wednesday, and Friday. Sometimes if there was enough escapement up the rivers, we would get to fish extra time. Talk about sleep deprivation and bloodshot eyes. The nights were the worst. Most of us would make a set just before it got totally dark. The name of the game was to set far enough away from the main rips, but close enough so you would have a good catch. Fortunately the nights were short. During some of the summer it doesn't get totally black dark. I would stand in the doorway of the cabin and strain my eyes and ears for a nasty rip that might be sneaking up on me. If the wind wasn't blowing, the only noise was fish hitting the net near the cork line. The excitement helped keep me awake.

All of the Snug boats were 32 feet except the *Not So Snug*. She was only 28 feet, and her capacity was much less than the others. Thankfully she had a bilge pump. It saved my buns a couple of times. One evening I was in the middle rip, and the weather started getting snotty. I could see fish hitting the net, so I didn't want to pull it in. In a short time the wind was blowing a gale. My stern kept rising way up on a wave, then slamming down, drenching me with green water. When I did start pulling the net, I soon realized that an intelligent person would have done so an hour earlier. I couldn't stop to pick the fish because I would have lost the momentum, and it would have been like starting all over again. With the wind now up to 35 knots, it took forever to get that net in. I had so many fish that the humongous pile of net and fish had my stern squatting big time. I didn't dare head southwesterly toward Snug Harbor, because the sea was coming from the northeast. I had to chug into it to try to get into the lee. The boat did only seven knots going with the tide on a flat sea. This was a wet, slow roller-coaster ride. There was getting to be lots of water in the bilge, so I had to tie the steering wheel in place so I could go below and turn the handle that engages the bilge pump. Yes, it sucked her dry. Of course I had to go down and disengage it too. This became procedure about every half hour. I was going three knots maximum, but by dark I was getting into calmer waters. When I got close enough to the beach, I dropped anchor and picked the gobs of fish out of the net and put them in the fish hold. As tired as I was, I grinned as I picked. Yep, just "a'pickin' and a'grinnin.'" I had more than 900 red salmon. It was my best day to date.

When I pulled up to our tender, the Chisik Island, Gabe smiled when he saw how low the boat was squatting. "Looks like ya did purty goode," he exclaimed in his Norwegian accent.

Not wanting anyone to think that I was bragging, I just replied, "I caught a few."

During those first years of my fishing career, we sold the salmon by the fish, not by the pound. Red salmon averaged more than seven pounds, and we were paid $1.40 for each one of the silvery gems. Dogs (Chum salmon) were worth 90¢ each.

It was a tough way to put in my first season as a "drifter," but it was rewarding. Joe Fribrock kept a list of all his boat fishermen and how they stood in amounts of fish caught. He kept the list in the store where everybody could see it. Joe took pity on me and asked me if I would like a real boat the next year. I was so happy when he said that I could fish the *Snug 3* that I would have done a back flip if I could have conquered such a maneuver.

I learned so much that first year with a boat. Running a boat by oneself requires dexterity and quickness. I honestly had no idea of the complexity of all that would be required of a boat operator. I didn't think a whole lot about it because I was so happy to have a boat to fish. You have to tie up to the pilings and docks with bow and stern lines. This is a feat that goes beyond most people's imagination. The pilings that served as moorings were thirty yards offshore, and were two feet in diameter. Most often the tide current would be running when you were approaching them, and usually there would be other Snug boats tied to some of the pilings. Also, remember that we had no deckhands. You were the skipper, deckhand, and cook. There was nobody to help. As you eased up to a piling, your bow-line had to be handy so that you could put the transmission in neutral and run out of the cabin to the bow, then swing the loose end of the bow-line around the fat piling and quickly tie it to the bow cleat. You would have to leave enough slack to be able to reach the stern piling. Then you ran back to the cabin and touched the shifting lever into reverse until you were almost to the stern piling. Then you put her into neutral and ran to the stern and did the same that you did on the bow. The first time I attempted this boat rodeo maneuver, I made sure that I had my lines in place and easy to get to. I also went to the very last pilings so that if I screwed up I wouldn't bump into any other boats. Besides that, I didn't want any of the "Outside" fishermen to see me if I fell into the water while trying to reach around the obese pilings. I remember how tense my body was while stretching my short arms around those pilings. Even on a brisk spring day, I wiped the sweat off my brow when I finished. Miraculously I never bumped anything too hard, and I didn't make a single "splash" scene.

You learn to row or "skuttle" a small skiff or "punt" to and from shore. I might note that it is super important that you do it like the old-timers. My grandfather had taught me this skill, so I had no problem with rowing. The difference was that all the seasoned Washington fishermen stood up and faced the bow of the punt while rowing. Important as anything was to wear a white, flat fisherman's hat and a tattered shirt and jacket that had the sleeves cut to elbow-length.

The boats were equipped with four-cylinder Ford diesels. It was my first experience with such a critter, so by the time I figured out where the oil dipstick was, it needed two quarts. Of course I had to learn how to make long and short splices in lines. (You don't dare call lines "ropes"!) Most of the Washington State high-liners wouldn't give me the time of night, but a few of them prided themselves on their knowledge and showed me some mariner stuff. A bowline was the most important knot to learn, because it doesn't cinch up, so it is easy to undo.

The Snug boats didn't have a galley or a head, but if you did have such luxuries, you would never refer to them as a kitchen or a toilet. Another thing was to learn and speak fishermen jargon, especially when using the radio. "How on that" was an expression that was used when you wanted to know what someone thought about what you had just told them. When the tide was coming in, it is the "flood." When it is going out, it's the "ebb," and when it's between tides, it's called "slack tide." Fortunately some super sleuth figured all this stuff out and published it in a "tide book." They say that the tides in Cook Inlet are second only to those in the Bay of Fundy at Nova Scotia. I can't emphasize enough what a 25- to 30-foot tide is capable of. When the tide is low, boats cannot get into or out of the Kenai and Kasilof rivers. If you made an attempt, you could get stuck in the mud and cause you to lose several hours of fishing. Because the tide switches from an incoming tide to an outgoing tide every six hours, it causes "rip-tides." The rips, especially the one that forms in the middle of the inlet, cause very turbulent water, as you can imagine. Add wind to the recipe, and you get some of the most wicked water known to man. Now add fog, and it has cooked up a condition that no mariner wants any part of. Almost always it produces a "confused sea" whose waves come from different directions. Waves in a rip can slam your boat from several directions. There were times when I fished the old planked-hull boats that I thought sure the planks would give way. The waves sometimes hit with such viciousness that it would turn the boat ninety degrees and then slam the vessel from a totally different direction.

Even on a fairly calm day, monster tides will move a boat thirty miles up or down the inlet in just six hours. If I happened to be fishing near the southern part of the inlet near the fishing closure, I might have to "buck the tide" for hours and hours in an attempt to get back to my home base. Going against the tide meant that the boat only gained one or two knots an hour.

When a person is vomiting, it is referred to as anything but vomit. I never got into the "gaggin' contest." My stomach never got riled. I absolutely never called Barf, nor Ralph, nor chummed for bait; nor did I puke my guts, or toss my cookies. Thank God for that, cuz I've watch others puke till the green bile came up, then dry-heave until they turned inside out. There was a big guy that came up every year and fished a Snug boat. One day we were lying on the beach in front of the cannery store when he asked me if I got sick. He told me how lucky I was after I told him that I never did. He said that he "heaved to" every day he was out there, even if it was calm. I haven't a clue why he continued to fish.

Doc Isaak's brother Ed came up from the States and begged me to take him out. He only had a week stay, so needed to go pronto. I pointed out to him that I was in the peak of the season, so would have to stay out the full 24-hour period. He replied, "No problem." Actually it's more like 36 hours, because you have to leave port in the wee hours so that when the period opens, you will hopefully have gone to where there are some fish. We hadn't been out of the Kasilof River more than ten minutes when Ed raced out and hung his head over the rail and urped up multi-colored morsels. I felt sorry for him, so I offered him something for breakfast. Yikes, he made another beeline for the rail. I'm not sure, but I think he called ralphhh that time. Anyhow, it was a fair amount of used food that he hurled. He was a slight man to start with, so I figured that he couldn't produce much more of the yummies. Wrong! He was out to set a record. I lost count, so I can't prove that he deserved the gold medal, but there was little doubt that he rightfully should have laid claim to some kind of a title.

When I made my first set of the day, the fish were hitting all along the net as it was going out. I filled the boat in six or seven hours. After delivering to our tender, which was anchored outside the river, I headed out and deck loaded the boat with more fish than the first time. I even had fish in the cabin. Slime and fish gurry—what a beautiful sight! Ed was now in the dry heave process, but I just didn't know what to do for him. He was such a gentleman. He would tell me between up-chucks that he was fine, and for me not to even think about going in. This guy was a man above all men. When I took him ashore that following night, he thanked and thanked me for taking him out. Most people would have begged me to push them overboard and let them die.

My youngest daughter, Nahanni, reminded me of a time when she was working on our fishing boat and had eaten a whole bag of Cheetos. The sea got progressively rougher, and she let loose with the ugliest orange puke! Not only was it ugly, but when she dashed for the rail, she didn't have time to think about the wind. One of the laws of the sea is never to pee or puke into the wind. Three guesses what happened to that poor little fart.

During the fifty some years that I now have been at sea, I've witnessed many world class gagging contests. I've seen big stout men, and a few women, feed the fish more than I could have believed that a human stomach could hold. My only regret is that I didn't film or video the greatness of all the super barfs. I could have made more money showing the video than I did with fishing.

Snug 3 was a dream boat compared to the *Not So Snug*. I couldn't believe how nice it was to fish a boat with hydraulics. The cabin even had a diesel stove that kept everything warm and dry. On the cold windy days, the salt spray would trickle down my neck and I would get chilled to the bone, so it was wonderful to go into the fo'c'sle and warm up. From down there, I could look out the aft door and watch my net. Then when I felt that it was time to pull it in, I would go to the stern and step on the treadle board that would engage the hydraulics and the reel brought the net in. Wow, what a difference from pulling it by hand. It allowed me to put all of my energy into picking fish, a chore at which I was getting faster. I had developed more confidence in my ability to catch fish, and I was determined to get my name moved up on Joe's list.

Fishing *Snug 3* wasn't all fun and frolic. All of the Snug boats were basic no frills, bare bones fishing vessels. Although there was a bulkhead that kept the fish from coming into the cabin, the gurry still went from stem to stern. The same was true for the salt water that would come in when you were picking fish or when rough weather deposited hundreds of gallons of water in the boats. There were no sealed decks or compartments to keep the water from filling the cabin and the fish hold. There was one small pump that ran off the engine, and it often was my salvation. There were two "rough sea" events when I nearly sank because the pump got plugged with fish gills and other parts. When that happened, I had to go down to the engine and take the faceplate off and then take the impeller out. Most of the time that would give me access to the junk that was plugging the pump, but sometimes I had to remove the hose also. All of this took time, and as I mentioned, there were two times that I nearly sank before I got the pump back together and pumped the water out. Both of those times the sea was lapping over the rails by the time I got the pump working.

During the first few years, I didn't realize that you could put too many fish in those boats. I had heard stories of guys filling their holds and then throwing fish down in the cabin because they brought up so many in their net. I didn't know that it had to be perfectly calm to pull off such a stunt or that you had to go very slowly so that you didn't swamp your boat. Sometimes the learning curve allows for zero mistakes.

At the end of my third year, I was at the top of Joe's list. I was a high-liner. I realized that I enjoyed competition. I was not content to leave the net in the water if it wasn't catching much. I was constantly looking for the "father lode," and most of the time it paid off. Some of the homesick fishermen from Outside left early each season, but I always stayed until the last fish went upstream to make out with a spawning female. Some of the tough old salts were quick to inform "lesser" fishermen that there was no time for sleep. "You can sleep in the winter" or "you can sleep when you die" was often heard from the old mariners. After I had fished 25 years or so, I found myself quoting those sayings to young, inexperienced fishermen. When the fish were there, you fished as hard as you could, and that meant 24 hours a day.

I knew that Joe liked me because every time a better boat became available, he would offer it to me. The last boats that he had built were the *Snug 24* and *25*. He gave me the *24* or *Two Dozen*, as he called it. If Joe were still around, I'd make it a point to give him that hug that I wanted to do when he gave me my start. A tall, slender man with a heart filled with love, his life ended prematurely in 1979. How bizarre it was that he died of a massive heart attack at age 54.

During the early years of my fishing career, I learned the importance of picking fish as fast as possible. If a fish was tangled badly, I would literally tear it out with my hands, even if it meant ripping the head off. My fingers got stouter and my hands were as tough as an old moose steak. The longer it took to pick a net, the longer it was out of the water. The old-timers always said that you couldn't catch fish with your net out of the water. I was determined to pick fish as fast as anyone so that I would be a high-liner. This philosophy seemed great until I found myself swinging my arms at night. The pain in my arms would wake me every hour. From my armpits to my fingertips, the tingling pain stole my sleep. If I got up and swung my arms for five minutes or so, I could get another hour of sleep. I didn't know it at the time, but I had carpal tunnel syndrome, big time. I just thought that it went with the territory. I suffered for more than twenty years before I found out that there was a name for the condition. I had both wrists operated on, and I've not had any problems since.

One of the other hardships that took its toll was rowing my skiff to and from my mooring in the swift Kasilof River. On many occasions I had to row as hard as I could to get to my boat, which was moored upstream from where I had to launch my skiff. The current would roar out at eight to ten knots and test the best of us. There were times that I would barely make it before my arms gave out.

Many times, yes, many times, my wife would wake me from a sound sleep and yell at me to stop rowing. I would be sitting up rowing in bed as fast as my arms could go. I was really glad that she would wake me, because usually I was losing ground.

Some of the worst events that took place during the years I fished the Snug boats occurred during storms. During the most violent northerly I'd experienced in Cook Inlet, one of the Snug fishermen came on the radio with a mayday. The storm had come up so violently and suddenly that all of us were taking a beating. It was getting almost impossible to pick our nets. Every so often a huge, white, cresting wave would hit the stern and dump its load in the boat. Then I would have to run to the engine room and put the water pump into gear. Fog had set in so thick that I couldn't see fifty feet. Previously, I had taken a land bearing, but none of us had any idea how far south the storm, accompanied by a huge ebb tide, might take us.

When the mayday came on, Toad said that his boat, the *Keta*, was breaking up, but he had no idea where he was. It was the first mayday that I had heard, and it gave me chills. It was a terrible feeling because I had no idea which direction he was from me. I began pulling the net in, but it was a painful, pounding chore. Every few feet of net that I gained, I got drenched by huge green waves hitting my stern. The few fish that I had were so tightly squished that it was super tough to get them out of the net.

The outside radio speaker blurted out another mayday! Bart, another fisherman from one of the Kenai canneries, had taken a green one through his windshield. He was cut badly and his boat was taking on lots of water. Again, no one had any clue to his whereabouts because none of the boats were equipped with any electronics in those days.

Unbeknownst to any of the fleet, Toad had a stroke of good luck. Just before his boat sank, it washed up on a small island at the entrance of

Chinitna Bay. He jumped off and barely got wet! We found out later that Bart was able to pump the water out of his boat and he also had survived.

When I first spotted land after traveling northeast for hours, I couldn't identify it because of the fog. Without a fathometer, I didn't dare go closer. I figured that I had been blown south, so I headed north. It was all I could do to hang on to the wheel. Several hours went by and I still didn't recognize the shoreline. I was beginning to wonder if I had gone too far north. If I could have seen the mountains in the background, I would have had a better idea of my bearings. I had been pounding against the angry northerly for more than six hours when I noticed the beach appear to the west. I was apprehensive, but followed the shoreline. The sea was calming. I faintly saw something white to the starboard. I couldn't believe it: there was my safe haven, Snug Harbor.

Another Cook Inlet storm that I remember well was a strong southerly. Again, the fleet was not having fun, and again there was a mayday. Although the sea was mountainous, there was little fog. The mayday came from a small bow picker, and he knew his position. He was just north of Humpy Point. I was close and had just picked up my net, so I headed to where I thought he must be. Sure enough, he was within a quarter mile of the beach. I got alongside him and tied my buoys between us to absorb the pounding. His little boat was really low in the water. I hollered for him to break out his side window so we could put the intake hose from my pump in to pump the water out. I told him NOT to let anything get into the hose that would plug it up. I had pumped a good steady stream for a minute or two when suddenly it quit. It was plugged. Soon the boat began to sink, so I hollered for the guy and his deckhand to jump over to my boat, and then I cut the lines. She sank like a rock. I took those two soaked, dismal guys into the Kasilof River, and they just walked away not saying a word.

Kasilof's population was primarily fishermen, and everybody knew each other. We were a tight community of mariners that watched out for one another. Gillnetting salmon in Cook Inlet is normally fairly safe, but on one particularly rough day, a heart-wrenching cry for help came over the radio. The ten-foot sea was tough to fish, but the tough guys go out no matter what because it's what they do. All of us recognized the anguished sound to be Poopdeck's. His real name was Clarence Platt, but nobody called him by his real name. He had been down in the engine room adjusting the hydraulic belt when he got his hand caught in it. It ripped all but one of his fingers off! He gave his location as "a couple miles outside the sisters." The sisters are two huge rocks that stick out of the water near Clam Gulch. I pulled my net in as quickly as I could because I knew that I must be close by, and Poopdeck was a good friend. Within ten minutes I spotted his boat, which was rocking violently because the wind made it ride crossways to the rough sea. Billy and Jack Duncan, Grant Fritz, and George Ryden were already there, but there was no way that anyone could approach Poopdeck's boat because of the danger of a devastating collision. None of us had a deckhand, so there was no way to attempt to have someone jump over to Poopdeck's boat. The Coast Guard informed us that they were sending a helicopter to help, so while we stood by, we positioned our boats on the windward side of Poopdeck so that our boats would break the sea and make it somewhat calmer. When the helicopter neared, someone suggested pumping diesel oil on the water. A couple of us were able to accomplish this by putting our water suction hose into the diesel fuel tank. Oil of any kind smoothes the water on contact. It made enough difference that the helicopter was able to lower a man down to put Poopdeck in the hoist and lift him into the helicopter. They saved his life, but Poopdeck had to fish the rest of his years with three fewer fingers. He claimed that the one remaining finger made a "good fish pick," and it was excellent for picking his nose.

George Ryden was a man of many talents, one of which was skiing. During the winter, George was on the ski patrol at Alyeska, a ski resort south of Anchorage. He was the first guy I knew that built his own boat. Welding came easy to George, so he built his boat, the *Skilak*, with steel. The *Skilak* was 36 feet and appeared to be very seaworthy. George fished salmon in Cook Inlet during the summer, and then tendered fish from Cottonwood Bay, which is located on the southwest part of the inlet. I was also tendering from Chinitna Bay, which is north of where George was hauling fish. I had just gotten to Per Osmar's cannery in the Kasilof River with a load of fish when someone came on the radio and said that George was missing. No one had seen him since he departed Cottonwood with a full load of salmon.

There was still no sign of the *Skilak* by the next morning, so all of us fishermen from Kasilof went out searching for him. The Coast Guard joined us, and we set up a grid for each boat to scour. After a couple of days of extensive searching, it appeared that the *Skilak* had gone to the bottom. Shortly after the mishap, we formed a Coast Guard Auxiliary flotilla at Kasilof.

The early 60s didn't produce very good salmon returns. All of the local fishermen had to get jobs after the season. I had joined the labor union in 1963, which made it easier to land a job. I always had work, but so often it would take me away from home.

Oil had been discovered in northern Cook Inlet, and they erected several platforms at each drill site. Of course they needed a pipeline from each platform to shore, so when the project began, I went to work as a laborer. Harold and Toot and some of my other local friends got on the job too. We were shuttled out to a herky-sized quarters barge that was anchored in the middle of the inlet. It had housing for all of the workers, and I'm guessing that there were 150 or so. The workers included pipeline welders and helpers, crane operators, laborers, and a bunch of "coon asses." Well, that's what they called the guys that came up from Louisiana to run the job. Until this pipeline in the inlet started, nobody had ever attempted laying pipe in the big tides of Cook Inlet. Coon asses know how to do pipelines. There was a slight obstacle working with these gents from the Okefenokee Swamp though. None of us Alaskans could understand what they were saying. They had their own language. It had French mixed with something else.

Even for these guys that had done nothing but lay pipe all their lives, this would be their greatest challenge ever. How could they keep the lay barge from being swept up or down the inlet? The thirty-foot tides would be a horrendous bit of nature to overcome. Until the day that we were taken to the lay barge, all of us Alaskans were skeptical about the success of the project. As we approached the site we were amazed to see that the lay barge was very close to one of the stationary oil platforms and that it was being held in place by three anchor cables on each side and three of the biggest tugboats in existence. The tugs were all pushing against the south side of the barge.

We had been transported on the open deck of a 100-foot steel vessel, and upon arrival were instructed to jump from our rail to the rail of the barge. It appeared a bit dangerous, but one of the Louisianans clambered up and over to the barge with the agility of a spider monkey. Quite intimidating, but we followed without hesitation. A real Alaskan fears nothing, right?

After a short orientation, we were assigned duties, and we began laying the first underwater pipeline in Cook Inlet. It was totally awesome to watch such expertise in motion. One man orchestrated the operation from a tower above the main cabin with the same professionalism as a symphony conductor. When the tides were at full force, the tugs were at full power, and as the tide was nearing high or low water, they had to slack off accordingly. Precisely at high or low water, they would switch sides and push from the opposite side. When they performed this feat, they would throw a heaving line to a few of us laborers, and we would pull their huge bow lines to the sturdy cleats on the barge and make them secure. The heaving lines had a ball, referred to as a "monkey fist," and when it came hurling over to us, we had to keep a close eye on it so it didn't hit us. It wasn't easy to see at night because the bright lights from the tugs would be shining in our faces. Sure enough, one hit me square in the right eye and gave me a dandy shiner.

Even though we couldn't understand most of the instructions from the coon-ass bosses, we figured out what had to be done. We would hook cables on each end of one of the heavy cement-covered twelve-inch pipes that were stacked on deck, and the crane would lift it and set it in place for the welders to adjoin to the previous pipe. Then the anchors would be adjusted to pull the pipe into the silt-laden inlet water. To accomplish this feat, some anchors had to be winched in at the same time that others were winched out. To my knowledge, no anchor cables were ever broken, which was remarkable.

Our shifts were thirteen hours a day, seven days a week. We got no breaks until a line was finished. This made a problem when I broke my finger. I was hooking a cable on a full drum of fuel when a boss got in a hurry and rolled it over my finger. Yikes, that smarted! I told him that he broke my finger, but he just shrugged his shoulder and walked off. I had a buddy splint it with some Popsicle sticks, and it stayed that way for several days until we finished that line. Then they sent me to Anchorage on a helicopter to get it straightened and splinted again. Within a few hours, I was back on the job.

We were working more than ninety hours a week, so we were all getting financially well off. The pipeline jobs attract gamblers, and this job was no exception. Every night six to ten guys would play poker. It was super entertainment for us non-gamblers. Some of these guys would lose their whole check plus gold nugget watches and anything else they owned. Scuttlebutt had it that one of the guys said he would let his opponent sleep with his wife if he lost the hand. The guys were on the other shift, so I never found out what the outcome was.

When the job was over, I told my daughters that I was going to take them to Anchorage to buy them some new clothes. They were ecstatic, to say the least. It was so much fun watching them trying to decide which rags would look best on them. Fortunately for me, the stores closed at 9:00, so the shopping came to an end. I took my happy family to a nice restaurant and let them gorge themselves with their favorite food. It was rare that we splurged like we did on that trip, so all of the girls were quite giddy on the trip home.

There were several feet of snow in Turnagain Pass, and I had the car heater fan on its highest setting to keep the windows from frosting. The road had snow pack, but it was good winter driving conditions. I was going down a long, gradual hill when my headlights picked up the forms of two moose in the road. I immediately started pumping the brakes. If I pushed the brakes too hard, the car would slide. I could tell that one of the moose was a big cow, and the other was its calf. They were facing each other and had both lanes blocked. On my left was a huge drop-off, so I kept to the right, but there was no way I was going to stop in time. Just before I reached the point of impact, the cow moved into my lane and the calf went into the left lane. The snow was so deep that the critters couldn't get off the road. When I hit that big mama, her front legs went over the right side of the car, and her hind legs went over the left side. Her body smashed the windshield into a million pieces, all of which came into the car. Our car stopped in the deep snow. The moose was standing behind us and appeared to be fine except for a stomachache.

No one made a noise except for Laurie. She let out a bloodcurdling scream that made me think she had been badly injured by the flying glass. After examining everybody, I found that I had a couple of small facial cuts, but the kids and my wife were fine. Laurie was only scared, so I calmed her and then got out to survey the situation. Other than being stuck in the snow and not having a windshield, we were okay. A car was coming from behind, so I blinked my brake lights to warn him to slow down. When he got close, he could readily tell what had happened, so he stopped to help.

He offered me his shovel to dig out of the deep stuff, and then he said he would take my family to Summit Lake Lodge, which was only a few miles away. I took him up on the offer, and as they drove off, I began the task of shoveling. Within a half hour, I was able to back out of the snow bank and head down the road. It was 20° below zero, so my face was just about frozen by the time I got to the lodge. The fellow that owned the place handed me a cup of hot chocolate and asked me for the keys to my car. My family was nice and cozy by the huge fireplace, and we talked about how lucky we were that nobody was hurt.

The lodge owner came in and told me to come with him to his shop. He had taken a piece of Visqueen plastic sheeting and duct-taped it to the windshield frame. His goodness was so Alaskan. I offered to pay him for everything that he had done for us, but he contended that anyone would do the same. He was so right. Alaskans always help those in need. The Visqueen worked great and got us home without tearing.

———◦◦◦———

During the late 60s, I took my 20-foot skiff to Prince William Sound to harvest kelp with herring eggs. The Japanese had a passion for the stuff, which they referred to as Kombu Kazunoko. I got Vern Savage from Seldovia to tow my skiff behind his 70-foot boat, which he would be using as a kelp tender. Named the Celtic, it was a deep-draught World War II ship that had been used to haul garbage. I ran the boat most of the way, and in return Vern thanked me and didn't charge me a penny for towing my skiff to the sound. I was a pioneer in that fishery, but had learned that the kelp was harvested by use of a grappling hook, so I had welded a few hooks together, which proved to do a great job. The kelp was found in waters that were ten to twenty feet deep. I tied a line to the grappling, and heaved it and heaved it, each time bringing in ribbon kelp covered with white herring eggs. I delivered load after load to the tender every day. The Japanese technician aboard the tender smiled every time he saw me come alongside with my big red skiff.

Anyhow, the following year I took my Snug boat, and Seth Wright, whom I had met the year before. There was another reason besides kelp that we were both excited about going over there: seals! The year before, I couldn't help noticing that there was an abundance of seals in the sound. We arrived a week or so before the herring did, so we hunted. There was a three-dollar bounty on seals because there were so many that they were eating themselves out of house and home. I had brought a small skiff for the occasion, and I would drop Seth off on a rock so he could get a rest for his rifle. Seth and I were born hunters, and Seth was a real marksman. I don't remember seeing him miss. We made enough money from the seal hunting to pay for all our expenses. Both of us suffered from tossing the grappling so much once the herring came, but we left with muscles and money.

We didn't get away from Prince William Sound soon enough, though. There were still several feet of snow even down to the beaches, but I knew it was time for the bears to come out of their dens. On the last day of kelping, the wind was coming up, so we headed for shelter at a small cove on Montague Island. It was getting dark when we dropped our 40-pound Danforth anchor. We were fifty feet from shore, and there was plenty of shelter with the gigantic spruce trees and mountains in front of us. There was a reef 150 feet behind us. It seemed to be a perfect place to sit out the wind. Just before we got to our anchorage, I heard a skipper on a big boat talking to another skipper, both of whom were anchored in a bay twenty miles east of us. He was recording fifty to sixty on his anemometer. Somehow, the wind was finding its way over the mountains and trees, and hitting us like there were no obstacles in its way.

Seth looked out the window and said in a loud voice, "Blow if you get a chance!"

The legendary god Kushtaka must have been listening, because it did blow! It blew so hard that it ripped the windshield wipers and the stove stack and everything except the cabin off. All of a sudden I could tell by the feel that we were dragging anchor. I started the engine and told Seth to pull the anchor in while I jogged into it. He went out, and as he was creeping along the side, the wind blew him off! I put the shifter in neutral and ran out there. It almost blew me off too. Seth was half in the water and half out. I grabbed his arm and pulled him up on deck. I scampered back inside as quickly as I could because I knew that we were in danger of going on the reef and would surely die if we did. I put her in gear and turned the wheel hard over. Seth had crawled to the bow and was pulling the slack anchor line. With the blackness of the night and all the rain hitting the window, I couldn't see land at all. I just pointed the bow toward the magnetic heading for the beach. The only light that I had was a flashlight. I could see that Seth had gotten all of the slack line in, but couldn't pull the anchor chain to the surface because it had a ton of bull-kelp on it. He tied it off on the cleat and came inside. I asked him if he thought he could take a knife and cut the kelp off. He courageously tried, but again almost got blown off. When he got in, I told him that he was to stay in because I didn't want to go back home by myself. I jogged on my position as best as I could by the compass.

I did good for an hour or two, but then came the most feared noise: *clank, clank.* Oh no, the anchor chain was wrapping around the prop! I had gone ahead too much. I immediately put it in neutral, and then touched it briefly in reverse. *Clank, clank* again. I shined the flashlight out the side window and saw that we were broadside to the sea. Not good! I turned the wheel and held my breath when I gingerly put it in gear. Wow, no clanking! I barely idled towards my heading. I was praying to God, but didn't know if He could hear me because of the wind noise. I guess He did, because it was definitely a miracle that I managed to keep us alive for the remainder of the night. At the first sign of daylight, the wind subsided slightly. When I was sure that we weren't going to go on the reef, we both went out and pulled anchor. I couldn't believe the massive amount of bull kelp that was on the chain and anchor. Both of us used sharp knives to cut it and get the anchor up. We found a better beach just a short ways to the west, so we dropped anchor again.

I turned the radio on just in time to hear the same skipper talking to his buddy, and he commented that during the night his anemometer pegged out at 125. Had I known at the time that Kushtaka could be warded off by copper, urine, or fire, I would have peed on him—except that the wind had been blowing so hard at the time that I couldn't have peed over the side if I'd tried.

We slept for a few hours, but even though the wind had died, I got up to see if all was okay. The first thing that I saw was a brown bear standing on his hind legs and rubbing his back against a tree. Well now, wouldn't that be a bonus to get a nice bear. I got the binoculars and took a good look. I thought he was no more than eight feet, but I needed to get a closer peek.

I guess that I was muttering out loud, because when Seth heard me, he jumped up and said, "You don't really see a bear, do you?"

"I surely do, and I'm going to put the skiff in the water and shoot him if he's big enough." I snapped up my 30.06 and quietly rowed to shore. I realized then that the trees were giants there and would dwarf a ten-foot bear. He was on all fours now and headed toward me. I got down on one knee, and when he was about 75 feet away, he turned broadside. I aimed the scope just behind the shoulder and squeezed it off. He let out the biggest roar and came right at me. Damn! I racked another round in and shot at a mass of fur, which was all I could see in the scope, he was so close. He dropped a few feet in front of me, and I remember letting out a sigh of relief. He looked much bigger now. I rowed out and got Seth, who was more excited than I was. It took us forever to skin that gargantuan, because he was too big to roll over. We measured his hide, and without pulling it tight, it squared 10 ½ feet. He was a beautiful chocolate color, and even though we saw him rubbing, his coat was thick and in good shape.

As we headed southwesterly toward home, the Gulf of Alaska reminded us that the sea has a way of keeping us on our toes. Long before we reached Gore Point I could see the black line of rough seas ahead. I knew that we would have to batten down the hatches because the wind and waves would make traveling uncomfortable. The wind was only blowing thirty knots, but the rip at the point was standing on end, and we fought 25-foot foamy waves. It took us forever, but when we got around the point, the sea mellowed dramatically.

That was an ending of a super adventurous trip that surely we would never forget. People sometimes wondered why I didn't quit the mariner lifestyle, but the thought never crossed my mind. Events like the one that I just described seem to have a luring affect.

Seth got his own boat and fished the inlet for salmon also. He was genuine, a fun buddy, and he enjoyed outdoor life to the limit.

Cook Inlet didn't have that many storms during the summer months when we were fishing. As a matter of fact, there were lots more good days than bad. The greatest times were when I had big catches. The first time that I "deck loaded" was the first year that I fished *Snug 3*. It was about the fifteenth of July, which is generally when the red salmon run peaks out in Cook Inlet. The fleet came out of their respective ports during the wee hours. Radio reports from all the major ports were the same. The wind was southerly and the sea was four to five feet. It made tough going for the fleets that came out of Kenai and Kasilof rivers because they had to travel more slowly into the sea as they headed south. Even though a five-foot sea is not that bad, it does make it hard to see salmon when they jump out of the water. Visibility was much better for us Snug boats because we had the sea on our tail and didn't have the spray on our windshields. You could tell by the radio conversations that tensions were high. It was nonstop chatter on all four channels.

I had been traveling for only two hours when I started seeing jumpers amongst the waves. I slowed to an idle to get a better look. Within minutes I could see jumpers in every direction. We still had half an hour before we could put our nets in the water, so I made sure that I had every-thing ready.

One of the Snug boats cruised up to me as I stood on deck drinking my last half-cup of coffee. "See any jumpers?" he asked.

Trying not to sound like I had seen much, I answered, "I saw a couple." I didn't like the guy because he usually acted like I didn't exist. I couldn›t believe that he hadn›t seen all the jumpers. He took off, and the last I saw him he was a speck on the horizon.

It seemed like it took forever before it was time to fish, but finally the hour hand was straight up. I threw the buoy out and the first couple of fathoms of net that I had pulled off the reel. Not only did *Snug 3* have a hydraulic reel, but she was also equipped with a throttle and shifting control in the stern and in the cabin. I eased the control into forward and began reeling out the net. Before the first fifty feet was out, fish were hitting the cork line. By the time I got the whole 150 fathoms in the water, the net was smoking with red salmon. I had never seen anything like that, and I remem-ber hollering, "Yes, sweet mama!"

I can't say how much time went by, but probably not more than thirty or forty minutes, and all the while salmon kept splashing when they got gilled in the net. I decided that I had better pull some of the net in because I had heard fishermen talk about their nets getting so heavy with fish that the net sank. When that happens, it is almost impossible to get the net back. I picked solid grapes (salmon), and when I had half the net in, I decided to put it back in the water and go to pick grapes from the other end. By then the sea was calming. All the time I was picking fish from the far end, fish kept slamming the near end. I was so happy that I never felt any exhaustion. I picked half of the net and then changed ends several times. The only time I took a break was when my good friend Keith called me on the radio. He said that he could see me with his binoculars from where he was and could tell I was doing good, and that he was too. We both knew better than to give away our position on the radio, because the whole fleet would descend upon us. I couldn't believe how fast the day had gone by when Keith said that we had better pick up our nets because it was getting late. The tide had pushed us a long way up the inlet, so we would have to go to Kenai to deliver our fish.

When I finished picking the last fish it was 6 p.m., and that was when the period came to a close. It was only when I brought my buoy in that I noticed that *Snug 3* was squatting so badly that she had only a few inches of freeboard. I didn't realize how lucky I was that it was glassy calm. I was leveling the boat by pitching fish forward into the cabin when Keith and his dad, Vern, came over to see how I had done. They insisted that they tie their boats to both sides of mine to keep me afloat. Their assistance got me to the tender where I made one of the biggest deliveries ever.

Without a doubt though, I will state that "Big Saturday" takes the honor of first place when it comes to big catches. The day took place many years, a wife, and several boats later. We had been having a mediocre season and were shut down by Fish and Game until such time that they were sure of having enough escapement. We sat and waited. Three days went by with no word. We took our 43-foot boat down to Homer to make some minor repairs. My boy, Eric, was with us at the time. Even at fourteen years old, he was a good fisherman. We were at our float in the harbor when a fellow fisherman ran toward his boat, hollering that there was an emergency opening. Luckily I had fueled up when we got to Homer. Off we went at full bore. I knew that the fish would be way up north, so my twin engines were screaming. The opening was to start at noon. Most openings are on weekdays at 7 a.m., so this one was a rarity.

By then I had three radios, and they were all on, but I couldn't hear anybody, which was an indication, of course, that all the boats were a long distance away. I kept my nose pointed north. The black smoke was billowing out the stacks. Finally after three hours of full bore, I began to hear some chatter coming from one of the radios. I faintly heard one of my Kenaitze Indian friends, Gordy Baktuit, tell Georgie Peterson, another Indian friend, that he was seeing popcorn. That meant that he was seeing bookoos jumpers. I knew that he had just come out of the Kenai River, so I held my course and arrived at the scene at 11:45.

I had a white-line recorder, and it was showing me numerous dots, indicating gobs of sockeye salmon under me. At straight up noon, I let the net fly out the stern. It was a flat calm, sunny day. There wasn't much action on the cork line, so I was soon getting nervous. I watched intently. I could see the net wiggling the full length. All of the 150 fathoms was wiggling! The cork line didn't have much splashing going on, but I had plenty of experience, so I knew that the fish were hitting lower on the net.

I took the Zodiac down and put her in the water. I paddled out and snapped buoys on the cork line. There are not many things worse than a sunken net, and too many fish can sink the whole thing. In a short time, the net began to sag. I grabbed the video camera and got some shots of the corks going down. I told my wife to get ready to pick. Never having seen a net so full of "grapes," she didn't realize that it could present a problem. The period was just a six-hour opening, and it takes a long time to pick a full net. These red salmon were huge. They were close to a ten pound average, and the net had grapes from one end to the other. We were definitely "a'pickin' and a'grinnin.'" I sang my grape pickin' song. Yes, I was a tad bit happy.

When we were done, our 43-foot boat was lower in the water than anybody else's. We had to put the last fifty feet of net on the reel fish and all so that we had the net out of the water by the closure at 6 p.m. I was really glad that I had Eric and Winnie aboard. Eric pitched all the fish into the hold, and Winnie picked fish like a pro. When we pulled into the Kasilof River to deliver, our boat was squatting big-time. It took a while to transfer more than 25,000 pounds of prime bright red salmon. That, my friends, was a mother lode and was what it is all about.

Meanwhile, today is one of those days that aren't fit for man or beast, or even a snowman. While I write in my cozy log house, Kushtaka is having a wind party. It's snowing and blowing a gale out there.

The day was unusually warm which allowed me to pick the red salmon without cold weather clothing. This was during the mid-sixties.

One of the Snug boats that I fished during the 60s and 70s.

I had been fishing a few short years when the "people of steel," Bob Chabot and his Amazon wife, Vita, cruised into Snug Harbor with their new state-of-the-art boat. Until that time, no one had ever laid eyes on a fiberglass boat with twin engines. Most of the seasoned fishermen made comments about the stupidity of the design, but they would have to eat their words when the Chabot's consistently caught more fish than most of them. The Double Dare was fast, allowing this muscular, tall, lean couple to excel by getting to the fish quicker. It opened the eyes of many, including me, and I vowed that I would someday have a boat of my own, and it would be fast!

After fishing the Snug boats for a dozen years, I finally bought my own boat, which I named the *Variant*. She was several knots faster than the Snug boats, and she even had a flying bridge. *Variant* was not a cute or seductive name, but a name that she would live up to. She was equipped with a davit and a hydraulic winch, which would allow me to fish crab and long-line halibut more efficiently. I've since told several people about the importance of christening a boat with a proper name. If you're thinking I could have stood some improvement in thinking up a cool name, you're right.

It was like when I named my kids. I didn't have good foresight or imagination when I named the first five, but as I matured through the years, I did much better naming my last child. She was a water baby, so it was fitting that I gave her water names. NAHANNI DESHKA IWALANI YENTNA WILLS is what appears on her birth certificate. Great name, huh?

Perhaps it's a good idea never to name a boat after anyone, because it's sort of like getting a tattoo. Once you've done it, you might be sorry later. This is just another reason to give serious thought to that new boat that you are about to get. Write lots of names down and look at them for a while before selecting the best one. You might even ask some of your mariner friends to select their favorite name from your list. I did that once but didn't like the one that got the most votes, so I chose the one that appealed to me the most. Ha!

I've had several boats during the course of my life, and I have to say that I most enjoyed the name of the last commercial fishing boat that I had. I named her *Bronze Maiden*. She was as beautiful as a smooth-skinned, in-shape, young South Pacific lady like my wife. I had her custom built from stem to stern, inside out. She was fast and sleek. She was also trouble free

Fueling our PA-12.

and a great sea boat. I loved her and took good care of her. When I got her, I suddenly realized how far I had come in the boat world. From the 6-knot wooden *Not So Snug*, to the fiberglass 20-knot super modern *Bronze Maiden*.

From salmon fishing, I entered into other fisheries, which included halibut, crab, herring, and others. If it wiggled, I fished it. This is what I did for forty some years of my productive life.

Chapter 6

A Baby Boy and a Shake

In the wee hours of January 1, 1964, my wife went into labor. I took her into Soldotna and called Dr. Isaak. We met him at his office, and after making my wifie comfortable, Doc instructed me on how to help. Then Doc and I talked hunting. Her screams sure made it hard to concentrate on our storytelling. After a few hours, out came a head. I pretty well knew that it would be another girl. After all, I already had four. Well, darned if it wasn't a boy! Yep, it had a penis. We hadn't even talked about a name for a boy. That would take some thought. It's somewhat like naming a boat. You want a name that makes you feel good, one that you can live with for a long time, one that sounds strong and noble, but doesn't put too much of a burden on the kid. Cute names don't get it, and we didn't want the kid to have to fight all the time, so names like Pansy and Marion were out. If we used one of the heavy-duty names like Oluf or Zeus, he would have to grow to be as big as a log. Such an outcome was doubtful, considering his fairly short parents. It's tough naming a kid. It's especially tough when you were expecting another girl. The best we could come up with was Eric.

Eric was almost three months old when an earth-shattering event happened. I had allowed someone to talk me into giving a Good Friday sermon at our new Lutheran Church, a first for me, and I was fairly nervous about it. I had just finished eating some moose meat and taters, and had picked up Eric, who was then three months old, and taken him to the living room where I had started going over my sermon when it struck. I've never been able to do justice in relating the event, but I'll give it to you the best I can.

Our log house began to shake. It started as a slow rocking motion and quickly developed into the most violent earthquake ever recorded on the North American continent. I held on to Eric with one hand and the wall with the other. My wife and the girls were still at the kitchen table, hanging on for dear life. Our car, which was parked by the house, hopped down the hill. The tall spruce trees began swaying, and in a short time the ground was rolling and the tops of the trees were almost touching the ground. The lake, which is 75 feet from the house and had been frozen to a depth of five feet, was now filled with monstrous ice cubes. The cubes were churning as if in a special-effects movie. It was a jumbled mess. A crack opened a foot or so outside the living room window. But it soon closed. I couldn't believe that the house hadn't already collapsed on top of us, but there was no way that I would go outside either. The cement block chimney for the wood stove banged back and forth so hard that I was sure it would soon come tumbling down. During the next four to five minutes, the quake was relentless. I felt that it was THE END OF THE WORLD! It seemed like an eternity. A couple of our girls were renowned for screaming, but I didn't hear anything except for the outrageous noises that the house was making. That doesn't mean that they weren't screaming, only that I was so consumed with the ravages of the quake that I didn't hear them. Finally the ground waves subsided. The house still creaked and groaned, but it too was quieting. It was strong and endured.

The girls came and surrounded me and hugged me tight. They probably wondered, like me, if it was over or if there was worse to come. For several hours there were after-shocks that shook more than most quakes, but nothing like the first one. We had all survived by huddling inside the house, so we didn't know if we should venture outside. There would be no sermon that evening!

Our Reflection Lake homestead was approximately 150 miles west of the epicenter of the quake, and yet it would be hard for anyone to convince me that a quake could get any worse. It measured 9.2 on the Richter scale. It was, without dispute, the mother of all quakes. The tsunamis that were born from it killed people near and far. People more than 2000 miles to the south in California died from the tsunami. The one that hit Seward, Alaska, was ninety feet tall, and caused all of the boats to be scattered a mile inland. The lower third of the town was demolished, and the railroad was no more. Kodiak also had boats so high and far away from the water that it was hard to believe that it was possible.

In the aftermath, the only communication that Alaska had with the rest of the world was ham radio, and there weren't many of those. It was several days before the outside world learned of the devastation. Anchorage was in shambles. In the southern part of town there were houses that looked like the ice on my lake. Some were nearly upside down. Right in downtown there were parts where one side of a street was twenty feet or so lower than the other side. All of the bridges between the Kenai Peninsula and Anchorage were gone or beyond repair. Towns were without sewer and water lines.

There was a bit of good news. The quake struck at 5:24 p.m. or thereabouts. Because of the time of day, not too many people perished. School was out. Workers had gone home. The death toll might have been many times over if it had occurred two hours sooner.

Railroads, buildings, roads, sewer and water lines all had to be rebuilt. Within days, I went to work for the State Highway Department and replaced some of the bridges with army Bailey bridges, a kind of light, very strong prefabricated truss bridge that can be constructed quickly with relatively little manpower. Then I went to Seward and worked on the water and sewer lines. Duane LeVan and I had the job of scooting through all the sewer lines in Seward and inspecting them for damage.

For those of you that haven't scooted down a dark two-foot diameter sewer pipe, let me put a little light on the subject. I was equipped with three items before going down one of the access culverts: a headlamp, an auto repair creeper, and a large round camera. These were the only tools we needed to document the damage that the quake had inflicted on the pipes. There was no need to show proof that we were college grads with a 4.0 grade average. Actually the only requirements were that we were small enough to fit in a two-foot pipe, and that we weren't claustrophobic The bosses were not small enough to get in there to retrieve us if we panicked and got stuck.

For the most part, the smell wasn't as bad as I thought it might be. I think that the 90-foot tidal wave that followed the quake went into the sewer system and cleaned a lot of the sewage out. My headlamp never went out, but a couple of times my calves cramped from pushing the creeper with my toes. Sometimes a line would be as short as fifty feet; others were several hundred feet. The long ones made me wonder if I was ever going to see the light again, especially if my creeper got stuck in a large crack.

I not only made some much-needed money, but met lots of "real" Alaskan folks, many of whom have been friends ever since. So, as the saying goes, some good comes from the bad. I finished working just in time to go fishing. Although it wasn't a great season, it was my best since I started.

When the fishing season was over, I built an addition on our house. The family was growing, and I could see that the girls would soon be disgruntled if they had to share a bedroom with a boy. While I was working on one of the bridge jobs, a fellow told me that I'd better stop having kids or I'd "screw myself out of a place at the table." Both my wife and I agreed that we had produced more than our share of kids. After all, we filled a whole pew at church. We had four lovely girls and one baby boy that was doomed by having four older sisters.

That Thanksgiving I shot a super-sized moose. He was only 100 feet off the road, but the snow was nearly four feet deep. I dumped the guts and then headed home to get a saw and my pack and some linen bags to put the meat in. When I got home, Woody was there visiting. He was more than willing to come and help me. When he saw the size of the antlers, he said that they would make a great handhold. He went on to add that we could cut the critter in half, and then drag it out a half at a time. I told him that there was no way that we could drag or push or whatever a moose so big. He insisted, so we cut it in half, and it was like I thought: we barely budged it. It would have to be done piece by piece, as always. Take the front shoulder off, then the ham, then the back strap and the ribs. Then roll it over and repeat the same on the other side. Lastly, dive in and retrieve the heart and liver.

I guess you can tell that 1964 was a tad more than memorable. The best reason for celebration was that I had a boy named Eric, plus we had 700 or more pounds of meat for all seven of us to gnaw on. The smell of moose steaks frying has always been one of my favorite olfactory delights.

Speaking of smells, coffee comes to mind. Before coming to Alaska, I had never had a cup of coffee. I tasted it once, but it didn't appeal to me. Whenever we visited any of our new Alaskan friends, they would pour us a cup. I guess they assumed that everybody drank coffee. To avoid offending any of them, we would politely drink some. When our cups were half empty, they would refill them. We soon began to enjoy the stuff, especially on a cold morning. Now the fragrance of fresh ground and brewed coffee is also amongst my favorite smells. For the past fifteen or so years, I've ground fresh dark roast beans daily and brewed some very strong coffee. Two cups a day is plenty, but oh, so good.

We bought a cow from Zeke Shadura, our neighbor to the south. It was on a Sunday that the transaction occurred, so we named it Sunday. We had all the milk that we needed for the whole family, but we were going to need hay for the coming winter. I heard that Bud Tri had some for sale, so I went to his place and bought a big stack of the dried grass from him. Even though Bud had only one arm, he was constantly working. We became good friends, and as winter neared, Bud proposed that he bring his sawmill to my home- stead and make lumber. I had a small dozer, so I could cut the trees and pull the logs to the mill, and Bud would make the lumber. We shared the lumber 50-50. It was awesome to watch him handle those big logs with only one arm.

One time I took my Jeep pick-up to Bud's to get a load of hay. I loaded the truck to the hilt and then tied it down with lines going every direction. On the way home I had to stop at the Kasilof Post Office to get our mail. We generally went there once a week. Charlie and Isabelle Heckel ran the office, and they always shared all of the local gossip with us, so it became a weekly source of entertainment. The first thing Charlie said when he saw me drive in was, "You have a pretty fair JAG on your truck."

I hadn't heard the word "JAG" before, so I replied, "Yep, it's a good- sized load."

"No, Jerre, it's not what we call a load. I think that you could've gotten some more on, so it's just a JAG." Charlie also informed me that he and Isa- belle had voted against statehood, and he knew one other couple that did the same, but now everybody that came in claimed to have voted against it. It seemed that they didn't like the results of statehood.

Bud bought a small plane and took just enough lessons to allow him to take off and land. Even with one arm, he seemed to do fine. One nice, sunny, summer day he got in that little plane of his and took off from the Soldotna Airport. He came directly over our place and buzzed our house. We waved as he pulled up and continued south. It looked like he was pulling it up too steep, but the trees blocked our view, so we thought that he went on to his place. Later that day, we found that he stalled out and crashed into Zeke's lake, just south of us. They eventually found his plane and body in fifty feet of water. I was so sad, because we had been close friends, and Bud confided in me and told me all about life at home. He left behind a nice wife and a bunch of kids. Bud was a good buddy. He made me realize that even though life is a bitch at times, you can make it, even with one arm.

Sometime in the mid-sixties, I heard that there was a Shangri-La over on the west side of the Alaska Range. It was called Twin Lakes. I had been seriously contemplating getting some remote land and building some cabins to use as a base camp for guiding, so I hired Bud Lofstead to fly me over there with his float plane to check it out. It was a super bright, sunny day when we departed Kenai. It was my first time to fly through Lake Clark Pass and over the Chigmit Mountains, which are a part of the Alaska Range. Bud was already noted as one of the great bush pilots, and I could tell that he was totally comfortable flying. We flew through a notch in the last mountain, and Bud throttled back. Immediately on descent, I could see Twin Lakes directly ahead. The beauty nearly took my breath away. The panoramic view of the turquoise lakes, mountains with many hues of brown, and majestic glaciers blew me away. It was all so different from the Kenai Peninsula.

Bud commented that he didn't know how I found out about the spot, but it surely couldn't get any better. I had him fly around both lakes before I decided where I wanted to land. As we cruised along in slow flight, we spotted sheep, caribou, moose, and a brown bear. All four species within a half hour! It was a buffet of browse for moose and a perfect residence for lichen-munching caribou. The lakes were a special shade of light turquoise and crystal clear. It was difficult deciding where I might want to land. Both lakes offered choice locations for a guide camp. Bud knew that I was concerned about his hourly rate, so he looked over at me and told me to take my time making up my mind. He said that he wouldn't charge me much. He was enjoying the opportunity to look over the area himself. Finally I decided on a nice cove on the north side of the upper lake. It was the sunny side, and there were sheep straight up the mountain. The cove would offer some shelter from what appeared to be prevailing northerly winds.

When we made our final approach to the flat calm lake, it was hard to tell when the floats would touch the water. Bud eased the plane down gently and greased it on so smoothly that I could hardly tell that we had landed. We taxied to the cove, and after taking a much-needed leak, both of us admired the awesome beauty and solitude. Other than two uninhabited cabins on the other side of the lake, there was no sign of humans. Within one minute I made the decision that this would be my new home away from home, my Shangri-La.

At the time, the Department of Lands had a program that was referred to as Trade and Manufacturing Sites. The program allowed a business to be conducted on forty acres or less, and if the land was utilized properly, title would be granted. I staked out forty acres that covered the cove and surrounding area. Then I went to Anchorage and filed on it as a guiding location.

I built two log cabins and acquired another plane with floats. I was in business. The hunters that I brought there all enjoyed the beauty and comfort of the place. I was going to have my dozer flown over in a boxcar plane when I could afford it. I was going to build an airstrip with the dozer. It was possible to land on the lake in the winter when the ice was two feet thick or so.

Before I had a chance to carry out the plan, another tragic event took place, making it impossible for the airstrip to become a reality. I'll tell you about that later. I was running out of time to "prove up" on the T&M site, so the land department gave me only five acres. At least I still had my cabins and the cove. I could live with that.

In the meantime, Bud carved out a T&M site at the upper end of the lake. He never charged me much for the initial flight to the lakes. He was as much a gentleman as he was a great pilot. There were several times when he flew my clients to and from the lakes and hauled meat back to Kenai. Bud taught his two boys, Vern and Craig, to fly, and for many years they have had a successful air taxi service.

Some of the other great bush pilots that I had the pleasure to fly with are Andy Anderson, Don Johnson, and Gene Kempf. All three of them loved to fly at low altitudes when the weather allowed, and they all enjoyed seeing the whites of the critters' eyes when they buzzed them. They didn't terrorize the animals; they just made a pass so I could see what they looked like close up.

Chapter 7

Laughter, the Main Ingredient

They say that a good laugh is good medicine. It's true, and it's always a treat to be around happy-go-lucky people that tell jokes or just say funny stuff. On the other hand, a little sniveling goes a long way. We all do our share of griping, some more than others. I try to keep it to a minimum, and if I do have a problem, I've learned that it's not good to be around other negative whiners. When I started my big game guiding in the early 60s, I worked with Ray McNutt and Larry Folger. Larry couldn't talk without being funny. Even when he was going outside to relieve himself he would say that he was "going out to swing a big deal." He kept the hunters and us guides laughing till our stomachs hurt.

One fall I teamed up with Keith Specking to guide. Keith was a really pleasant gentleman to be around. He always guided with horses. All of his hunters got the moose, bear, and goats that they came for. One night Keith came back to camp with his hunter just after I got back. Except for the campfire, it was pitch black out. The cook had dinner ready, so we gathered around the fire and filled our plates. Suddenly, Keith bellowed out, "Who the hell put onions in the salad!" Wow, even the mellow, sweet-talking Keith sniveled a bit. Even though I guided with Keith only one season, I could tell that he was a man of integrity. He was a serious person, but his sense of humor cropped up now and again.

Then there was Toot Halstead. He had the same makeup as Larry. I never could understand how a person could come up with so much funny stuff. It was nonstop. His mom was the same way, always laughing. He and his brother, Tuffy, grew up in Seldovia, which is across Kachemak Bay from Homer. He was a fisherman, and we worked on several jobs together. Toot was no saint, but his humorous nature was a natural cure for anything ailing you. If he was going out to pee, he would say that he was "going to the nushnik" (outhouse), or if you were going out to the nushnik, he would tell you to mention his name and you would get a good seat. When the Alaska Native Land Claims Act was happening, Toot would say that he didn't have any Indian in him, but that he had been in a lot of Indians. One time I said that it was nice out, and Toot said, "Yes, I think I'll leave it out." Toots ex-wife Patty is a Kenaitze Indian, and sometimes Toot would sing out, "Unna-muck-sookie-ay," and Patty would just shake her head. I asked him what that meant, and he said he wasn't sure, but it seemed to attract the women.

Bobby Correia, a lifelong friend, has the same qualities as Larry and Toot. He can laugh at his own mistakes. Most of us try our hardest not to let others know that we made a mistake, but Bobby gets a kick out of any screw-ups that he does. Anyhow, I have learned a lot from these guys and others that seem to laugh at life. I think that all three of the fellows I mentioned were born with laughter and a smile whereas I had to acquire them. It would surely be easy to go around with an angry heart, especially when so many people think nothing of lying, cheating, and stealing. The three guys that I mentioned, taught me by example the importance of laughter and good humor. These are traits I've tried hard to pass along to my children.

Bobby and I became good hunting buddies. We usually went after Dall sheep, the toughest of Alaska game to acquire. Neither of us had hunted the Brooks Range, so we drove to Fairbanks, and from there we flew on a small commercial plane to Fort Yukon and from there on the mail plane, a Cessna 206, to Arctic Village. The fellow that welcomed us aboard looked too young. That seemed like a red flag, but that little plane was the only way to get to our destination. Within fifteen or twenty minutes, fog was obscuring visibility, so we found ourselves flying barely above the treetops. I was in the seat next to the pilot, so I felt compelled to make conversation. The first thing that came to mind was "How long have you been flying this mail plane?"

"I just came to Alaska a week ago, so I've made this trip a couple of times. I'm from New York, so this is all new to me," he replied.

Suspicions confirmed. Now I felt totally out of my comfort zone. I asked him if he knew where we were. The fog had closed in all around us and visibility was getting close to zero. Suddenly there was a creek meandering beneath us. The Cheechako pilot said, "Now I think I know where we are. I believe that's the creek that I flew over the other time I went to Arctic Village."

I guess I was supposed to be relieved to hear him say that, but I was still puckering as he tilted his wings each time we came to a bend in the creek. After ten minutes or so of following the creek, we broke out of the fog. I heard Bobby let out a sigh of relief. I glanced over at the pilot's hands, and his knuckles were pure white. We wasted no time getting out of the 206 when we got to the village.

Ernie Viens had the only air taxi service in the Brooks Range, and he was expecting us. After a short walk on the boardwalk, an old Eskimo couple hollered at us and invited Bobby and me in for a bowl of "boo stew." As we flew towards the Brooks Range with Ernie, there was comfort in our hearts and stomachs. Ernie was an accomplished bush pilot. He landed on a small gravel bar on the Canning River.

The weather had turned from downright crappy to bluebird, so we took our time making camp. The first mountain that we climbed found us eyeball to eyeball with nine nice rams. The sheep just stood there while we brought our guns to our shoulders. Our trigger fingers squeezed off simultaneous rounds. It was the shortest sheep hunt I'd ever gone on. Both rams were more than full curl. Packing the meat, horns, and cape from a mature ram is just as tough as packing a moose hindquarter. Side-hilling down the steep slope required several breaks, but the thought of having two nice sheep eased the pain.

When we reached the camp, we just dropped the packs and sprawled out on the moss. After we had a drink of creek water and rested a bit, we went into the tent and ate a granola bar. Then Bobby got something out of his duffel and announced that he was going to roll a joint. Until that very moment, I had seen pot only once. It didn't matter to me. After all, we were a zillion miles from anybody. After taking a hit, Bobby handed the thing to me. I sucked a lungful and proceeded to cough my guts out. Bobby laughed so hard that it got me laughing too. After a couple more drags on that joint, everything seemed so funny that we couldn't stop laughing. Then something caught my eye outside. The front flap on the tent was open, and I could see some animals about 75 yards from us. It was a bunch of bull caribou. We had unloaded our rifles and laid them out of the way in the tent. The scene must have been hilarious, two guys fairly screwed up and both trying to get out the tent at the same time. Somehow we were able to find ammo and load the rifles. Bobby almost knocked me down while exiting the tent. I don't know how we accomplished it, but we each shot a big bull with one shot apiece. Neither of us could believe what had taken place. Again we laughed until we hurt.

The day before Ernie was to come and pick us up, Bobby started cussing. "That slow-moving, pipe-smoking jerk. He couldn't care less if he picks us up on time." Ernie was due the following day at noon, but Bobby was convinced that he wouldn't show, and he needed to get back to sign divorce papers. It was barely getting light out when Bobby woke me and told me that we needed to break camp and be ready, even though Ernie wouldn't come on time. I had no idea that divorce court was so demanding.

Morning arrived in the form of a bluebird day. There wasn't a breath of wind, and the sky was completely void of clouds. Nonetheless, Bobby kept saying, "That no good son of a gun isn't coming." He would listen intently for the drone of the plane. At 11:45 he turned to me and said," I told you, he wasn't coming!"

Three minutes later we heard the humming of the 185. Ernie landed and taxied up to us, and Bobby ran up to him and shook his hand like he was an old-time friend. Within a few seconds, Bobby became a happy camper again.

One of the last hunts that Bobby and I went on together was for deer on Shuyak Island. We invited Robby Carrol to go along because he is another humorous fun guy to hunt with. He can't hit a bull in the butt with a banjo, but with his red beard (more gray than red) and gravelly-sounding voice, he is a picture of a real Alaskan outdoorsman.

Shuyak had an abundance of deer, so the legal limit allowed five deer per person. My hunting partners met me in Homer where we loaded our gear into my 28-foot boat. Mandatory items included beer for Robby and Redman Chewing Tobacco for Bobby. The sea was relatively calm as we blasted past the Barren Islands and down to Shuyak. We laughed continuously at Robby's yarns. You would think that he would have had to be 150 years old to have come up with so many tales. Even though most of the stuff that he spewed out was the truth stretched considerably, he had an uncanny ability to keep a straight face, so we could only guess at what small morsels of his stories were true.

We pulled into a small, protected bay and dropped anchor, grabbed our rifles, jumped into the inflatable raft, and paddled to shore. Bobby offered me a wad of his Redman as he stuffed a gob in his mouth. I declined. We came to the mutual decision that I would hunt in one direction and they would go the opposite way. We would rendezvous before dark.

It was early fall, so I figured that the deer would be near the highest elevations. I made a beeline to the top of a nearby hill, and sure enough, just before I broke into an open meadow, there was a nice big buck bedded down. He had no idea that I was looking at him through the scope on my 7mm magnum. I had to hurry with gutting and dismembering his fat body, because it would soon be dark. Does and young bucks aren't very big, but the mature bucks are close to 200 pounds. I boned some of the meat so I would be able to carry the whole thing in one load.

When I got to the beach, the guys had built a "white man fire" and were warming their backsides by the blaze. Robby made a comment that I had gotten lucky, because they didn't see anything. We paddled out to the boat and had ourselves an extravagant freeze-dried meal and a beer. Then the guys took their tent to the beach and made camp while I slept on the boat. It was a sleepless night for Bobby and Robby because a couple of brown bears kept rubbing against the tent. It was barely light out when I heard them boarding the boat. Robby said that I was going to have to put up with their farts and snoring because they weren't going to share a tent with a bunch of hungry bears.

The next two days were a repeat of day one. I returned both days with another big buck and they had diddlysquat. On the fourth day, Bobby said he was going with me. Just before we got to the top of the hill that we were climbing, I told Bobby that I would go around the fringe of the brush and he could go the other way. Only a few minutes had passed when a barrage of shots came from Bobby's direction. When I came into the clearing, there were dead deer everywhere. He limited out within twenty seconds! It was like he wasn't taking any prisoners.

Robby, on the other hand, had no intentions of climbing the hills, but he didn't care whether he stumbled on a retard deer or not. He knew that we would share our deer, and he enjoyed standing by the fire with a cold brew.

The last day of the hunt, Bobby offered me a chew, and I surprised him by accepting. I had never done chewing tobacco, so it was a shock when I stuck it in my left cheek. Within seconds I got buzzed! I tried not to show its effect, but I had a tough time walking a straight line as I departed. When I got out of sight, I spit that nasty stuff out and sat on a log until I felt like I was able to hunt without doing bodily damage to myself.

Bobby and I hunted together several times, and each hunt was of the highest quality. Both of us have sheep heads on our walls that remind us of the great fun and laughter that we've shared.

Guiding was another one of those things that was a bit on the rough and tough side, but was more fun than flying for the first time. I never was an assistant guide per se, because I took the Alaska guides exam and became a full-fledged guide and started my own business. When I guided with Ray and Larry, we were on the Alaska Peninsula. Most of the guiding was for brown bear and moose. Both species were plentiful, so it was just a matter of being able to select the largest and best critter for each client. The hard part was packing moose meat and the heavy bear hides. Fleshing and salting took considerable time also. Ray was an excellent Super Cub pilot. Weather is born on the Peninsula, and it was a common occurrence to deal with forty- to fifty-knot winds. Sometimes when Ray was coming in for a landing, he would actually fly backwards. We would have to be right on the spot when he touched down so we could grab a wing strut and tie it as quickly as possible. The Cub had big tundra tires, so it could land almost anywhere out there in the pucker brush.

After that first year I bought horses and guided on my own. I chose an area on the Kenai Peninsula that nobody had hunted since the early 1900s when the great Andy Simons guided hunters there at the headwaters of the Killey River. You wouldn't believe how wild and exciting it was. I hired Eileen, a local woman, to do the cooking. Her whole family was great in the culinary field. A good cook is mandatory if you want your clientele to be content.

Numerous bears, both black and brown, had never seen man, so were terribly aggressive. When we had moose meat hanging, there was always a bear or two hanging around, trying to get it. I slept with my gun at one side, and a flashlight on the other—still do to this day. One night something woke me. There was something close and it was breathing hard. I flipped the switch on the flashlight, and there stood a big bear right next to my feet. I hadn't closed the flap on the tent, so he took the liberty of joining me. He made no attempt to leave, so I slowly picked up the gun and released the safety. I put the barrel of the 30.06 close to his chest and squeezed the trigger. The 220-grain bullet blew him out of the tent the same way he came in. I guess you can imagine what a commotion it made with the others in camp. Eileen, who was on the far side of the tent, sprang up, but only a small squeak came out of her mouth because she was so startled.

Harry, my assistant guide, hollered out, "Did you get him, Jerre?"

I got him all right. I blew his heart into many pieces. I made a point of keeping the tent flap closed after that.

I've had many other close calls with bears since then. Once, while on a sheep hunt, I was fighting my way up through a tangle of alders. All of a sudden I heard a bunch of crashing in the brush above me. Before I had a chance to react, a big black sow with two cubs came down on me. The sow knocked me down, but just kept on running down the mountain. I was unscathed, but lay there until I couldn't hear them anymore. The sow was probably as startled as I was when she knocked me down. If she had been intentionally attacking me, she would have munched on my bones.

I had several encounters while guiding. If you are being charged by any of the animals that "bite back," whether it be a bear, elephant, or a big cat, you need to have your act together. A false attack is when a bear charges toward you and then stops abruptly. When this happens, you don't always have time to determine whether the bear is going to follow through with the charge or bluff and stop. Hopefully you have time to shoulder your rifle, or at least bring it up to your waist. You don't want to kill a bear unnecessarily, but it takes nerves of steel not to shoot until the last possible split second. Ursus Arctos Middendorffi is the largest of the animals in North America that bite back. Alaska has more of the big teddies than all of the rest of North America, so when you are stumbling around in their back yard, it's a good idea to carry a heavy-duty protection apparatus. There was only one time that I had to shoot a bear under this type of circumstance. It was on the trip that I call the "Mr. Scruffy" hunt.

Spring bear hunts can often get nasty, the reasons being that the bears are famished after hibernation and they are mating. Both of the aforementioned conditions pertained when I first saw Mr. Scruffy. He and another boar were fighting for the rights to a pretty blond sow. They were two hundred yards above me on the same mountain. Both boars were good-sized, but one seemed a bit larger than the other. I was by myself, so I was well aware of the fact that I needed to have my act together. I was halfway up the mountain in a place where several large rocks were scattered about. The breeze was ever so slight and was in my favor. I edged up to a rock that was just the right size to allow a perfect rest for my 7mm magnum. I have better bear guns at home, but the 7mm was my favorite and the one in which I have the most confidence. All three bears were lying down, taking a break. The boar that I wanted was perfectly broadside to me. I carefully placed the crosshairs just behind his shoulder and aimed a slight bit low because I was shooting uphill. I squeezed the trigger and sent the 175-grain bullet on its way. Instantly, the bear began rolling down the mountain.

When he got on the same level as me, only about 100 feet away, he went out of sight behind a small mound. I was confident that the bullet hit its mark, so I stayed put for a while. I looked up the mountain, and saw that the other boar was coming straight at me. When he was getting too close for comfort, I sent a round to the side of him, and he turned slightly and ran by me and down the mountain. I had racked another round into the chamber to be ready in case he didn't turn. The sow seemed content to remain up the mountain and didn't even get up.

Any time I'm guiding other hunters for bear, I always make sure I have extra ammo ready and in an easily accessible place. I reloaded and made sure I had a few more rounds in my right coat pocket. Again, I waited and regained my composure. I kept watching the sow Fifteen minutes went by and she was still lying down.

It was time to check out the bear that I had shot. I eased the safety forward and proceeded over the mound that obscured my vision. Ever so slowly and quietly I made my way. The sight that I was about to see was so unexpected that I froze in place. My dead bear was being shaken like a rag doll by a monster-sized bear! This was a real DOUBLE CELESTIAL HERCOMITE! I had no idea that there was another bear in the area. Fur was flying, and my dead bear was just about totally off the ground. I was completely shocked by the size and power of this bruin. I slowly backed out of sight and back to a big rock. I was sweating, and I don't think it was from the sun. What now, Jerre? Alaska law says one bear per person, so I didn't want to shoot this giant, but he was destroying my bear's hide. This was a serious problem, and one that I had never had to deal with before. I waited for five minutes and took another peek. He was still engrossed in tearing my bear to shreds. Again I backed off. I needed to make a quick decision or I wouldn't have anything but bits and pieces. I opened the gun bolt just enough to make sure that a round was in the chamber. The magazine held three of the round nose bullets, and the chamber contained the round that would be the first to greet the bear if he decided to charge. I put two more rounds between my fingers. I probably wouldn't have time to use them, but it gave me a little more confidence. My thumb eased the safety forward, but I had to be sure, so I tilted the rifle and glanced at it to visually make sure that the safety was off. A mosquito persisted to buzz my ear, but it was no time to be swatting at bugs. I put the stock up to my shoulder and eased forward. I was prepared for the worst, but was hoping that upon seeing me he would drop my bear and run away. When I got to the point that I could see him, he still was clamped onto my bear, and fur was still flying.

I hollered, "BEAR!" The R part of the word hadn't left my lips when he charged me so fast that I had no time to try to shoot beside him. I had to kill or be killed right now. I had put my scope on the lowest setting, which was three-power, and had it aimed at his chest before I called his name, but when he charged, all I could see was fur. He closed the distance from 75 feet to 20 feet in a blink of an eye. All I could do was stand my ground and let her rip. When I shot him, he barely turned ten degrees from my position, but didn't slow down a bit. He was a blur when he blasted by me just a few feet away. I didn't have time to rack another round in before he blew past me. The decline of the mountain was my friend, because he would have had a tough time stopping and coming back. Unbelievably, I watched him run full bore down to the bottom of the mountain. Why didn't he drop dead? His stride never faltered, and after several minutes he went out of sight.

The sow was still lying down in the same place. The shooting didn't seem to faze her. I kept an eye on her nonetheless. I had to take a minute to shake my arms and fingers to relax a bit. I eased over to my dead bear and noticed why the bigger bear reacted like he did. The snow was deep in the dip that he was in, and he had been in the process of digging a big hole where the remains of a caribou carcass lay buried. I guessed that he had his head down in the hole and didn't hear my shots. My bear, which I have named Mr. Scruffy, came rolling down precisely where the big bear was digging. It must have really startled the big guy, and he wasn't about to let any bear (dead or alive), steal his find.

After skinning Mr. Scruffy, I measured his length and width and he squared 9'2", and yet he was dwarfed by the big bear. Even with the skull out of the hide, it was almost impossible to lift the hide. I dragged it across the snowfield and then lashed it to my pack. I barely staggered back to camp. I hadn't been there more than a few minutes when another seven- or eight-foot bear walked by my tent. He glanced at me, but went on his way. I had seen enough bears for the day.

If any of you folks reading this are bored or have a case of cabin fever, I'd suggest that you go on a spring brown bear hunt. I guarantee it to get you out of the doldrums.

Jon Berryman, the pilot that flew me in there, showed me a place not far from where my camp was where three hunters had had some severe bear problems the previous fall. They were moose hunting and had harvested one moose. The bears came and relentlessly harassed the hunters and stole all their meat.

Bear season is only open every other year in this area, and the bears seem to have learned that nobody can shoot them on the "other" year. In fact, just like the Kodiak bears, they come running if they hear a shot. It's like a dinner bell going off. On the Alaska Peninsula, a gunshot means that you might have killed a moose or a caribou; on Kodiak, a gunshot tells the bears that you probably got a deer. Most deer hunters that have hunted Kodiak can attest to that.

The three hunters tried to keep the bears from taking their moose meat, but nothing worked. They first tried the "shoot in the air" trick, then shot in the ground close to the bear. When that didn't work, they hollered and waved their arms. They even shot a flare gun into the fur of one bear. Nothing fazed the brazen bruins. It wasn't long before the hunters feared for their lives. Bears brushed by their tent every night. They claimed that there were

Mr. Scruffy with his prize at Christmas time.

six or seven bears that terrorized them daily. I guess that if they had ever slept you could have said it was a nightmare.

When Jon came to pick them up, there was nothing left of their camp. The bears had torn up the tent, the sleeping bags, and had eaten all of their food. They even bit holes in the cans of white gas that they used for their stove and lanterns. The hunters almost knocked Jon down scampering to get into his plane.

When I got home with Mr. Scruffy's hide, I decided to do the taxidermy myself. He deserved to look stately, so I mounted him standing up. He's a handsome dude.

I was on a caribou hunt later that fall, and I used the same ammunition that I used on the bear hunt. I shot a young boo that was standing broadside seventy yards away. The bullet entered the front part of the rib cage but didn't exit, which meant that the ammunition was defective and it could have cost me my life. I heaved the remaining cartridges and never bought that brand again.

A couple of times in my guiding career, I had to go into the brush to finish off a wounded bear. Both times I felt the hair on the back of my neck and arms stand up. It's sort of like being in the water and having a shark circling you. Yes, that happened to me too, but I'll tell you about that later. There was a time that I was going to write a book about bear maulings. I even interviewed eight or nine people that had gone to battle with bears. This included Jimmy Second Chief from the Glennallen area. Unfortunately a personal matter got in my way, and I never followed up on the book.

Bear meat can be delicious, but it is best late in the fall when they have berries going in one end and coming out the other. If a bear has been fishing, forget it. The meat has to be cooked well done, because it's like pig meat in that it can give you trichinosis. We used to render out the fat and use the lard for piecrusts and biscuits. Rendering it slowly in the oven at 150 degrees or so made it better than store-bought shortening.

There appears to be an abundance of black and brown bears in much of Alaska now. Right here in Homer people are continually having bears coming onto their porches and sometimes right into their homes. You don't dare leave any garbage or dog food outside because it is like inviting a bruin for a free lunch.

My son-in–law Charlie and I went deer hunting last fall and we encountered more brown bears than we could count. We actually saw more bears than deer. We had prepared for it by bringing an electric fence. Yes, they work, and you get to keep the deer that you worked so hard for instead of giving the bears your hard-earned meat. Plus you can sleep at night without griz bears brushing by your tent. I've witnessed both a bear and a moose get jolted by an electric fence, and both times the animals made a fast departure.

I wouldn't dare leave the bear subject without sharing one of the best true bear stories ever. In 1960 when I was working for United Geophysical, one of the guys was having a problem with a mischievous bear. Like most of us at the time, he didn't have electricity, so he had to keep perishables outside in a hole in the ground. A bear locked onto the goodies, and would come by at night and devour every morsel. After the second time he was robbed, the guy stayed awake all night with a flashlight and a 338 Winchester. All he got was sleep deprivation because either the bear never came or he ran off when he sensed that the guy was watching for him. The guy decided that there was a much better way to deal with the thief without losing any more sleep. He borrowed a couple of cans of blasting agent from work and set it outside far enough away that the explosion wouldn't do any harm to his cabin. He wrapped the cans with lots of bacon and then tied a bunch of empty cans to the explosives. Then he ran the wires through the cabin window right next to a set of batteries. The idea was that when the bear rattled the cans, it would wake the guy and he would touch the wires to the battery, and PRESTO: end of bear. Well, the bear did come, and he did grab the cans of blasting agent, but somehow he kept quiet while eating the bacon. Like Yogi Bear, he was smarter than the average bear. Unbeknownst to the guy, he carried the explosives just outside the cabin and dropped them. The rattling cans woke the guy, but the bear had run off. When he touched the wires to the batteries, it blew him and his bed out the other wall of his cabin. When neighbors found him, he was still in his dilapidated bed, and the whole wall of the cabin was gone. United Geophysical had to hire a replacement.

It was spring and time to net some fish again. I spent more time watching other high-liners so that I could adopt some of their ways and means. Commercial fishermen are a different breed. They will brazenly get on the radio and ask others how they are doing, but are reluctant to say anything if they are doing well. It took me a while to understand why they were like that, but I eventually realized that the whole fleet was listening to your conversation and that they were all eager to come and keep you company if you were catching great numbers of fish. Some guys couldn't stay off the radio while others almost never said a peep. Koke was one of those quiet guys. Kaarlo Kokko was his real name. Even though I never heard him on the radio, I noticed that his name was always on the top of the list that Joe Fribrock kept in the store at Snug Harbor. I had heard that he fished near Kalifonsky Beach a lot, so I made a point to look him up. Koke was a large man with the biggest hands I had ever shaken. He was a real "gentle Ben." When I found where he fished most of the time, I soon understood why he did so well. Most of Cook Inlet's fish are bound for the Kenai and Kasilof rivers. Koke didn't waste time out in the briny deep. He fished as close to the beach as he could. It made total sense, but you really had to know what you were doing, or you could snag a submerged rock and lose your whole net. I began working at it and found that I could make good catches when most of the fleet was scratch fishing. One time I lingered too long in the shallows, and when the tide swung, I snagged a rock with my lead line. It stripped about twenty fathoms of net before I got it loose.

Jimmy Linderman was another fisherman that tried fishing in close. For the most part he was successful. One day, though, I sadly watched him towing on his net in an attempt to keep it from being devoured by a riptide full of "net gobblers." The black smoke bellowed out of the exhaust stack as he pulled for all he was worth. The logs and trees won, and Jimmy lost his whole net.

One of the Danish guys that fished Snug boats was fishing in close to the beach, and I watched him wrap his whole net around the "sisters," those two house-sized rocks that you can see for miles. The Danes wore aprons instead of rain gear, so it was almost amusing to watch him standing on deck, obviously thinking that he was going to miss the rocks as the tide moved him down the inlet—another net lost.

Upper Cook Inlet is cluttered with oil platforms, and when the big tides are flooding, it's easy to find yourself dodging the stationary structures. One sunny but windy day, I barely got my net in before making contact with a leg of one of the platforms. The boat that was a little south of me didn't react quickly enough and wrapped his whole net around the platform legs.

Our Homestead at Reflection Lake.

Not all the rip tides had logs and junk in them, but they still posed problems. If you got sucked into a rip, there was always a chance that other boats would be sucked in too. Then the fun would begin. The rips have a way of turning you around in circles, so you can imagine what a mess it causes when you are twisted up with two or more boats. It's sometimes hard to figure out whose net is whose. Often the worst happens, and the net goes under the boats and gets tangled around your prop and rudder. Ugh! This dilemma is referred to as "web in the wheel." During my early years, I had this happen twice, and both times I had to go overboard with a knife, swim under the boat while holding my breath, and cut lines and web as fast as I could. It was a task that would take your breath away because the water temperature was about 45°. Usually you had to go under four or five times before you got it all cut out. The water is murky, so for the most part, you had to feel what you were doing. By the time you got the job done, you were so cold that you had to summon up some supernatural strength to get back on board.

Later in my fishing career, I bought a dry-suit and a mask and snorkel. Those items made the job easier, but I still almost died under the boat while cutting the net out of the prop. The sea was quite rough when I screwed up, but I had to get the net cut out of the prop or I wouldn't be able to move the boat or catch any more fish. When I went under the stern, the waves slammed the boat down on my head and almost knocked me unconscious. Not good. I came out and hung onto a buoy that we hung over the side. My wife was with me, but she couldn't do anything until I cut the line out. I went under again and tried to stay lower so the boat wouldn't send me to Davy Jones's locker. I had to use both hands to cut the line, so I couldn't keep myself from hitting my head on the bottom of the boat as the waves slammed it up and down. I had to go under a third time to get the line out. By then, I was totally exhausted. I was strong, but the task had sapped my strength. With Winnie pulling for all she was worth, and me using my last remaining ounce of energy, I made it aboard. After that episode, I vowed never to attempt that job again, so I took extra precautions to keep from getting web in the wheel.

One of my neighbors built a new boat for himself and incorporated a removable hatch in the stern that would enable him to access his prop and rudder without going into the water. It was a great idea except for one small detail. The first time he got web in the wheel, he opened the hatch and began the task of getting the line and web out. His son, who was fishing with him, noticed that his dad wasn't moving back there. He called to Dad, but there was no response. The boy smelled exhaust, so he dragged Dad out of there. Luckily, the fresh air revived him. He hadn't thought to shut off the engines, and the exhaust had nearly done him in. He had what we refer to as a wet exhaust. It is piped out underwater at the stern of the boat. It was a terrible way to learn a lesson, but it could have been much worse.

During the early years I wasn't making much money fishing, but I loved everything about it. Then 1966 came along, and we had our best year ever. Deck load after deck load. At the end of the season I had enough money to buy some lumber and supplies to build an addition on our house. We really enjoyed the extra space, especially the kids. When winter came on, I got a good construction job and made some more money. We were in tall cotton—for a while.

Chapter 8

Good Comes from a Disaster

April 7 of 1967 changed fun and frolic to doom and gloom. Our daughter Laurie had tonsillitis and had to stay home from school that day. I needed to go to town for some chicken feed. When I got back, Laurie came running out of the house, screaming, "The house is on fire!"

I saw smoke coming out the open door. Right away I could tell that the fire was in the attic. I ran inside and immediately saw that the trap door we had for access to the attic had blown open and wispy, blue flames were coming out. It was hot! I hooked up a hose and sprayed up there, but it didn't seem to be doing any good. I got a ladder and climbed up on the roof with an axe and the hose. While I was chopping a hole in the roof, I yelled at my wife to go to a neighbor and call the fire department. I began hollering as loudly as I could, hoping that my nearest neighbor, Zeke, might hear me. I inserted the hose through the hole and sprayed it in different directions, but it wasn't enough. I scampered down the ladder and filled a bucket with water from a puddle, ran back up the ladder, and poured it in the hole. I repeated this procedure many times. When my wife got back, she got another bucket, filled it, and had it ready to thrust into my hands. We made a two-person bucket brigade, thus speeding up the process considerably.

In a short while I could see through the window that the fire was spreading. I decided to go into the house and see if I could salvage our important papers, some pictures, and maybe some guns. Surely the fire department would be there soon. I took a deep breath and crawled to our bedroom where our papers were kept. I grabbed what I could, but I couldn't hold my breath long enough. I had barely started to inhale when I just about choked to death on the toxic fumes and smoke. I don't have a clue how I got out, but I did. I realized that I was lucky I didn't lose consciousness. Then, as I was reviving, the windows blew out, and I could see our bear rugs and everything we owned go up in a blazing inferno. The fire truck that was supposed to save our home had gotten stuck in our road. Our beautiful log home, which we built by ourselves, was burning to the ground, and there was nothing we could do. We had had a strong wind the night before, and we figured that it separated the stovepipe in the attic where we couldn't see it.

My wife and daughter were crying harder than I'd ever heard anyone cry. My strength and youth were useless. I had allowed my family's home to be destroyed. There never is a plan when such a disaster happens. When the other kids got home from school, there was no home. The sadness was overwhelming. There seemed nothing that we could do to comfort each other. I was too stunned to cry, or perhaps I didn't want my tears to make my family think that all was hopeless.

Even though neighbors were scattered miles apart from each other, the word somehow spread that our house was gone. By mid-afternoon enough neighbors had come by that all the kids had temporary places to go until I could get my head together. I tried to sleep in the car, but it was useless. Whenever I did doze off, I had flashbacks of being in the fire, and then I would have panic attacks. When dawn broke, I walked over to the still-smoldering ashes and kicked around in them, looking for anything that was salvageable. A terrible, overwhelming feeling of sadness smothered my body, and I fell to the ground. Tears burst from my eyes, and I wailed so loudly that it surely would have scared anyone, had they heard me.

I don't know how long I had been crying when I heard a voice. I remember thinking that it was God talking, trying to console me. When I opened my eyes and looked up, there stood Morris Coursen, not God. Morris was the best "cat skinner" in Alaska. A cat skinner is a person that runs big bulldozers. Morris's family attended the Lutheran Church that we built in Soldotna. At the time, Morris didn't care much about church, but later got baptized and went to church regularly. Church or not, he was a godsend.

He sat down next to me on a partially burned log. He graciously waited for me to settle down a bit before he spoke. I'll never forget how courteous and tactful he was. He had a suggestion, he said, and if I didn't like it, I should just forget that he had mentioned it. "Why don't I bring my D-7 Cat over and dig a big hole and bury these ashes, and then I'll level a spot to start building a new house."

His words totally blew me away. What a wonderful offer! He knew that it was important to stop me from feeling sorry for myself and occupy my mind with something productive. Here was a man that possessed more compassion and understanding than I could have believed. Just as quickly as I agreed to his offer, he touched my heart with another one. He had two big school buses, which he and his family used when they fished their sites during the summer months, that we could use. One bus was for cooking and eating; the other one was for sleeping. He insisted that it was a meager offer, and he hoped that he wasn't offending me. I was taken aback by the more than generous offer. I politely asked if it wouldn't be an inconvenience to him. He quickly replied that the buses would just be sitting around doing nothing.

The next day Morris came roaring down our homestead road with his D-7, and he did just as he said he would. He dug a herky-sized hole and pushed the charred rubble into it and buried it. It was a done deal. I have to admit that I had spent the morning kicking around the ashes. I found my old 45 ACP pistol with which I'd spent many hours practicing the "quick draw." The fire was so hot that it had bent the barrel. I threw it back into the ashes.

Morris was so good with that Cat that I believe he could have shaved a shrew's hair with the blade. Just as quick as he finished burying the remnants of our log house, he started leveling the spot that I had marked for the site of a new house. When he finished the perfectly level spot, he shut the Cat down and said that he would leave it for me to use. I told him that I had never run a big Cat, only a small dozer. His reply as he was leaving was that if I could run a small one I'd have no trouble with the D-7. I do declare, Morris Coursen was one unbelievably kind and generous guy.

Breakup had begun, which meant that our road would soon be a mucky quagmire, and it would stay a mess for a month or so. We got the buses in, and I parked them between the lake and the building site. The kids were so happy to be back together even though they had to walk out to catch the school bus each morning and back in the evening. The days were longer by then, so at least they didn't have to walk in the dark. Cindy was the smallest of the four girls, just a first grader, so she was always tuckered out when she trudged in behind the other three girls.

Fortunately, the root cellar, which contained our potatoes, wasn't damaged, nor was the tent where most of our moose meat was hanging. So it goes without saying that we dined on "taters and moose meat" often. All of our canned goods were gone, including the homemade jellies and jams, but some of the neighbors shared theirs with us. I made a makeshift oven on top of the propane stove that was in the cooking bus. My wife burned the first couple of loaves of bread that she attempted to bake, but she soon learned to adjust the flame so the kids and I had bread for our lunches again. Living in those two buses was like a luxurious camping event. The kids squabbled a bit about which bunk they slept in, but it all worked out.

While breakup was in progress, I was laying out the forms for the footings for the new house. Bob Holt, one of the church members, drew up plans for a nicely designed three-bedroom, two-bath house. He even incorporated a sunken living room and a fireplace. Together, he and I figured out the dimensions and how much lumber I would need. The local lumber supply company gave me an outstanding deal, so as soon as the road was drivable, I hauled the whole kit and kaboodle in. The word got out that we were starting the house, and people came from near and far to help. There were never fewer than ten people each day for the first six weeks. Sometimes there were twenty or more. There was still ice on our lake, so some of the help landed their planes on it. Women came and kept our bellies full and helped carry lumber to us carpenters. Before we knew it, the roof was on and the house was enclosed.

Jack and Beulah Reffet, a couple that had a nearby restaurant, held a fund-raiser spaghetti feed event for us and gave us all the proceeds. At the J Bar B that night, people slipped money into our pockets. A church in Sterling gave us a check for $100. I'm hesitant to mention names for fear that I will forget someone. Money and help poured in. I thought that I was going to have to get a loan to be able to finish the house, but with all the help, I didn't have to. It was a good thing too because I had gone to the local bank and inquired about a loan, and the head man for them wanted me to put up the whole homestead as collateral. I had to politely tell him, "That will never happen."

The house was nearing completion, so we decided to show our appreciation by having an open-house party. I was still working on the living room ceiling at 1:00 a.m. the day before. What a grand time we had! People cried happy tears for us, and we shared the same.

During the summer a man came to our house and asked if he could drill us a water well. I told him that we sure didn't have the money for one. He said, "Oh, I wouldn't charge anything except for the pipe and pump, and you can pay for that whenever you have it."

Well, I don't know how I could beat a deal like that. He drilled an 82-foot well, so for the first time while homesteading, we had running water. Yay!

After fishing season, which was a little better than average, I had another guy help me build a fireplace. After the cement blocks were in, I did all the rockwork. I put a cantilevered hearth to sit on, and the mantel turned out quite nice too.

In those days, three bedrooms seemed fantastic and out of this world, but with five children, there still was a tad bit of grumbling. Five kids isn't a big family, but if we had one more, we would have had one too many for a basketball team and not enough for a football team, so it was agreed that there would be no more babies. I was so proud of my family and loved taking up a whole pew at church, but one pew is enough.

Today happens to Saint Patrick's Day, so I will drink a toast to all the super, giving people that were so gracious and helpful to us: "To you that helped us in a time of need, I salute you. May you live to be 120, have good health, and die a quick, painless, death"!

I must also mention that since that outpouring of help in our time of need I've made a point to help others that have experienced similar disasters. It's true: some good comes from bad.

Chapter 9

Moving Up a Notch

In regard to my fishing career, that nasty word "mediocre" needn't plague me anymore. I was catching more fish than most of the Cook Inlet drift gillnetters, so why not spread my wings? I knew of a couple of fishermen that were long-lining for halibut, and it excited me. At the time I had use of the Snug boat year around, so I gathered all the fishing gear that was required for catching the flat fish: twenty skates of ground line, each skate 1800 feet long or 300 fathoms; 1200 hooks; eight anchors; and the same number of flagpoles and buoys. I was in business.

The spring season was opening soon, so I purchased ten boxes of herring for bait. Baiting hooks is anything but fun, especially by yourself. If you're doing it with other fishermen, you can tell stories as you bait, which makes the experience more pleasurable and helps to pass the time. I wasn't very good at baiting, so I never got my master-baiting card. Nonetheless, I filled the hold with ice and off I went. It was 75 to 100 miles to the fishing grounds, so you can imagine how long it took to get there with a boat that did six or seven knots. I think it was on that trip that I began talking to myself. I'm not a great singer, but there was no one out there to complain, so sing I did.

I had a fair idea of how to make a set, but there is nothing that replaces actual experience. When I began the first set, I quickly found myself wishing that I had four arms or a deckhand, but, like I said before, nobody used deckhands in those days. After the buoy, flagpole, and anchor went out, it was a simple matter of snapping pre-baited hooks onto the ground line while steering the boat. I had lined up some landmarks so that when I came back I would be able to find the set. For each set, I had tied seven skates of ground line together with sheet bends. A fellow fisherman that had been halibut fishing for a couple of years gave me a few clues on how to do it. Chuck Simons referred to himself as a Mongol. Mongol or not, he was a good fisherman. He told me to snap the hooks onto the ground line twenty feet apart, so twenty feet it was. After making the last set, I headed back to the beginning of the first one. I was antsy, so instead of waiting for a few hours, I picked up the buoy and began reeling it in. I couldn't remember if Chuck had told me to pick going into the current or with it. Well, I found out quickly enough, because there was some tangled line. There were also some good-sized halibut that caused some panic. The 150-pounders would come in flopping around like crazy. I thought, these fellows could break a leg real quick if I get in their way. The two gaffs that I had were a little on the short side, so I had to really stretch to sink the sharp point in their heads. Whoa, this was as exciting as all get out! It reminded me of the proverbial "Mexican fire drill," whatever that means. I had made a "butt beater" just for the occasion, and it was a lifesaver. It was like a short bat and I would use it on the heads of the big fish just as soon as I got them in the boat.

The learning curve of that first trip was awesomely steep. When I got home, I slept most of the next two days.

The fish buyers wouldn't buy a halibut if you hadn't gutted them, gilled them, and put ice in the stomach cavity. I also learned that when you put the fish in the hold, they must be white side up and have layers of ice between them. There was a lot to it, but halibut fishing was rewarding. By doing the halibut fishery spring and fall, I felt like I was becoming more of a full time fisherman.

Once in a while in the spring, halibut fishing would have to take a back-seat while I guided brown bear hunters. One spring hunt that really sticks out in my mind took place a year that I didn't have access to the Snug boat. I had bought a twenty-foot skiff from John Hulien. She was fire engine red and built with natural knees and cedar planking. Natural knees are almost unheard of now. When old-timers made a boat, they would search the spruce forests and find roots that were L-shaped. They would cut the tree and proceed to cut the stump all the way through the root. These natural knees were the frame that the planking was attached to. At the time, I had as much fear as I did sense, which was close to none on both counts. So I loaded all of my camping supplies and food into the skiff, and off I went seventy miles down the Alaska Peninsula. The rip tides in the middle of Cook Inlet can be treacherous, but, like I said, I didn't know fear.

I had made arrangements to have Gene Kempf fly my clients down to the bay where I had my camp. Gene was a remarkable bush pilot and could land his Super Cub on a dime. Well, the trip down there and the hunt went fine, but the trip back was another "save your butt" kind of trip. It started out calm and looked like it would be smooth sailing. Wrong! A northerly began to snort, and by the time I reached the middle rip, all I could see was white water. Not good, but I was committed. To turn around would have been suicide. I kept the throttle at half speed in order to keep the bow up and the water splashing in to a minimum. Constant bailing kept me from freezing my buns and too busy to think about fear. I just concentrated on angling across the inlet and getting back to the Kasilof River. Luckily, no planks came loose from the constant pounding. I'm sure I looked like a drowned rat by the time I got to the river, but what the heck, I made it.

Yep, I should have gone halibut fishing, but I notice a pattern when I think about my life in general: it appears that I have more "wild hairs" than the average person. It's not particularly something that I'm proud of; it's in my makeup. People are born with certain traits. Some are born to sing or play musical instruments. Others are born to be leaders, and there are those that seem to be on the planet to do harm to others. Anyhow, I have a few wild hairs. Some of them have caused some close calls and excitement, but no matter what, for the most part, I've enjoyed the ride. There have been times that I've almost felt guilty for having so much fun commercial fishing and getting paid for it.

Halibut fishing was more lucrative on average, so I quit spring guiding. It not only put more money in my pocket, but the sea—how it attracted! It was as seductive and alluring as the sexiest woman. It was like a giant magnet, and I a small metal object. But there was something about it that constantly puzzled me. How could it suck me into its wild core and then at times make me want to get off at the next stop? There were times when I enthusiastically greeted terra firma, but in a short period of time I would find myself lured back into the clutches of the sea. As for the 'butt' fishery, it wasn't the most exciting of fisheries, but it had its moments. Besides, I was my own boss. Right or wrong, I made all the decisions. I've worked with jerks that couldn't make a good decision even if not doing so meant going blind and losing their extremities. I sometimes beat myself up for doing the wrong thing, but I usually got over it and tried not to make the same mistake again.

During the second or third year that I fished halibut, I found myself setting gear on a flat calm, sunny day. It was May, and the snow-capped mountains on the west side of Cook Inlet were showing off their beauty. In front of me was a volcano named Iliamna. To the south was the volcano called Augustine, and a short distance to the north was Mount Redoubt, another volcano. Of the three, only Iliamna was puffing smoke.

During the years, I've witnessed all three of these mountains come alive and blast off at one time or another. Mount Redoubt must have heard me mention her name, because she just blew her top last night. So far, no big deal though, just a little ash fallout.

I was enjoying the warmth of the sun as well as the grandeur of the mountains. I took my shirt off so my white Alaskan skin could absorb a bit of Vitamin D. I couldn't take my rain pants off because of the slime and gurry, but the sun surely felt luxurious on my upper body. It's not often that the sea is mirror calm, so after I set all of my gear, I sprawled out on the deck and let the boat drift. I closed my eyes but didn't allow myself to go to sleep, because ships sometimes go up and down the inlet. If they hit my little boat, they wouldn't even know that they'd run over such a small morsel, and everybody would wonder what became of me.

I let a couple of hours go by and just couldn't wait any longer. I had visions of big slabs on every hook. I had drifted eight to ten miles north of my first set. The tides were not big that day, only fourteen feet, but it still took me more than an hour to get back to where my landmarks lined up. My flagpole and buoy were nowhere in sight. I checked my logbook to make sure that I was looking in the right spot. I got my binoculars and scanned the area. With the conditions as nice as they were, it should be easy to see the flag. Not.

I went a mile further to the south: nothing; back to the north: nothing. I went to the south again. This time I chugged two miles below where the set should have been. There was plenty of scope on the buoy lines, so I knew that the tides hadn't sucked them under. Again I took out the binocs and searched. Finally, I barely saw a flag hanging limp on the windless water, but it was too far south to be mine. I hadn't seen any other boats, so I proceeded south to check out the flag. Before I got there, I noticed several black fins on the surface. It was a pod of killer whales. I could see my flag and buoy moving, so I knew that one of the whales had done a no-no. One of them had gotten tangled in my ground line or had tried to make off with one of my halibut and got caught. Before I reached the set, the buoy stopped moving and the whales swam off. The guilty whale luckily got loose. It surely did make a mess of my line though. There were places where there were thirty or more hooks sucked together and gobs of tangled line. It took me hours to untangle everything. There was zero halibut. The other two sets had a fair amount of fish, but I figured that I had better leave the area.

Most days I could run the sets twice, and sometimes it would take three days to load up. Then it would be the long trip to Homer to deliver. I didn't have an autopilot in those days, so I had to stay on the wheel for the duration. I would deliver my fish, clean the boat, and rest for a night, then do a repeat: bait up, take on ice, and go to sea. It was a hard grind, but it was a living, and it wasn't without excitement.

When my boy, Eric, was ten, he asked me if he could go with me on a halibut trip. I agreed, thinking we would have a nice father-son time together, but while pulling a set, a hook caught on the bottom of the transom, and when it released, it hit me in the eye with the force of a flying sledgehammer. It knocked me down and bloodied my eyebrow and eye. It was an hour or two before I could see with that eye and then it was blurry. When we resumed pulling line, Eric hollered that a monster halibut was on the next hook. I stopped the reel and grabbed my 357 magnum. I shot the big gal (the biggest ones are all gals) and rammed my harpoon through her. I then sunk a gaff into her head, but realized that I wouldn't be able to pull her in from the cockpit. I tied the gaff to the fairleads and got up on the rail. I told Eric to stand back. I put every ounce of effort into it and finally got the biggest part of her over the gunnels. When she flopped in, I landed on the edge of the reel and thought I'd broken my back. It knocked the wind out of me, so I didn't move for a while. Eric was scared and didn't know how to comfort me. When I was able to breathe again, I slowly moved into a sitting position, which gave Eric instant relief. He told me later that he thought I was dying. We had to call it a day, and headed to Homer to unload. The weather got snotty and I was hurting, so I dropped anchor near Anchor Point so that I could rest for a bit. I kept seeing lightning flashes with my bad eye, and my back was stiffening. After a couple of hours, I gathered my strength and, with Eric's help, pulled the anchor. It was a good thing that I took that little guy with me because I don't know if I could have gotten home by myself. He took the wheel, and helped me tie to the pilings when we got to Homer. It took a week or so, but I healed fine. My eye cleared and I have good vision to this day.

Eric had the makings of a fisherman. He enjoyed the sea and never got sick, but following in my footsteps was not his destiny. Perhaps the timing was not right. The electronic world was beginning to pop, and he took to it like Bill Gates.

Sometime in the late 60s, I went to Prince William Sound again to seine herring. That fishery is the most exhilarating of any, and that year was no exception. The seiners and processing tenders gather and await the arrival of the small silvery fish. Every sea predator joins the assembly to get its share too. Most of the fishermen have a "spotter," which is a pilot with an eye that can spot a school of herring from the air no matter what the conditions are. There are great spotters just like there are great fishermen. Put the two together, and you can get rich in a day; that is, if you don't make a mistake and tear a big hole in your net, or collide with another boat that wants the same school of fish that you do, and if your spotter pilot doesn't crash or lose his plane in a snowstorm. As you've gathered by now, many things can go wrong, which they quite often do.

The gathering of the fleet is an awesome sight to see. At first there are just a few boats, but within a couple of days it's as though a city has been born. Some of the protected bays have twenty or more boats tied together. Small single-engine planes are coming and going. Skiffs make trips to the beach or to the tenders, which also act as grocery stores. If the herring don't show up in a reasonable time, the guys get bored and do all kinds of wild things. Some of them put their survival suits on, and their seine skiff tows them around on a hatch cover or any kind of a makeshift water ski. Jumping rope is not just for girls. Contests are held to see who can jump the most times both frontwards and backwards. One of the boats had some talented singers on board. I never knew who it was, but they entertained the fleet with some raunchy songs that they sang over the radio. They called themselves Milky and the Spawners.

I watched the McLay family dig butter clams in a unique way. The dad, Jake, would run his deck hose into the gravel and wash the little fellers out, and the mama, Mid, would pick them up and put them in a bucket. They would steam them and invite anyone and everyone.

We can't forget Herring Rose. She would get on the radio and, like Tokyo Rose during WW2, seductively try to get the seiners to leave the fishing grounds. She would come up with things like "Hi, fellas, where do you think your sweetie is sleeping tonight?" It definitely got to some of the fishermen. They would have their spotter pilot fly them to town. I'm sure that Herring Rose's tactics worked to some extent, and that some of those guys missed the opening. She was more than likely some ambitious fisherman's wife or girlfriend.

Then, usually without notice, Kushtaka, the wind god, would have a fit. When it is springtime in Alaska, you can be sure that there will be a storm or two. I'm talking about hurricane force. The only warning that we sometimes got was from Peggy. She gave the marine forecast over the vhf and single-sideband radios for many years. They didn't have the sophisticated methods that exist now of determining how the weather was developing, but she was right most of the time. If you heard Peggy say, "Storm Warning," you could be quite sure that she was right, so you had better get prepared.

The spring storms were capable of blowing 75 to 100 knots, and that's exactly how hard it blew while we were serenely tucked away on anchor. With the wind came snow, tons of it. Most of the time it blew sideways; consequently the snow didn't accumulate. That particular spring day when the wind peaked, the noise it created was joined by a plea for help, a mayday. The tender G.W. King, which was an 85-foot wooden scow, had broken its anchor line and was going on the rocks. The crew was spared, but in a short time the boat was smashed to pieces by the enormous waves that relentlessly pounded her aging hull.

As night approached, the wind subsided, but the snow came on like you wouldn't believe. Some of the spotter planes were on floats and were tied to the stern of some of the seine boats. Most of that city of boats thought they had outlasted Kushtaka, but the snow built up so much on the wings of the planes that one or two of them sank during the night. Some of the seine skiffs that weren't set on the decks of the bigger boats ended up on the beaches. The lucky ones weren't broken to pieces. I believe this was the same year that the sixty-foot boat called the Ruff and Ready went high and dry on a pinnacle at low tide. It was quite a sight to see. Talk about precarious positions. It would have fallen off if there had been the slightest movement, and it surely would have been upside down, so the crew sat tight. High tide came along peacefully, and she floated off and went on her merry way.

The herring came as predicted. The usual predators came with them. Sea lions fished ferociously 24 hours a day. When they surfaced, their mouths overflowed with the shiny morsels, and the seagulls dove for the leftovers. Even at night, because of the phosphorescence in the water, you could see the sea lions moving under the surface. Whales surfaced in all directions. Seals were everywhere. Springtime in Alaska is when the predators get fat, which prepares them for reproduction.

When the opening was announced on the radio by the Department of Fish and Game, all hell broke loose. Thirty spotter planes swarmed above, concentrated in a small area. The pilots had one hand on the mike of their radio and the other on the stick. Their eyes were going crazy, watching their boats, the fish, and most important, the other planes. The job of a spotter pilot is right up there with winter crab fishing when it comes to danger. The seine boats and their skiffs are banging and pushing, vying for position. When each skipper hollers to his skiff man to pull the pin, he has committed to his whole season. There can be no mistakes. There are no holds barred. The more experienced skippers know all the aggressive moves. Every year there are boats that catch hundreds of tons, while others get the weenie. No pantywaists, twinkies, or diaper babies allowed! One of the guys wore a hat that said it all: "GO FOR THE GUSTO OR GO THE blank HOME." Uncouth but true.

On the average, the fleet spends a month on the fishing grounds waiting for the fish to arrive, but are allowed only two hours of fishing time. We managed to stay out of trouble and scratched up eighty tons for our efforts. Not great, but not bad, considering the fact that some guys didn't catch a fish and lost everything they had. It was a wonderful feeling to make some money in the early spring after going through a long winter. The experience was invaluable, and at the time making money was paramount.

Moving up a notch or two gave me some priceless experiences, but it didn't come without some losses. To date, the things that I've shared with you are barely the tip of the iceberg, so to speak. I didn't realize it at the time, but the occupations that I chose happened to be categorized as a "hazardous to your health" type of lifestyle, but had my way of life been more laid back and complacent, it probably would have caused restlessness.

As soon as the Prince William Sound herring season finishes, some of the fishermen make a mad thousand mile run to Togiak to take in the later run of herring. Togiak is in Bristol Bay which means crossing the Bering Sea to get there.

A good friend of mine that I had guided with the year before was one of the pilots that spotted for some of the boats that went to Togiak. Dick Moll was one of the best spotters, and was a fine gentleman. He and a pilot from Seward crashed into each other and no one survived. I was so saddened when I heard about the accident. Dick's son Mike took over the spotting business and became a great spotter like his dad.

Lots of the guys that I hung out with were also pilots. Quite often someone would brag that his plane was the best performer in Alaska. The remark would always spark arguments because bush pilots are continually upgrading their planes with more horsepower, bigger flaps, shorter props, and larger wings. Every year more and more pilots hopped up their planes, always leading to more bragging.

I don't know who the organizer was, but someone got tired of listening to the same old claims every year. The word spread, and everybody who was anybody gathered one day at Kalifonsky Beach when the tide was low. Basil Bolstridge had one of the many Super Cubs that were represented. James Isaak brought his puny J-3 Cub, and there was a Citabria Scout, a Maule, and an Arctic Tern. The event would be referred to as "The B.S. Eliminator."

Wind would not be a factor because there was none. It was a balmy 55° and flat calm. Some of the guys were so anxious to show off the performance of their craft that they clamored to go first. Not everyone knew all the tricks of getting off the ground quickly. You had to have good brakes so that you could "give her the gun" and static the tail up, and then take your feet off the brakes and let her rip! There wasn't much difference among the first half dozen attempts. All of them were between 50 and 75 feet, which is darned good.

Several people joined in taking the measurements. There would be no cheating! Even so, a couple of the first competitors were still arguing about which one had the shortest tire mark when it got down to the last couple of entrants. While they were squabbling, James Isaak taxied to the line. There were a few snickers in the crowd because James had a fraction of the horsepower that most of the prior entries had. James was young, but his dad had taught him well, and the kid had also done most of his flying on and off the beaches. On the wings of the bright yellow J-3 was written "JESUS IS MY LORD." James did everything right. He even made sure that he had very little gas in the tank. There was no electrical system to weigh the plane down, and James himself probably didn't weigh more than 140 pounds. With full throttle and the brakes on, the sand blasted behind him. He no more than released the brakes when he was airborne. The distance was an unbelievable nineteen feet. The crowd was totally awed, and they cheered James as he came back for a landing. Being a lot like his mom and dad, James wasn't much for "strutting his stuff," so he modestly sauntered off to the side.

The last plane taxied up to the line. It was a Super Cub that belonged to Basil Bolstridge, but Basil wasn't the pilot. At first glance it appeared to be a little girl! As it turned out, it was a 100-pound woman. She could barely see over the instrument panel. I never did know her name, but will refer to her as Miss Smallgood. When the little lady punched the throttle to the hilt, the plane came to attention like a horse that had been hit with a willow switch. The tail gyrated up, and when she released the brakes, the tires left the ground within a few feet. When measured, it was less than the length of the plane. She had beat James by one foot. Miss Smallgood won the "B.S. Eliminator" trophy, which was not in the form of shiny metal, but was instead all the smiles and cheers, and a five-minute hug from Basil.

Most of the entrants were unaware of the alterations that Basil had made to achieve 100% bragging rights. The gas had been drained from both tanks and then only a cup or two put back in. Everything that could be stripped

James Isaak preparing for the B.S. Eliminator contest.

from the Cub had been. Of course the lightweight woman that possessed short-field takeoff skills was the ingredient that made it happen.

I always savored my time with the kids. Sometimes in the evenings I would help them with their homework and then teach them songs like "The Little Old Lady That Swallowed a Fly" or tell them my version of the pea that wanted desperately to get eaten. They all seemed to love being scared, so I often hid and gave them a "boo" when they found me, or I'd make up some scary stories … but never right before bedtime. Cheryl and Suzie were the oldest, so when we referred to them, it was "the big girls." Laurie and Cindy were "the little girls." You would have thought that Eric, who was five years younger than Cindy, would be picked on all the time, but usually the girls got along with him fine. He was always pretty easygoing and didn't seem to be a pest to the girls, so there were very few problems. Suzie was the most high-spirited, and was the first to try new things.

The big girls approached me one day and begged me to buy them some horses. I tried to convince them that a guinea pig or two would be much better. Cheryl had puppy dog eyes, and Suzie had a tactful, convincing way about her. I had never owned horses before, but thought that I had a pretty good idea of the work involved in their upkeep, not to mention the money. But I was a pushover, even after lecturing them on the responsibilities and stressing that they would have to do ALL the work involved. Actually, I didn't have any more clue as to what we would be getting ourselves into than they did.

I was about to learn how demanding and painful it can be to be a horse owner. I guess that a person who was raised around horses would have an inkling how to go about such a thing. In my case it wasn't just another "wild hair" that prompted me to become a horse owner; it was those manipulating daughters of mine. A neighbor just so happened to have three horses for sale. When the girls heard about it, they pleaded for me to buy them. Cheryl's eyelashes fluttered and Suzie begged. How could I refuse? The guinea pig thing didn't even come close to working. Next thing I knew, we were building a corral. Yep, we were the proud new owners of Bo Weevil, Brownie, and Smokey.

We didn't have any fenced-in fields, nor did we have any hay crops, so we had to buy hay, and we had to constantly stake the horses out so they could have a new grassy spot to nibble on each day. One day the girls were moving the horses to new grounds when Smokey got frisky with Cheryl. She was about to tie his line around a tree when he lunged and took the end of her finger off. I heard her screaming a quarter of a mile away. When I saw the damage, I wrapped her finger in gauze and rushed her to the doctor. The rope had nipped the end right off, so the doctor just sewed the skin over the end.

When our house burned, the horses inhaled some smoke and Bo Weevil went down. I had to build a tripod and raise him with a come-along. To do this, I put one line behind his front legs and another near his rear legs. I tried to use some rags as padding so the lines wouldn't chafe his underside. The rear line cut off his bladder, and he went unconscious and fell out of the lift. It was up and down for weeks. I had my hands full with other important stuff, so it wasn't easy to make time for the poor horse. If you'd seen his condition, you wouldn't have given him a five percent chance of survival. One day I glanced out the window to see how he was doing, and the horses were gone, including Bo Weevil! The first signs of new grass were beginning to show, and the horses were no longer satisfied with dry hay. We found them several days later five miles away. I had to tie them behind my car and herd them all the way back home. The girls were so happy when they saw me driving back with the three horses following.

Our homestead became a real menagerie. We had chickens, geese, rabbits, a cow, horses, and five sled dogs outside and a few guinea pigs and a cat in the house. Animals and kids go hand in hand, but the feed for the tribe was costing a bit much.

After observing my kids, grandkids, and other people's kids, I've come to the conclusion that 99% of the time the novelty of caring for an animal wears off within six months. I'm sure a few kids are exceptions to this rule, but so few as to make it a risky proposition to imagine that the parents won't pretty quickly inherit the responsibility of feeding and caring for the pet. Maybe it's a form of payback: nature's way of getting even for what we almost surely did to our own parents when we were kids.

I really can't complain too much. On a scale of one to ten, my kids were about a six when it came to the feeding and caring for their critters. On the whole, animals are wonderful for little people. They have a way of teaching kids about life, and animals don't care if you are nasty to others or talk with your mouth full or pick your nose. Just feed and water them, and maybe give them a little pat or scratch every now and then, and the animal is a devoted companion.

There are a few other lessons kids may learn from their pets, for example, the finer points of mating and birthing and how to bully others to get more than their share of the food. If you've wondered where your kid learned to be a push-and-shove kind of person, it's not always the genes. They might have learned from that pet rooster or goose that will attack anything that wiggles. Maybe your daughter learned her table manners from the 4-H pig she's raising. Well, I'm kidding, of course (mostly). There may be a few things you would rather your kids not see, but definitely the kids learn a bunch of good from their animals, which is something to keep in mind when one becomes fed up with feeding and caring for the kids' pets.

I was taken aback when the boys started coming by. All of my daughters and my son are good-looking, so I shouldn't have been surprised to see the stream of boys that trudged more than a half mile to our homestead to "play" with our daughters. I would tease them by telling them that our daughters couldn't come out unless they helped split and haul firewood or did some other chores. Ha, never once did I get any work out of any of those drooling boys. You'd have thought that I would have seen it coming. When I was twelve, I drooled and slobbered when any girl got within an arm's reach. I thought that I was controlling the situation with my girls quite well, but truly I was clueless. Years later when the girls were married and had kids of their own, I was informed that they all had slipped out the back windows of the house and got together with the boys. Four beautiful daughters and I was totally naïve. They did away with chastity belts years ago, right?

During the mid-sixties and early seventies, there were times that I didn't have a job, so it was fitting that I do some trapping to supplement our income. I happened to cross paths with Gene, whom I hadn't seen since working with United Geophysical shortly after coming to Alaska. Both of us had planes, and neither of us was working at the time, so we teamed up and did some trapping.

Gene was extremely smart, but never made any attempt to act superior. He also was very meticulous and methodical. I, on the other hand, was more a "get it done now" type of person. As different as our personalities were, we got along well and seldom had disagreements. I surely learned more from Gene than he learned from me, but overall we had great times trapping and flying together. I brought to the table my previously-learned skill at trapping and skinning. Gene, on the other hand, read up on the subject and, through trial and error, became a very good trapper.

I had built a log cabin at Twin Lakes on the west side of the Alaska Range, which became our base camp. The cabin was 14'x20' and quite comfortable. I had built a log table, chairs, and bunks, all of which lent to the comforts of home. The barrel stove that I built was the most important piece of handiwork because it not only kept us warm when it was 60° below, but we also did most of our cooking on the flat surface.

Each evening we would put our planes "to bed" by placing a catalytic heater under the cowling and then cover the whole engine cowling with homemade insulated covers. This course of action allowed the engines to start the next morning, even if the temperature got down to -40°. We made a rule that we wouldn't fly if the thermometer got below -40°. It proved to be a good rule because people and machinery tend to break when it gets colder than that.

During mid-winter that year, there was a sudden change in the weather. Overnight the temperature went from sub-zero to 40° above. A huge low system had moved into south-central Alaska and was causing shirtsleeve weather. The snow was melting and there was water standing on the lakes. Trapping became difficult, so we decided to take a break and fly down to Lake Iliamna to see what the locals were up to. We took Gene's plane and left my Champ behind. Iliamna is huge, so it takes much longer to freeze than the smaller lakes. When we circled the north end of the lake, it was obvious that the warm air had melted lots of snow and ice there too. All along the shoreline, water was standing on the ice. Three guys were on the shore, so we made an approach to land on the ice and visit with them. When you land on glare ice, it takes forever to stop because there is no way to brake. Gene touched the skis down nicely and throttled back. Then, in a blink of an eye, there was open water immediately in front of us! Gene reacted by hitting the throttle full bore. The skis skimmed across the water and we managed not to sink. There was ice on the other side of the fifty-foot stretch of water, so when we got to it, Gene yanked the throttle all the way back, but we still ended up on the grassy slope.

Thanks to Gene's quick reaction, we didn't have a misconbloberation. There was no damage done. When we got out of the plane, the three guys came over and congratulated us on the show. When we introduced ourselves, one of the guys said that his name was Crapashets. I thought I'd heard him wrong, but he smiled and said that I'd heard him right. We had a good visit and then departed without skimming open water.

Because Gene was more meticulous than I was, I sometimes got a little impatient when we were pre-flighting the planes. Eventually I learned the importance of a thorough pre-flight. The chances of metal fractures and other problems might be detected if a good inspection was done prior to flying. We used skis on the planes in the winter, and they don't have much "give," compared to tires. Both of us were good bush pilots, so for the most part our planes stayed in one piece.

One sunny, calm winter day we took Gene's PA-12 to check the trap line. Maybe the weather was too nice, because it led Gene to land on a small lake to see if there was much "critter" sign. Gene's depth perception was a tad off, and he "landed" six or eight feet above the smooth ice of the lake, which meant that the plane stalled out and hit the ice a bit hard. The landing gear on the right side broke on impact, and the wingtip dragged on the ice until the plane came to a stop.

This was the mid-sixties, and there were no other planes flying around. We were many miles from any civilization, so there was no one to call on for help. I could readily tell by Gene's language that he was slightly mad at himself. When we got out and looked over the situation, we put a plan together. We always carried small "Swede" saws in our planes, and we used them daily. I went to the edge of the lake, cut a few spruce poles, and hacked them into various lengths. I cut a notch in the top of each pole so we could prop it under the wing strut. Then we chipped a divot out of the ice to put the bottom of the pole in. I got under the wing and pushed up while Gene put the shortest pole in place. Then, after a short rest, I got under the wing again and Gene placed a longer pole. We repeated this procedure, with Gene inserting a longer pole each time, until the plane was level. After we pulled the landing gear back into place, we used trapping wire, duct tape, and quarter-inch line to hold it. We referred to this as "Jerre-rigged." Even though it looked skookum enough, neither of us breathed when we took off or when we landed by the cabin. It probably would have stayed together all winter, but Gene flew back to Kenai and got it repaired.

During the winters that we trapped together, we learned to appreciate our surroundings. Because there were almost no other planes flying around, we had an abundance of fur to trap, and there was always bookoos of caribou. Most of our trips back home included "meat in the seat." Our families would enjoy a boo or two every time we came back. They also loved to see all the fox, wolverine, wolf, and lynx furs that we had harvested.

Quite often I would bring along whole fillets of smoked salmon for Gene and me to munch on. The floor of the cabin was gravel, so it was easy access for an ermine that couldn't resist the tantalizing aroma of the salmon. He would invite himself in while we were playing cribbage and jump as high as he could in an attempt to reach the hanging morsel. One of us would give in to his begging and lower the salmon just enough for the little white critter to jump up and latch onto it. He would hang on for dear life, even if we raised it several feet off the ground. He wouldn't stop eating until his little belly was swollen. This little ermine circus was a welcome diversion because I was so bored from beating Gene so many times at crib. On one of his trips back to the Kenai Peninsula, he got his chess set and brought it

Gene's PA-12 with a broken landing gear.

back to Twin Lakes. I had never played the game, but Gene patiently tried to teach me. Within an hour he gave up on me and I never saw a pawn again.

One evening when we'd finished skinning and stretching the furs we had caught that day—and of course when I'd finished "diving for pearls" (doing dishes)—we somehow got on the subject of women's work. While in our giddy mood, one of us decided that we should make a "squaw manual" and list all of their duties (don't take offense ladies; it was all in fun): things like splitting wood, changing oil in vehicles, sheet rocking and spackling, and for sure chewing hides to make them supple. We laughed the night away, thinking of a hundred different things that would be listed as "squaw work." I wouldn't dare mention most of the subjects that we came up with that night. It's probably a good thing that we never put the Squaw Manual in black and white. Someone might have taken it seriously. Tears continued to roll down our cheeks as we dozed off that night.

Almost all of the trips to Twin Lakes required flying through Lake Clark Pass. The Pass is as moody as a midlife crisis. Most of the 200 or so times that I've flown through the pass, I've witnessed one of the most scenic

Just being able to breathe the crisp, clean Alaska air is a gift.

places on the planet. There are jagged mountains on both sides that rise to eight thousand feet. Several eye-popping glaciers with blue tones are nestled between the multi-colored mountains. Emerald and turquoise lakes punctuate the landscape. As they say, it is a sight to see.

When her mood changes, though, hang on to your seat and pray, because the pass can get nasty! I've flown through there when I thought the turbulence was going to tear the wings off my plane. It seemed that it would wait until I got halfway or more through before it turned on its charm. One time in particular I was bouncing around (with my seat belt as tight as it could be cinched) and all of a sudden a downdraught hit me and pushed me toward the ground. I pushed the throttle all the way forward and held the stick back as far as I dared. Still the ground was screaming up at me. I was holding on to the bottom of my seat with one hand and the stick with the other. It was like I was trying to squeeze blood out of the stick! The sky was an ugly grey, a complement to the mood of the wind. The downdraught pushed its thumb on me like I was a little toy. I think I was less than 100 feet above the ground when she took her hand off, but then her sister, "Little

Miss Up-Draught," got into the act. In an instant I was shooting upward just as fast as I had gone down. First I had lost 1500 feet, and now I was gaining so much altitude that I was being slung up into those wicked-looking clouds. I had to yank the throttle back and push the stick forward. Fortunately there were occasional breaks in the clouds that enabled me to determine whether I was upside-down or not. When my altimeter read 6000 feet, the wind stopped playing with me. Gosh, my wings were still intact! When I emerged from the pass, the air was as smooth as a baby's butt. It was then that I realized that my butt was as tight as the proverbial bow fiddle and my knuckles were white. I relaxed both parts and continued home.

Two years prior to the down and up event, the Lintz brothers experienced the same type of downdraught, but it squished them to the ground. Paul survived with a broken back, but unfortunately his brother Dave didn't make it. There are several other planes that litter the landscape in the pass, and they are reminders that it can be cruel in there.

Chapter 10

Changing Times

I had some marital problems in 1971 and found myself in the woods, screaming at the world. For some strange reason, that was how I dealt with it. I was hoping that God would hear me and make the problem go away. This was one of those times in my life that I refer to as "a skating season in hell."

I went away on a construction job in the bush, which is almost funny because my time away from home surely wasn't the best thing for a marriage. Alaska had become my mistress and I plead guilty of being gone fishing and working away from home so much. The work gave me some temporary relief, but my personal situation was one that seemed to have no closure. I carried it on my shoulders for several years, and then I finally got strong enough to call it quits. The time for divorce had come. I'm not trying to play the part of a martyr, nor am I claiming to be exempt from fault. It was a terrible decision to make because of the kids and because I was so attached to the Reflection Lake homestead. An ocean of happy and sad tears had been shed there. It was there that I learned about the land, and I loved every inch of the 120 acres. I had so much pleasure watching the kids frolicking in the lake and playing with their animals. Damn, there wasn't much that I didn't love about those years on the homestead, but this was one of those times in my life that I felt that there was no other solution and that I must leave all the material things behind. At least nobody could strip me of my memories.

Perhaps what I needed right then was to be alone. Trapping was the first thing that came to mind, so I called Gene Kempf and asked him if he

These sheep would have been a meal for the wolves if we hadn't come along.

could fly me to my trapping cabin at Twin Lakes. I had sold my plane, so I would do the trap line on snowshoes. We loaded Gene's Super Cub with my food and supplies, and off we went. When we cleared the last mountain and began the descent to the lake, I spotted something on the glare ice. A closer look revealed a mama sheep and her lamb. The mama's legs had gone out from under her, and she was doing the splits, front and back. The lamb was okay, but it couldn't do anything but watch its mom in her helpless state. Gene landed the plane, and we lifted Mama until her legs were under her. She was too weak to support herself, so Gene and I had to put our coats under her belly and shore her up by holding onto the sleeves. It was at least 300 yards to the beach, so we had to stop and rest several times before we got her there. The poor little lamb didn't know what to think, but it followed along. Once we reached the secure footing onshore, Mama stood on her own, and after a few minutes she regained enough strength to head up the mountain with her lamb. She stopped and gave us one last look and then trudged on. It was a wonder that the wolves didn't find her before we did. I saw her the following fall straight up the mountain from my cabin.

It didn't take long to get settled in, and I enjoyed the solitude and serenity. Twin Lakes is surrounded on three sides by mountains, which provide majestic beauty, but also block the sun. It would be six weeks before I would see a glimpse or feel the warmth of it.

Shortly after I arrived, the weather moderated, so for the next three weeks the temperatures were unusually warm. Generally the mercury in this part of interior Alaska plunges to 30° below or colder at this time of year, but shortly after I arrived, the weather changed, and for the next three weeks temperatures were unusually warm, with highs 40° or better each day. The warm weather made trapping on snowshoes almost impossible, as the mushy snow made it so difficult to get to the traps. Besides, furbearers don't move around much unless it's cold enough to make it necessary for them to hunt widely for food, so the likelihood that my traps would yield bounty was small. It was easy to heat my cozy Twin Lakes log cabin, but as the days went by, I felt a bad case of cabin fever coming on. I had very little iron set out, and my catch consisted of only a handful of furs. Staying busy was no problem. Hunting rabbits and ptarmigan for meat, combined with daily chores, kept me occupied. I had time to make a couple more log chairs that I had been putting off and to enlarge my supply of firewood. For the past week I'd had a strong urge to walk down-country to one of my other trapping cabins.

One afternoon I hit my thumb with a hammer while building furniture. That was what it took to make me give in and make the 25-mile hike to another cabin that I owned. I threw my tools down and began gathering the bare necessities for the trip. It would take only six hours or so to get to my other cabin at Snipe Lake. There wasn't a whole lot to do when I got there, but I just had to get out and do something different. I didn't take much in the way of food because I planned to return in a day or two. My pack was light at 25 pounds or so. As it neared 1:00 p.m. I slung my 7mm magnum on my shoulder and bade farewell to my main cabin, which is located 125 miles southwest of Anchorage at Twin Lakes. The upper lake, where my cabin sits, is seven miles long and the lower lake is five. Both are about one mile wide. The lakes are nestled among the rugged but beautiful Chigmit Mountains.

I left a note on the table for anyone that might happen by, telling them my whereabouts and when I expected to return. It was rare that anybody visited me, but once in a while some of my flying buddies dropped by to see how much fur I'd accumulated.

Because I started so late in the day, I knew that the latter part of the journey would be in the dark, but it was only partly cloudy, so the half moon would give me enough light to find my way. I knew the terrain well, so I had no concerns about traveling at night. After all, I had hunted and trapped this area for a dozen years.

As I approached the short stream that connects the two lakes, I thought about the grayling and lake trout that I had caught there before. I didn't want to take the time to fish on this trip, but it would have been nice to have a fresh fish to cook when I got to the other cabin. The stream is also a natural place for furbearers to check out, so I decided that when the weather got colder, I would make several sets there. Just three days before, I had shot four ptarmigan in this same spot. By the time I reached the west end of the lower lake, I was perspiring a fair amount. Traveling was good, so I was "making tracks." Caribou travel faster when they are feeding, but I was happy with my progress. "I'll never forget the time," I mused as I crossed the end of the lake, "when old Swihart landed his ratty Super Cub in the hummocks in pursuit of some caribou." Later that day he "pranged" one of his landing gears.

I gained some altitude to where the wind had blown the snow off the mountainside. There was a caribou trail for me to follow, which made it easier for me to walk on the snow. It was almost like a paved road, so I could jog in places. If the conditions remained like this, I would reach the other cabin in less time than I had anticipated. After about four more miles, I was nearing "Lookout Knob," a hill that rises about 500 feet above the surrounding country. I dubbed it with that name because it's a natural place for predators to look for prey. When on top of this knob, one can see for miles in every direction. I would skirt it this trip though, as time wouldn't allow me the pleasure of viewing the country from the top. It was the time of year when daylight hours were at their shortest, so dusk was settling on the land. Even if the day is clear, the mountains block the sun from shining in that valley. There were about six or seven weeks each winter when I didn't get to feel the warmth of the sun's rays at all. It was completely dark at 4:30.

I would have to move to a lower elevation to keep a straight line to Snipe Lake where my cabin was located. Traveling was getting increasingly difficult by the time I got to the lowlands. The snow was only four inches on the level, but every dip or ravine contained two to five feet. Most of it was soft, and I found myself sinking up to my waist, so my progress slowed to a snail's pace. The soft snow was tiring me by the minute. My legs were telling me that they wanted to stop, but I didn't even have a tarp to use as a makeshift camp. I trudged on, but the conditions didn't improve. The half moon slipped behind the clouds, and my body tensed because I couldn't tell when I would encounter the next dip. I wasn't in survival mode, but I was wishing that I had traveled during daylight hours. This was getting to be a long, drawn-out jaunt. I was down on myself for breaking my number one rule: "When in the wilderness by yourself, be safe!" Even my lightweight pack was feeling terribly heavy. I took my coat off and put it in the pack because I was so hot. It was time to take a short break. I hadn't stopped since I set out, and I had covered about 22 miles. I scooped up a handful of snow and savored the cooling effect as it made its way to my stomach. I rubbed some on my forehead and hair, then put another handful in my mouth. Darn, I got a "boing." Some people call it a brain freeze. I donned my pack and slung my rifle over my shoulder. The clouds continued to obscure the half-moon, but once in a while I could barely make out the snow-covered Snipe Lake. It appeared to be no more than a half-mile away. My cabin was on the opposite side, which was another three quarters of a mile.

I was trying to focus my eyes on the ground to avoid getting in the deeper snow, so I didn't notice anything unusual until suddenly a wolf let out a low, short howl. It was close. It startled the dickens out of me, but my reflexes reacted and I snapped my rifle to my shoulder. The wolf was dark but visible in the snow and was only thirty feet or so in front of me. There was another shadow a short distance behind and to the left of the first one, and then I saw movement to my side. Darn, I had been stalked!

The wolf's head filled the picture in my scope. I lowered the barrel a bit and squeezed the trigger when I thought I had it aimed at its chest. Oh man, I forgot to push the safety forward. The wolf was sneaking closer as I fumbled with the safety. Again, I put its chest in the scope picture and quickly squeezed the trigger. When the gun went off, I was blinded by the muzzle blast! After a few seconds, my eyes caught movement of wolves running on both sides. They weren't coming at me, but seemed confused by the blast of the gun. I wasn't able to put the scope on them, so instinctively I ran.

Adrenalin flooded every inch of my body and it was like I was totally rejuvenated. I kept glancing over my shoulder, but I couldn't make out any movement. If I could reach the lake, I could hold off an attack better. As I ran, half stumbling, I unsheathed my knife and fumbled for extra cartridges. The loudest, most bloodcurdling howling wailed out. There must have been ten or more of the hungry canines, and they weren't far away. The frozen lake provided better footing, so I lengthened my stride, going as fast as I could without making my heart pound too mich. If I had to stand them off, I didn't want the sights of my rifle bobbing up and down with every heartbeat.

The howling stopped. I came to a halt and held my breath so I could hear better. I didn't hear or see anything, but I knew that when they weren't howling they were probably on the move. I turned and ran towards the far side of the lake where my cabin was. Except for the rhythmic sound of my footsteps, the night was silent. I was three quarters of the way across the lake when the howling struck up with an excited tone. Then the chorus stopped, and I figured that they had decided to resume the chase.

I had two choices. Either I stood my ground and let my heart calm some before I had to start shooting, or I ran for all I was worth and tried to make it to the cabin before they got me. I ran! When I was most of the way across the lake, I glanced back and could make them out two thirds of the way across, and they were coming on strong. I was now in panic mode as I sprinted the remaining 200 yards to my safe haven.

Fortunately I never lock the doors on my cabins, because if someone wants to use a cabin, they will break in somehow. I slammed the door behind me and bolted it. I tried to look out the two small windows to see if the wolves were close to the cabin, but they were so badly frosted that I couldn't see anything. The eerie howling had ceased, but not the thumping of my heart. I was in desperate need of something to drink. I was so dehydrated that I couldn't even swallow. When my heartbeat got back to normal, I listened intently for any sounds outside. After an hour or so, I slowly opened the door. I stuck the barrel of my rifle out, but in the dim moonlight the wolves were nowhere to be seen. I quickly dipped up a pot of snow and hurried back inside. The firewood and kindling that I had gathered during the late fall were still there, so I started the wood stove and melted the snow. I took my clothes off and hung them to dry. The world seemed much better now that I was safe and had some water to drink. Although I felt triumphant, I was a bit shaken by the whole ordeal. I owed my survival to my 7mm magnum rifle. There was no doubt that the wolves had sensed that I was in a weakened state and therefore easy prey. Perhaps they had been unsuccessful on their quest for food, so were willing to take on a single human showing signs of weakness. Had it not been for the low howl that the one wolf let out, they could have overtaken me easily.

Hunting is the wolf's' sole occupation. He knows every trick associated with it. He is big, strong, and has an extremely sharp mind. These wolves could sense that I was alone and tired and weak just by the sound of my uncoordinated steps. I was a prime prospect for a carnivorous predator.

During the many years that I've trapped in this part of Alaska, I've never caught more than three wolves in a season. Only one or two weighed less than 150 pounds, which is my weight when soaking wet. The wolves in this part of the country are big. They are so smart that very few trappers catch more than a handful of wolves each season.

There was no sign of the wolves at daybreak. My daughter Cindy had told me that she and her husband, Clark, would like to use this cabin to trap from, but that they wouldn't be able to come until mid-season or later. They would appreciate a clean place to stay, so I tidied the cabin and repaired the holes that the squirrels had made, and then did a quick survey of the fur sign before heading back to Twin Lakes.

Before I was across Snipe Lake, I heard a single howl. Then the whole pack sang out. I could see them through the scope on my rifle. There were two blacks and seven grays. They appeared to be feeding on something near the same area where I shot one of them. When they saw me, they ran off and headed up the mountain. When I reached the area where they had been, I was awed to see the remaining fur and bones of the wolf that I shot. They had eaten their own.

As I continued back to Twin Lakes, I thought about the skeptics that lead others to believe that wolves don't attack people. Well, I'm here to say that they definitely do. I wonder how many hunters or trappers that have been placed on the missing list were the victims of a wolf attack. I have always had great admiration for the intelligence of wolves and still do. Now I have an additional feeling that is hard to describe, but I guess it's more of a feeling of fear, because I now know that there are times when hunger will cause them to prey on anything that wiggles.

After traveling for an hour, the sound of wolves howling rang out once more. I stopped in my tracks and listened. It was a beautiful, blue sky, silent day. Now the howling sounded romantic like the typical storybook description. I took my time going back to Twin Lakes, picking my way around the dips of deep, soft snow. Time not being of the essence, I took the opportunity to climb Lookout Knob. I relaxed and thoroughly enjoyed the grandeur of the scenery. The sun barely cleared the horizon. I hadn't seen the great orange ball for five weeks or so.

When I got back to my Twin Lakes cabin, I sat down outside and rested my back against the log wall. Looking back down-country, I thanked God for my 7mm magnum and an obedient, strong pair of legs. While relaxing, I thought about my friend Tom Walker. He is a great outdoorsman and a fantastic photographer and writer. Tom has had some profound experiences with wolves and has written about the intelligence of the canine.

Three weeks after my confrontation with the hungry wolves, the "camp-robbers" (grey jays) were tiring of listening to my babble. I was wondering if Cindy and Clark were at the other cabin yet, so I donned my snowshoes once again and began the 25-mile trek. The snow was soft, which made traveling slow. Even though I started early in the day, it still got dark before I reached the lake. I was getting a little edgy and was looking over my shoulder quite often. I could see a light in the cabin window as I crossed Snipe Lake. Cindy and Clark must be there. When I got closer, I could see a plane on the lake, so I knew that they had company. Apparently it had gotten too hot in the cabin, because the door was open. Nobody was expecting me, so when I stepped into the doorway, everybody let out a scream. I'm sure that I looked like a wild man, and I was carrying a gun. The two guys that were visiting were on the floor in their sleeping bags. When they saw me, they nearly jumped out of their bags, all the while screaming like little girls. Then Cindy recognized me and ran over the guys on the floor to give me a hug. I was about to tell them that I would have sent a smoke signal to let them know I was coming, but when I tried to speak, nothing came out. I hadn't talked for a long time, so didn't know that my voice was gone. Lucky for me, the two visitors had brought some beer and had a couple left. The beer brought my voice back, but then I got giggly. Both Cindy and Clark are full of the dickens, so we laughed the night away. Laughter has a way of curing the blues.

I returned to Twin Lakes the following day rejuvenated enough to make the remainder of the winter tolerable. My trap line was always productive; consequently I finished the season with a respectable catch. The fox population was overflowing, and I caught more wolverines that winter (and most winters I trapped) than most trappers catch in a lifetime.

When Gene had dropped me off, he'd asked when he should come back to pick me up. I was feeling so down at the time, that I told him not to bother coming back. Now March was upon me, and it was time to pull the traps. I hadn't seen anybody since mid-winter when I visited Cindy and Clark. Finally, one evening just before dark, I heard a plane, and it was headed towards my cabin. It was Ron and Steve, two lifelong friends from the Soldotna/Kasilof area, and they were flying Ron's Cessna 180. They landed and said they saw smoke coming from my chimney, so they stopped to say hello. I was ready to go back to civilization, so I asked if they had room for me and my furs. They had plenty of room in the back seats, so they agreed to accommodate me. I closed the cabin down as quickly as I could and loaded my furs and junk, and off we went. It was dark, but there was moonlight, so navigating was not a problem.

When we got to the east side of the Alaska Range, we ran into solid fog. Ron thought maybe we could get under it, so there we were, trying to sneak along just ten feet off the pan ice in Cook Inlet. The fog closed in on us just before we reached terra firma, so we had to abort and go back to the west side of the inlet. I was beginning to pucker a bit, and I was wishing that I had stayed in the comfort and safety of my cabin. We managed to get to the village of Tyonek. I didn't know it at the time, but we were running on fumes. Both fuel tanks were on EMPTY. It was late, so most of the natives were sleeping, but we finally found someone that could sell us a couple of gallons of gas. I was skeptical, but Ron thought it was enough to get us to Kenai or Soldotna. It looked as though the fog had thinned, so off we went into the night again. We made it, but I know that we couldn't have had more than a cup or two of fuel left.

The guys said that it was time to hit the Bear Den. It was 2:00 a.m. and the Bear Den bar served a great beer. When we walked in the door, I was unexpectedly greeted by my daughter Suzie. The guys didn't know that she was my daughter. One of them asked me to introduce them to this "hot babe." They pulled their little red horns in a bit when they found out that she was my daughter.

In the spring of '69 I took up running, and that helped my mental state to an extent. I found that when I ran, I thought only about running. A friend of mine, Joe Lawton, had run the famous Mount Marathon race. He told me how exciting it was and urged me to do it. I had watched the race, which takes place in Seward on each Fourth of July. It starts on the main street in town, then continues on a gradual incline for a half-mile or so before reaching the foot of the mountain. The mountain is fairly steep and the incline averages 38 degrees. The runners scramble to the top, which is 3033 feet, then blast down through the shale and a gulch with a creek and all the way back to town. The top runners do the whole thing in 45 minutes or less. I knew immediately that I had to do it.

To train, I would run miles and miles through the week, and on weekends I would run a mountain. I would always try to beat my previous time on each mountain. On my first attempt at the race in 1970, I received the bronze medal in my age category. That pumped me up so much that I still do it. More on that later.

I had gotten my own boat in the early 70s and had added another fishery to my mariner lifestyle. I bought 100 Tanner Crab pots, and outfitted the *Variant* with a "pot puller." I moved my operations to Homer so that I could fish daily in Kachemak Bay. Crab fishing was paying the bills until an oil company pulled an oil platform into the bay. They went right through my long lines of pots. I lost half of them, and they refused to pay for them.

Kachemak Bay is so beautiful that I just loved being there. The bay was teeming with King, Tanner, and Dungeness crab. Shrimp were everywhere, and halibut were abundant. The month of May brought thousands of tons of herring. I was able to participate in all of those fisheries. But like the song goes, "Those were the days my friend," and then there is the saying, "All good things must come to an end." Because of overfishing, combined with El Niño currents, and who knows what all, the fisheries in Kachemak Bay went away one by one.

Homer was not overflowing with single women in those days, and there was little to do at night. I wasn't one for hanging out in the saloons, but I didn't have T.V. or a woman, so I stopped by the Yah Sure Saloon a couple of times. It was humorously entertaining because Dennis Leach was the bartender, and he kept the place lively. Anybody that came through the door was invited to arm wrestle Dennis.

It was an extreme rarity for a stray woman to inhabit the place, especially if she was good-looking. The second time I went there I took a seat on the far side of the bar so I could watch the activities. As I sipped on an Oly beer, Dennis put arms down one after another.

All of a sudden the place went silent. A woman had come in the door, and she was alone! When she took off her coat, all the guys cheered because she was packing big guns. Guys were clamoring to get her to sit by them, but she politely declined and sauntered over by me and sat on the only vacant stool, which was next to me. She was great company because she enjoyed laughing as much as I did. After an hour or so I told her that it was time for me to go to my boat for the night. She asked me if she could come with me. Being the gentleman that I am, how could I refuse?

Several years later I ran into Dennis, and we reminisced about the rare sighting of a "new to Homer" female species. As he put it, "Guys were peeing on the trees, marking their territory!"

Nobody has figured how to take my super view across Kachemak Bay away from me. I never have tired of it. I will always make the claim that this is the most beautiful spot in the world, and I have traveled enough of the planet to know it to be true.

So I'm sitting here bragging on the beauty, but ironically there is an ugly ash cloud closing in on my utopia. Mount Redoubt blew its volcanic head off this morning and the winds are not in our favor. I can see the dusty stuff coming down on the snow now. The sky is very dark. I'm going to have to turn some lights on.

Kachemak Bay used to be the herring capital of North America. During the late 1800s and early 1900s, communities on the south side of the bay thrived from the abundance of herring. Many salteries sprouted up. The old-timers still talk about years when you could walk across the bay on herring. A bit exaggerated, but I'm sure that it was a great era.

But then the little fish disappeared. It's been that way as long as man can remember: one year they come in mass numbers, and the next year, nary a fish. For many years there weren't enough to count on two hands, but they returned in 1969 just as though they'd never left. Again there were great black balls of them. By the time I heard about it, the harvest was all but over for the year.

The following year I geared up and was joined by two other fishermen that were willing to take a chance. All three of us were greenhorns when it came to fishing for herring. We had never caught a single one before. We got an early start and made many practice sets before any fish arrived. Six or eight boats joined us after the fish showed. Nobody had spotter planes, so we had to figure out how to find the little critters. Aha, if we wore a certain kind of dark glasses, we could sometimes see occasional silver flashes under the surface. Other boats saw us set our seine, but they couldn't figure out why we made the set.

I had known for years that certain birds would tell you where fish are. Close observation told me that when it came to herring the gulls knew nothing, but the kittiwakes were the key to it all. If the kittiwakes were in a frenzy, there were herring under them. A couple of the other boats caught on too, but the rest of the boats caught zilch. After pecking away for three weeks, we had delivered 571 tons. Three happy guys we were, we were! Sad to say, there hasn't been an opening in the bay since then.

I bought some property that stretched down to the beach and built a house and a shop. When I build, I do most of the work myself, so it takes a while to have a finished product. That was good in a way, because staying busy kept me from being so lonely.

Bob Hoedel and I had worked on a couple of construction jobs together, and we had several things in common. Both of us were full of the dickens and enjoyed a good laugh. He had always lived in Homer. When I moved there, I frequently visited him, and we became good buddies. We always laughed, even about our divorces. All of the local musicians would gather at Bob's and play hoedown music all night. It was people like Bob that made the hurt ease from leaving the homestead. Unfortunately, several years later, Bob and his new wife, Venita, were killed in a plane crash. Bob's kids, Doug, Nancy, and Robby, are all chips off the old block. They all have the same sense of humor.

I had been in Homer only a short while when I began noticing some outstanding paintings here and there. These masterpieces were the work of Norman Lowell. I was drawn to his art, so I made it a point to go to his homestead and meet him. He and his lovely wife, Libby, greeted me like an old friend. They had homesteaded the same year that I had, and they had built a grand log home and a quaint studio in which Norman spent hours each day. When he showed me all of his paintings, I was totally awed. Every one of the pieces of art was so magnificent that I would have loved to have any of them. I could tell by the price tags that I couldn't afford the smallest one. I was hesitant to inquire, but I got up enough nerve to ask if he ever bartered. He claimed that he enjoyed trading and asked what I had in mind. I told him that I fished for salmon, crab, shrimp, and halibut and added that I didn't know if I could ever give him enough to trade for one of his paintings. He didn't hesitate to agree to a trade. I told him that I would like a "rough sea" scene, and he gave me an idea as to their favorite kinds of fish.

During the next two years, I hauled all kinds of fish to their wonderful homestead and enjoyed the friendship that they shared with me. When Norman surprised me with the painting, I felt so honored—by having one of his art pieces, but even more to have made friends with some great Alaskans. These two hard-working, modest people have now built one of the world's most outstanding studios, and thousands of people come each year to feast their eyes on the wondrous paintings.

I was making plenty of new friends, and my kids came down to visit often, but I didn't like sleeping alone. I missed the little things like having a warm body to snuggle up to at night or enjoying a cup of coffee along with the morning smile of a woman. Most important, I missed having someone to tell that I loved her.

At the time, Homer had a population of 3000, so it doesn't require a mathematician to figure out that the number of single women was close to none, especially in the winter months. Each spring some new blood would show up to look for jobs on boats or in the canneries. They were referred to as "spit rats" because they camped on the five-mile-long spit that protrudes out into Kachemak Bay. Quite a few of those women got jobs stripping herring roe, which made them the "stank" of all smells. The spit rat women were easy to spot, and not always by their smell. They all wore big wool sweaters, Carhartt pants, and for sure Xtratuf boots. These ladies lived and slept in their Xtratuf's. Some of the stores banned herring strippers, but the bars tolerated them as long as they spent money on drinks. Some of the fishermen referred to the gals as "stench skags." The smell was so bad that they claimed that showering couldn't get rid of it. There was only one Laundromat in town, and they refused to let any of the "rats" wash their clothes there. It made me feel kind of sorry for them, but at least they had a job. There were never enough jobs for all the rats that migrated into town each spring, so there were always empty-pocketed hitchhikers headed out of town.

As a single man with my own fishing boat, I managed to attract enough short-term female deckhands, which pacified my love life, or at least my lust life. Had the right woman come along, I would have considered marriage, but for me there are several things that have to come together, not criteria exactly, but certain qualities in a woman's makeup that are important, if not mandatory. A good body is where it starts. I've always kept in shape, so I realize the benefits of better health and wellbeing. I have always played sports, and to this day I run and play basketball. It's not easy to stay in shape, but the rewards are worth the effort. A woman that smiles often draws my attention too. Of course those women that I spent time with had their list of qualities that they were looking for in a man, and I'm sure that I didn't meet their expectations. All of us could go on about the list of qualities we would like in the prefect mate, but let's not get carried away.

Paperwork is one of my least favorite chores, but there always is and always will be that nagging pest. One day I was going through some of my important papers and noticed that my health insurance was about to expire. I hadn't been to a dentist for some time, so thought it would be a good idea to get the pearlies checked out. Off I went to Anchorage. The doc said my wisdom teeth were impacted.

"What does that mean?" I asked.

It meant they never came in like they were supposed to and they were sideways. He claimed that they needed to be removed. He said he would take them out one at a time, but I told him that we needed to do them all in one shot because my insurance was about to run out. He agreed to do it, but warned me that it wouldn't be pleasant and that I would need to have someone drive me home. Big deal, I thought, I can handle a little pain. I didn't think to ask how he would go about getting those buried smart teeth out. He had me lie back in a nice reclining chair, and he put a thing to my mouth and nose that put me to sleep instantly. The next thing I remember was my daughter Cindy telling me that we were almost to Homer. She helped me to my house, handed me my "pain pills," and asked if I was going to be all right by myself. Of course I was all right. Why wouldn't I be? She had to go back to Kenai, so I gave her a goodbye hug and proceeded to my bed. I had zero idea of what I was about to experience. YIKES! I woke up a few hours later with the most excruciating pain imaginable. It had to be right up there with childbirth. For the next four days, I got up only to take another pain pill. I couldn't have told anyone what day it was or where I was. Nobody came by, so I didn't have to tell anybody anything. When I was finally back on my feet—barely—I was a bit on the slow side. There was a small white packet on the kitchen table. I dumped the contents out. It contained many broken pieces of teeth that the dentist had chiseled out. There also was a note from the doc that said not to forget to remove the gauze from the holes. Wow, my mouth had been so numb that I didn't know there was anything besides my tongue in there. I lost a week of my life and about ten pounds. So, for those that wonder whether I possess any wisdom, I can show them the packet with the pieces of teeth to prove that I do indeed.

A friend of mine had broken up with her boyfriend and asked if it was all right for her to stay at my place. Oh yes, the timing and the company were just what I needed. She sure helped get me back in the groove.

It was dark this Saturday morning when I got up. Mount Redoubt blew again, and the Homer area is the recipient of her ash. There is a quarter of an inch of the nasty grey dust on everything. Nobody will be able to go anywhere because it is so abrasive to car and plane engines. Oh well, we've experienced these eruptions many times through the years. Augustine, Redoubt, Iliamna, and Spur have all dumped ash on us at one time or another. Maybe it will make the garden grow better.

A few paragraphs back I wrote about the prospects of getting married again. I didn't say that I was looking for a wife because I guess I thought that the perfect woman would just happen along. After all, several women had found their way to my doorstep. It took me a while to figure it out, but the right woman doesn't necessarily just pop into your life. Maybe, I thought, a guy has to hunt for one. After all, I'm a hunter and trapper, so it might be a good idea to set up a trap-line and use the right bait. Assessing the situation would take some serious thought and the use of imagination. Why not check out women in other parts of the world? Was this not a perfect time to travel abroad? I could start by driving down the Alcan to Seattle and see what kind of thoughts I could get from a travel agency. I've got to confess, there was another reason that I was zeroed in on Seattle. A girlfriend of mine had moved down there a couple of years before. She was so vibrant and fun; plus she had a great body and terrific looks.

I would have to take some clothes for cold weather and hot. There was no telling where I would end up, so I took my only two pair of shorts and a bathing suit. Alaskans seldom get to use tropical clothing, so you won't find their drawers full of shorts. The rest of the clothes that I packed were my everyday jeans and shirts.

I'll not use her real name, but let's refer to my Seattle friend as Kim. I hadn't seen her for a couple of years, so I didn't know if she was married or what. When I called her, she was thrilled to hear that I was headed her way and demanded that I stay with her. I sure didn't argue with that. When she lived in Alaska, she never ceased to amaze me by saying things like "I'd be honored to go out with you" or "My, you look handsome today."

There weren't many stops on my way down there, not even for sleep. I hadn't driven the Alcan Highway since I moved to Alaska, and it was quite improved. I surely didn't take in the grandeur of it all, because I was so anxious to see Kim. Maybe I was too anxious. I was driving late at night through the Lake Louise area when a big bull elk wandered onto the highway. By the time my headlights picked him up, I was almost on top of him. I slammed on the brakes and stopped a scant few feet away from him. He just stood there, totally unconcerned at my presence. He finally ambled off the road. After I calmed a bit, I slowly made my way to the next pull-off and took a much-needed nap.

When I was three or four hours away from Seattle, I called Kim, and she said that she couldn't wait to see me. She had given me good instructions on how to get there, and she was waiting outside when I jumped out of my car. The greeting was like a sensual movie. She wrapped herself around me and gave me the most passionate kisses. It wouldn't have mattered if there had been an audience.

The next three weeks were a romantic dream come true. I had been love-starved, but now I was getting a much-needed fix. We went for drives in her convertible sports car and sped around the countryside. The G-force would cause us to skid on the curves. When we were on the expressways, we would take turns driving and see who could hit the fewest turtles (the little diamond-shaped markers) as we changed lanes. All the while we had the stereo blaring Jimmy Buffett songs. We drove several times to Tacoma to check on the new boat that I was having built.

Both of us were a tad on the wild side, but we never had a disagreement. When I told her about my thoughts of going to the South Pacific, she sincerely agreed that I should do it. She even took me to a travel agency that she had done business with. Sure enough, the woman that she recommended was so helpful and kind. She asked me if I had heard about the Micronesian Islands. She had been there herself and loved every island. Micronesia takes in a vast area. Located between Hawaii and the Philippines, it's actually above the equator and consists of three major groups of islands: the Marianas, the Eastern Caroline's, and the Marshall Islands. She spent considerable time telling me about everything of interest, including the topless women in Yap. Not that I had any interest in that sort of thing.

I mentioned that I would like to go to Japan to see if I could acquire a market for Alaska shrimp. So we arranged the trip to take in all the islands with Japan as the last stop. There would be no timeframe. I'd just stay at each place as long as I wanted. I also thought it was a perfect opportunity to investigate the possibilities of a winter fishery at one of the islands.

I was saddened by the thought of leaving Kim, but we both knew that this would be a trip of a lifetime. She was completely supportive, but I could tell by her expression that she was as sad as I was when we parted. Our smiles were nothing but a cover-up that didn't begin to hide the tears that both of us wiped away.

Chapter 11

Micronesia

The woman at the travel agency did a wonderful job of describing the islands, but nothing could have prepared me for what I was about to experience. The first stop was Majuro, which is the main island of the Marshall Islands. When I got off the plane, the beauty of the women took me aback. They have the typical bronze skin of the islanders, but also long straight hair, which complements their features. I'm sure that I drooled. Everywhere I went there were more slender, model-looking women. They were so graceful and stately when they walked.

One of the first people I met was John Slattebo. John had the only air service in the islands. He and I clicked instantly. We both flew, and we loved adventure and good-looking women. For sure, John was not your average dude. When he wasn't flying, he was racing Hobie Cats and another kind of small one-man sailing craft that he referred to as a Laser. Of course at night he always had a houseful of women. He had built his house himself, and it was unique. You had to go up a cylindrical part to get to the octagon-shaped, one-room main living area. The octagon was horizontal and was kind of perched up on the cylinder.

The first time I was invited to John's place, I was slightly out of my environment. All the women were lying on big pillows, smoking. John told me to sit wherever I wanted, so I squeezed in between two gorgeous young women. The most beautiful woman in the house was lying directly across from me, but when John came in with some frosty beers, he nuzzled down beside her. The woman next to me had a super body, and she smiled pleasantly as she introduced herself. Her name was Nauma, and we hit it off immediately. I was handed an ice-cold beer, which I welcomed because it was fairly well hot up there. John displayed a generous what's-mine-is-yours attitude and insisted on sharing everything he had, including the delightful female company. Welcome to Majuro!

I was in good shape at the time from lots of running and wanted to stay that way, so each day I would pound out eight miles or so and then dive into the calm ocean to cool off. The island is an atoll surrounded by a reef, which protects the low island. John often asked if I would accompany him on long flights to the outer islands. I helped the elderly folks get into John's plane, an amphibious Goose. Sometimes he would have to pick up someone that had been injured, and I would help him with that too.

The Majuro people had a custom that was different but fun. All the men had a stick that was about a foot long, each one with its own design. If a guy liked a woman, he would go at night to the house where the gal resided and slip his "love stick" under the door. If that didn't get her attention, the guy would throw a bit of gravel at the house. Hopefully the woman wasn't married to a big, jealous guy.

There didn't appear to be a lot happening as far as commercial fishing went, so it was improbable that I would get involved with a winter fishery at Majuro, but I did meet some interesting people there, among them an adventurous couple from Germany. Klaus was a pilot for Lufthansa, and was married to Akiko, a beautiful Japanese woman. They rented a small skiff and asked me if I'd like to join them on a day trip. I gladly accepted, and off we went with Klaus at the helm. He had a perpetual grin as we proceeded many miles out to sea. All three of us wore our bathing suits with tee shirts over them. Nothing else, and why not: it was clear, calm, and sunny.

I'd never seen a tropical storm before, so I was somewhat shocked when one came upon us so fast that there was no time to find shelter. The sky turned black within minutes. Lightning was followed by cracking thunder—exciting for a guy who was used to Alaska's usually lightning-free storms—and then came the torrential downpour. The massive raindrops actually hurt as they pelted our bare bodies. Only five minutes of the beating rain and we were shivering uncontrollably. The skiff was filling with water, and we had nothing to bail with. We could no longer see land, but I had taken a mental note as to its general direction in relation to the wind direction. Akiko was getting hypothermic and we guys weren't far behind. I asked Klaus to stop so we could bail some of the water with our hands. While bailing, I noticed that the water seemed warmer than the air. I dove overboard and immediately began to warm up. When I announced my finding, Klaus and Akiko followed. It was actually pleasant. We just had to watch that the skiff didn't blow too far from us. The storm was short-lived, and I noticed that Klaus never stopped grinning. We became lifelong friends.

Majuro and its people were more than accommodating, and I never came close to having a bad experience. I could have easily settled in with these loving, easygoing people. Nonetheless, I had several other South Pacific islands to explore. When I left, I went in sadness, and many of the islanders were sad to see me leave. John and a few beautiful island women were particularly sad as they waved goodbye. While waiting for the plane to take off, tears made their way to my lap. I had an urge to tell the crew to let me off, but I resisted the urge because I knew that I could always come back.

Ponape, located in the Eastern Caroline Islands, was my next stop. As the plane circled it, I was awed by the dramatic change in topography. There was no reef to slow the waves, which had small whitecaps. I lack the ability to describe the color of the water, so I'll have to settle for saying it was a brilliant blue. The small white beaches were surrounded by mountains, and the whole island was lush with various green colors Coconut trees were everywhere and lent the island a storybook tropical look.

There were no fancy resorts, only a couple of small thatch-roofed guest cabins, just my style. It was hot, so I donned my bathing suit and headed for the beach. I had barely gotten in the water when a knockout island beauty swam over and introduced herself. She had the same qualities as the women at Majuro: long black hair down to her hips, perfect lips, bronze smooth skin, and that warm, "come-hither" smile. Katherine was her name. She seemed interested when I told her that I was from Alaska, although I could tell that she had no idea where it was. It didn't matter, because we were soon intertwined and making out in the water. She invited me to a party that night at her place. While in Majuro, I was informed that if you were interested in a woman you should simply go up to the damsel and ask her if she would like to "go around." There appeared to be no shame in instantaneous sex. Obviously the Christian missionaries hadn't gotten their message across. In the case of Katherine, she didn't have to be asked to go around.

As the huge sun touched the water, I was dressing for the party. My party clothes were the same as my leisure clothes, which were shorts, tee shirt, and flip-flops. Including the time it took to comb my hair, I was ready to head out in 42 seconds. After trekking the dirt trails for twenty minutes, I spotted a fire with a dozen or so partying islanders. Katherine greeted me, but there was no introduction to the others. I was the only white person at the party, but nobody seemed to care. There were a few plates of food, and my host told me to help myself.

Taro was the main dish; everything else was unfamiliar. Not that it mattered, because two-thirds of the people were female, and from what I could see in the dim light of the campfire, they were all keepers. There appeared to be a shortage of men at Ponape. Darn! Other women occasionally snuggled up to me, but Katherine made sure that I was hers for the night. I was still munching on the food when a local drink served in a half coconut shell was passed to me. It was milky-colored and had a strong but pleasant fermented aroma. I believe they called it Sakau, which is a form of Kava. Being the lightweight that I am, I cautiously sipped some of it. The taste was fine, but I detected a noticeably high alcohol content. More people showed up. Most were women. Everybody sucked up plenty of the milky drink. I had never heard the word "aphrodisiac," but this drink was definitely one. Most of the women looked to be 18 to 25, and I guessed Katherine was 28 or so. Within a short time, people were making out. Some guys had two women clamoring all over them. Without saying a word, Katherine took my hand and led me a few feet away, took her sarong off, and laid it on the grass. There was no pretense, no need for words, just pure shameless sex. Of course, being the clean-cut dude that I am, I ordinarily wouldn't have participated in such an immoral act, but I didn't want to offend Katherine. I don't know what she did to stay in shape, but she sure had stamina.

The next day I made contact with one of the local fishermen and told him that I would like to go out on one of the larger tuna boats to see how they went about fishing. Within the hour, the guy came back and told me to go to the dock right away. He'd arranged for me to go out with a Japanese crew that fished on a 50-foot rusty slab of a boat. The weather seemed never to change, and that day was no exception. It was hot and sunny, so I grabbed my sunglasses and jogged down to the dock. One of the crewmembers motioned for me to come aboard. None of them spoke English, but sign language would suffice. We chugged to sea at a speedy six knots. The good news was that it didn't take long to get to the fishing grounds. Within a couple of hours, we could see a small flock of birds diving. They were on the move, so the skipper headed thirty degrees to the left of where the birds were. With such a slow boat, they had to head off the school of tuna that swam below the birds. As we got closer to the birds, the crew threw some chum in the water. All of the crewmembers snatched up long bamboo poles, each of which had a single hook attached to twenty feet of line. Just as quickly as they threw the bare hooks into the water, the frenzied tuna bit them. Then the fish came flying into the boat. I had to stand back to keep from getting clobbered. It was a short but wild scene. When a fish hit the deck, it would come off the barbless hook, and the line would fly back into the water and snatch up another wild tuna. When the fish stopped biting, the crew threw all the fish in the fish hold while the skipper attempted to head off another flock of birds.

Within a few hours, we were chugging back to port with the boat loaded and the crew being fed bowls of rice. The rice had no goodies in it, just plain rice. I helped tie up the boat when we got to the dock. The skipper bowed to me and shook my hand with a smile, and I thanked him for taking me along for the ride.

Although I described Ponape as some sort of utopia, it didn't seem to have much to offer other than more or less constant partying. Perhaps I didn't spend enough time to see the total makeup and inner parts, but I elected to move on.

The travel agent had warned me about the men at Truk. She said that they were big and that they enjoyed fighting, especially when they had had a drink or three. I would definitely heed the warning. It was deep in my mind. A caution about big people that liked to fight was not to be dismissed lightly, but at the same time it seemed to have the same effect as a bad weather forecast when going to sea: sometimes a person just has to go. I surely would be crowned "twinkie of the South Pacific" if I blew by Truk without saying howdy.

On touchdown, the pilot slammed on the brakes and threw it into reverse so abruptly that my head almost hit the seat in front of me. The strip at Truk is the shortest of all the major islands. The approaches are clear of obstacles at each end, which makes it a little easier to hit the mark. The pilot must have been a Super Cub pilot in private life.

The travel agent was correct: the people are big and they like to fight. There was no nightlife except a bar or two, which I did stop by a couple of times. I generally enjoy talking with the local people as long as they don't get into politics. For the most part, these people were of a friendly sort, but there were two fights that broke out in my vicinity. Most of the men were big enough to pinch my head off, so I chose to be a spectator. I just stood back and watched. I drank Coke when I bellied up to the bar. That way I could make a quick exit if need be. Both fights were over in a short time, and right away everybody was happy again.

I had become a certified scuba diver several years prior to my trip, and I knew in advance that this was the perfect place to dive. Truk Lagoon is renowned for diving because two thirds of the Japanese navy and several Zero airplanes were sent to the bottom during World War II. I asked the desk clerk at the hotel if there was a dive business around. He told me to go to the dock and ask for Clark. The day that I found him, he and his Trukese wife were feuding. Clark acted like it was no big deal, but when we were driving along in his small truck, a car pulled up alongside. It was his wifie, and she threw several coconuts at us. They bounced off the truck and barely missed Clark. The words that she hurled at him were more violent than the coconuts.

We picked up another couple and made it to the dock without any more coconut episodes. After loading the tanks and other paraphernalia, we went out to where you could see some masts barely showing above the surface. The depth was 110 feet, and I've never seen such clear water. The dive was astounding. There on the bottom were all of the ships, Zeros, and ammunition, just as it was at the end of the war. All sorts of fish had taken up residence in the ships. There were bullets of various sizes everywhere you looked. We dove for two hours, but only saw a small fraction of the submerged relics. My ears hurt that night, so I was unable to do any more diving.

I decided it best not to mess with any of the women there because I didn't care to get my little head busted. Actually there weren't many of them that excited me to the point of a possible confrontation with one of the monster-men. Then one evening a middle-aged gent tried to get me to divulge my political stand. As tactfully as I could, I told him that I had to take a leak. Then I slipped out and made arrangements the next morning to boogaloo.

I had a culture shock when I arrived at Guam. This was 1977, and already the place had so many people and the traffic was so heavy that I knew immediately I wouldn't be sticking around very long. I have to admit, though, that there was no shortage of good-looking women to feast my eyes on. I also have to confess that I did fall in lust for a short time while there. I made a half-hearted attempt to see some of the island, but the traffic was too much, so off to Palau I went.

A Japanese fellow close to my age sat next to me on the plane. He barely spoke a few words of English, so we conversed a tiny bit, and he drew a picture of a boat and a fish on a scrap of paper. It was his way of telling me that he had intentions of fishing while at Palau. Then he pointed to me in a quizzical manner, and I smiled and nodded. He was asking me if I would like to go fishing. Hey, do Eskimos like muktuk? Yes, I'll go fishing.

For the most part, none of us knows what lies ahead or what the next day will bring. Little did I know what this serene, laid-back island might have to offer. From the very first step of my island journey, I became aware that any island on any given day could alter my life. I knew little about Palau Archipelago prior to my arrival, but it didn't take long to realize that it was far from average. One thing I did know was that one of the islands in this group, the island of Pelelu, was one of the most fought-over during World War II. Other than that small morsel, I knew nothing.

Apalonia greeted me at the reception desk of the small hotel where I would stay. She was more interested in me and where I came from than checking me in. She was an eight on the scale, meaning that her looks, body, and smile were above average. She flirted with me for a half hour or so before showing me to my room. There was no pretense as to her intentions. It took her all of three seconds to drop her dress and only a few seconds longer to take my shirt and shorts off. I resisted and struggled. Not really.

No sooner had Apalonia gone back to the office than there was a knock at my door. I wondered if she was coming back for more. I slipped my shorts on, peeked out the curtain, and saw the Japanese fellow that had accompanied me on the flight. He was ready to go fishing. Wow, that was fast. I was glad he didn't come ten minutes earlier. His smile was that of a kid with a new toy. We headed down a small road that led to the beach. How he arranged it so quickly I don't know, but an elderly Palauan guy was pouring gas into a small tank in his skiff. He was a thin but strong-looking fellow. He wore a loincloth and nothing more. There was no introduction, because neither of them spoke English. They conversed in Japanese, and I spoke "fisherman," so off we went.

The small skiff was equipped with an ancient ten-horse outboard, but it seemed to run fine. I figured our speed to be about eight knots. Immediately I noticed that there were no fishing poles. Within a few minutes, the old skiff man took a hand-line, put some kind of bait on the single hook, and trailed it behind us. He attached a rubber band to the line and put the other end on his big toe. Within a minute or two, the band broke and the old guy handed me the line as he throttled back. The tug on the other end was substantial but not overpowering. I knew better than to pull it in too quickly, so it took several minutes to land my first rainbow runner. It was a beautifully-colored eight-pounder about the size of a red salmon. My Japanese companion caught another one as we continued in a southerly direction.

The turquoise water was so clear that I could see the bottom, and it was at least twenty feet deep. It was getting shallower when the old Palauan brought the engine to a halt and dropped the small, rusty anchor in a depth of twelve to fifteen feet. The guys had brought three snorkels and masks. They gave me one, along with a spear of sorts. The spear was bamboo and had an old blade attached to the end of its forty-inch length.

They took off their loincloths and jumped in. Oh yes, the water was warm, but cooler than the midday sun. When the older guy dove, we followed. Upon reaching the bottom, I could see several giant clams. I had never laid eyes on such an awesomely humongous clam. The top shell was open, and the bottom shell was attached to the coral. All of them were open, revealing the massive amount of living meat inside.

The weathered Palauan jammed his small spear into a clam and, with many quick jabs, severed the muscle so that the clam couldn't close. He then cut all the meat loose, took it to the surface, and dropped it into the skiff. Was that cool or what! It didn't look like he had any intentions of taking the shell, so I gestured that I would like it. He nodded and smiled. He also motioned for me to dive and do the same as he had. I was surprised at how quickly the clam tried to close at my first thrust. I barely got the muscle severed before it clamped shut.

After I deposited my catch in the skiff, I swam a short distance away so as to avoid crowding the guys. I adjusted my mask, and when I placed my face in the water, I was startled by a very big shark coming at me—fast. Its tail was going back and forth really fast, but just before it got to me, it swerved. This thing was ten to twelve feet long, which I'm sure was big enough to eat me. Prior to that moment I had never had fear, but now I could feel all the hairs on my body come to attention and blood rush to my face. I lost track of him, but in a few seconds he came at me again. Like the first time, he swerved and, like a bullet, was out of sight. I took the snorkel out of my mouth and screamed, "Shark!" The guys just looked puzzled because the word "shark" didn't mean anything to them. They didn't understand what I was hollering about. I didn't dare lose track of the predator, so I put my face back in the water just in time to see the blur of that son-of-a-bitch whiz by again. I kept my face down but swam towards the skiff. I was sure that that bugger would grab me by the leg. What a helpless feeling! I didn't even think about trying to defend myself with the spear. When I got to the skiff, I shot up over the gunnels like someone had stabbed me in the butt. Jerre was nothing but a "worthless, day old weenie."

I didn't see the dorsal fin anymore, so I guessed the shark was done playing with me. He definitely taught me something about myself. Prior to that frightening experience, I had never considered Jerre to be a tough guy, but hadn't thought that I was a twinkie either. I concluded that henceforth I had better think things out ahead of time and have my act together so that in the future I could think of myself as a warrior, not a puny wet diaper. Perhaps if I would have poked the sharks nose with the spear, he might have went on his way.

As the old man pointed the bow toward Palau, I wondered if these two fellows realized that I had just had a harrowing experience with a shark and that perhaps they were in danger also. I guess it didn't really matter. I was enjoying the afternoon sun as the skiff slipped through the crystal clear water. We had enough clam meat for the whole island, and I had a nice fish for supper. When we landed at the beach, the old fellow offered me all the giant shells. I wasn't sure what I would do with them, but I was hoping there was a way to get them home. As we put them into the old fellow's car, I couldn't help marvel at their size and thickness.

On the way back to my room, I stopped by the restaurant next to the motel to see if they would cook my fish for supper. A middle-aged, slightly heavy woman greeted me. She oohed and aahed about the beautiful fish and said she would be happy to cook it for me. It was big enough for several people, so I told her to cook a small bit of it for me and to keep the rest for her and her crew. She hollered for someone named Winnie to take the fish to the kitchen. When Winnie came out, she really rocked me back. She was in her early twenties, had long black hair, and her smile sent me to the moon. Her bronze legs extended below the short shorts, and the tight blouse left no guesswork about her bust size. It was her flirty smile that was the main attraction though. My stare had to be obvious as I watched her backside when she headed to the kitchen.

I was almost back to my motel room when Apalonia slithered up to me with a book in her hand. Business was almost nil, so she had plenty of leisure time. Without an invite, the sex box followed me into my room. She immediately dropped her book and her dress. The women in Micronesia don't care about underclothing. You would have thought that she had been waiting for a month for me to show up. She didn't waste any time getting down to business. After I showered, Apalonia asked if she could borrow my tape recorder and some of the tapes that I had brought along. I showed her how to operate it, and as she went out the door, "Hot Chocolate" was blaring.

I dressed in my Sunday-go-to-meeting clothes. Yes, you guessed it, shirt and shorts, but it was the nicest shirt I had. Sauntering over to the restaurant, I couldn't help thinking about Winnie. I wanted to know all about her. I was wondering if she had a big, tough, handsome boyfriend or, worse yet, a husband. She didn't have the same facial features as the Palauan women that I had seen. Perhaps she was from a different island.

The day had already presented more excitement than an average month, so how could I expect anything more from the remaining evening hours? When I entered, there she was. She was setting the table, and when she saw me come in, she stood erect and gave me that sweet smile. The name "Jerre" never sounded as seductive to my ears as when she greeted me.

I got right down to business asking her a bundle of questions before the boss lady came over and politely told me to take a seat. She had already anticipated my thirst for a cold beer, which she placed on my table. Winnie had to work in the kitchen, so I didn't get to talk to her much more that night, but she had told me that she was from the Philippines and that she did not have a boyfriend. She came from a family of ten kids, so she came to Palau to work. I also found out where she lived. So far, so good, I thought.

After going to bed, I was having some sweet dreams when I suddenly woke with fire on my chest. I fumbled around, searching for the light switch. When I flicked on the light, I saw that my chest was covered with fire ants, hell bent on eating me. There was a horde of the little monsters all over the bed too. I killed ants for fifteen minutes. I didn't stop until every last one stopped wiggling. My legs and chest took the brunt of their vicious attack. I had "dumbed out" and put a piece of homemade bread from the restaurant on the bed, and that was what provoked the little soldiers to come to the feast. I showered with cold water, which soothed the pain a bit. I left the light on when I went back to bed.

The soft sound of Ackerbilk's clarinet woke me. Apalonia started her day by playing "Stranger on the Shore," which made a pleasant accompaniment to my awakening. My chest was still hurting from the visiting ants, but not nearly as badly as when they got their orders to attack. Some swelling and redness was evident just below my left nipple, but no big deal.

The thing foremost on my mind was to see if I could spend some time with Winnie. After showering and shaving, I headed straight for the restaurant. My flip-flops made a noise unlike the locals'. They were a perfect fit and comfortable, but they slapped the bottom of my heel, which announced my arrival. The restaurant owner greeted me with a cup of aromatic coffee and a smile. I ordered eggs and rice, the local favorite.

I was facing the kitchen when that lovely bronze maiden came out with silverware for me, and my eyes surveyed her body from head to toe. Her skin was unbelievably beautiful and soft-looking, and again she was skimpily dressed in halter top and short shorts. Her flip-flops made no sound whatsoever as she made her way over to my table. The authentic pleasant smile made an indelible imprint on my brain. When she said, "Hi, Jerre," it sounded as sexy as the day before.

I didn't waste any time asking her if we could get together. She said that she had the afternoon off so I would find her at her house. I lingered at the restaurant, talking to one of the local guys. He soon got on the subject of politics, and that is like stepping on my toes. Talk to me about sports or fishing or women, but not politics. It seems that those that follow the subject are very opinionated and are wanting to debate with someone on the other side of the fence. I excused myself and began touring the town and surroundings. I was told that there were giant crocodiles in the mangrove areas. I was definitely curious, but after my brush with that shark, I wasn't interested enough to penetrate the wet mangrove far enough to see one of the brutes. It was dark in the thick stuff, so I reminded myself that it was not prudent to poke around without my .416 Remington. Crocs belong on the list of "animals that bite back," so I figured that they were best left alone.

When I got back to my room, I hastily cleaned up and even combed my hair. I went around the backside of the office so Apalonia wouldn't intercept me. I hadn't run or walked fast for more than a week, but I now found myself in second gear. The anticipation of being with Winnie was tightening my stomach. I was bouncing along when I saw her one hundred yards away… accompanied by two guys. Darn! The smile still adorned her sweet face as she introduced me to her friends, Jesse and Ernie. I greeted them with a handshake, and they cringed as though I had squeezed their hands too hard.

Jesse noticed that I was gawking at Winnie. He said, "You like him?"

It took me a few seconds, but I realized that he was referring to "her." I was thinking, You bet your ass I like him, but I just nodded.

They had brought a basket of chicken and some fixings, so we went to a grassy spot near a bridge and enjoyed a picnic and conversation. The guys didn't speak English nearly as well as Winnie, but I soon learned that they were not her boyfriends, just Filipino friends. With that out of the way, I edged my way closer to Winnie. I questioned her about everything, including her age, her lifestyle before Palau, her likes and dislikes. She answered everything in a positive manner and then began her inquiry about me and Alaska. Other than my white skin, it appeared that we were quite compatible. I particularly admired the fact that she recognized that there was little future in the Philippines and had made the bold decision to go abroad for the chance at a better life. Coming from a family of ten children and a meager farm life, she felt that she didn't have much to look forward to if she stayed at home, which actually mirrored my life as a young adult.

I was invited to a huge party the next day. I gladly accepted because it meant that I would get to spend more time with Winnie. My, I didn't know that there were so many people in Palau! It was an outside event and was overflowing with people and food. Lots of beer, I might add. Palauans are happy people in general, but the Palauan men don't particularly enjoy the company of Filipino men. I thought everyone was in a merry mood until an egg-sized rock whizzed by my nose and struck Ernie in the left ear. Palauans are noted for their accurate rock throwing. I instinctively ducked, but looked for the thrower. The guy was winding up to release another missile, so I grabbed Winnie and departed the fine party. Bummer, I didn't even get a chance to eat. Winnie was scared and said that she had better go home. Amazing how quickly things can change from joy to disaster. Oh well, hopefully there would be another day.

We managed to spend time together every day after the party, and our meetings got progressively more enjoyable. As time went by, we both realized that something wonderful was transpiring. It was totally different from the time that I had spent with any of the other island women. This was not a frivolous affair, but both of us would need some time to absorb its implications.

In the meantime, my ant-bitten chest was hurting more and more each day. A bump was developing just below and to the right of my left nipple. It got to the point that it hurt from the contact of my tee shirt. There was one doctor on the island. When I went into his office, he said, "I see that you have a boil." Ugh, that's what I thought it was. A guy that I played football with in high school had a boil, and he told me how he screamed when they squeezed the goopy stuff out of it.

My hump was bigger than a golf ball and had to be lanced. The doc told me he had no anesthetic so I'd better clutch the armchair. I latched on to the chair and took a deep breath, and the doctor made a half inch slice in the top of the lump—"ouch". Then the doc got a serious look on his face and placed both hands on the boil! He squeezed with all his might. Damnnn! I was trying to be tough, but even though I didn't scream, I think blood came out of the armchair that I was hanging on to. So much pus came out of the hole that you could have filled a cup with it. I had just let out a sigh of relief when he squeezed it a second time. Then he informed me that I would have to come back in two days and get it done again. I did, and it hurt just as badly as the first time. I was left with a hole in my chest the size of a .357 magnum bullet.

The following day I gathered some boxes and tape, padded the giant clamshells with crunched paper, and carried them to the post office. The postmaster inquired as to the contents, and I told him that they were clamshells. He angrily grumped that I couldn't keep the local shells. I informed him that a local fisherman had given them to me. Apparently that was exactly what he wanted to hear, because he reversed his decision and agreed to let me keep them. I sent them parcel post, and they arrived in Homer six weeks later.

Yap was next on my itinerary, so Winnie and I agreed that I would spend some time there, and then perhaps we would know for sure if we were meant for each other. In the meantime, Winnie would contact her family and tell them about me. Maybe her parents wouldn't approve of a cold-climate commercial fisherman marrying their daughter, and I wouldn't blame them. Just the climate change would be a good enough reason to arrive at a negative decision. Then there was my occupation to give thought to. I had told Winnie that if I married again I would want my galley gadget (wife) to be on the boat with me. To me, that was a key element to a happy relationship. These were things that she and her family would have to mull over before I could expect the go-ahead. I hadn't really proposed to her, but the cards were on the table.

While on the plane to Yap, I was wondering if I was doing the right thing. Was I being an idiot for not staying on Palau with that bronze maiden? Time would tell, and it seemed that both of us needed some time to make sure. Because of my lifestyle and occupation, I knew that there were times that required instant decisions, but other times a man should give careful thought to the wellbeing of others. I was all too capable of making "wild-hair" snap decisions, but this was no occasion for Mr. Spontaneous. I knew that it wouldn't be easy for a person that had spent her entire life in the tropics to move to Alaska.

When I got off the plane in Yap, a slightly grey-haired man with the island smile approached me and asked if I needed a place to stay. After traveling through several islands, I knew that he was not trying to scam me, but was probably going to be of help. Sure enough, he had a small motel, and the price of a room was absurdly low, so I accepted and we hopped into his van. I made a feeble attempt not to stare at all the topless women, but he just smiled and politely clued me in about Yap's make-up and people. The motel was better than nice, and he and his wife treated me like a son.

There were some other things about this island that set it apart from all the others in Micronesia. When I was making my itinerary with the travel agent in Seattle, she had mentioned that Yap had an outstanding characteristic: stone money. Yes, round stones shaped like wheels. Some of the stones are as small as one foot and others as big as ten or twelve feet. The more stones a person owns, the richer he is. The larger ones weigh several tons. These peculiar stone rocks came from somewhere else because that type of rock doesn't exist in Yap. Even the most modest homes have some stone money.

After the initial "boob staring," I noticed that most of the people, both young and old, had orange mouths. As I strode down the small gravel road, I could see that the men, women, and children were chewing something.

I needed a cold drink, so I went into the first small store that I came to. Oh my, here we go again. There at the counter was a woman that would cause most men to drop their jaws. She was so attractive, and you didn't have to look twice to notice that she had a killer body. Her smile was a genuine greeting. Did all the island women have that come-hither smile? I got a Pepsi and went to pay her. I told her my name and asked what hers was. She softly replied that it was Loreeta. Her voice matched the graceful way that she moved. I also noticed that her mouth had a slight orange tint, so I tried to make conversation by asking what it was that everybody was chewing. "Betel nut" was her reply. She probably wondered how anyone could not know about betel nut. When little kids there got their baby teeth, they chewed it, and when people got old and lost their teeth, someone chewed it for them and put it in their mouth.

I'm sorry, folks, but I had to ask Loreeta if she would like to "go around" after she got done working. "Yes" was her simple, shy reply.

I know what you're thinking. I was the guy that was considering marriage with Winnie. I'm going to say that God was showing me all the options.

I'm sure that at the time my heart was in my pants and I was following my heart. I hadn't been single since I was seventeen, so I guess that I was taking advantage of my island experience.

While waiting for Loreeta, I meandered around and checked out the stone money and, of course, the half-naked women. Guys can't help themselves; they have to ogle boobs. I'm not sure, but I believe that it comes from the day we are born and start sucking. It's healthy, and I can't believe that there is anything wrong with it; otherwise women would try to hide them. Enough on the subject. Let's just say that God had his act together when he gave women breasts.

Loreeta took my hand as though we were longtime lovers. As we strolled down a trail toward the beach, I asked her if I could try betel nut. She took one out of her knitted bag and split it between her teeth. Then she took a "pepper" leaf and a small bottle of lime out of the bag. She sprinkled some lime powder on the half nut and wrapped it in the leaf. I got one half and she put the other half in her mouth. I watched and did what she did. I put it between the back teeth and began to chew. The saliva was overwhelming, but I noticed that Loreeta swallowed hers. I swallowed twice and bam! I got dizzy. I had to sit down. Loreeta giggled at my reaction. I had to spit some of the orange liquid out. I don't know how long I sat there, but everything was mellow.

For the next seven or eight days, everything I did, Loreeta did with me. She didn't care what we did, just as long as she could be with me. She even took me to meet her folks, and as it turned out, they were from Palau. They were so accommodating and pleasant. They obviously appreciated my caring for their daughter.

We had left Loreeta's parents' house and were walking back toward town when I heard a woman crying. As we got closer, the wailing became louder and louder. As we passed the house from which the crying emanated, Loreeta told me that the woman had lost her husband and that she was in the third day of mourning. The extremely loud crying is a ritual that all widows do when they lose their mate. My sorrow was heavy for this woman because of her love loss.

Perhaps Yap was a test for me. I loved Loreeta for the simple, beautiful person that she was, but I realized that nothing more could come of our relationship. I'm as Alaskan as they come, and I would have done injustice to even entertain the thought of taking her from the island. It was now time for the awful task of saying goodbye. Loreeta never said what was on her mind, so I didn't ask. Goodbyes to loved ones are terrible, to say the least. I didn't want her to come to the airport because I didn't want her to see the stream of tears that I was spilling. My heart was so heavy that I thought it would burst through the skin. As the old motel owner drove up with his van, I parted with Loreeta. She cried uncontrollably, but said nothing. We both knew I would not return.

The old guy said, "You fell in love, didn't you?"

I barely responded with a nod.

Winnie had equally wonderful but different qualities. I had decided that she had the right stuff to adjust to Alaska, but was there really a possibility of that happening? Was my vision only a dream? I would know soon enough because we were about to have a reunion. Ten minutes before we landed at Palau, I went to the restroom at the back of the plane and splashed cold water on my tear-drenched face. My eyes looked like two eagles' assholes in a power dive. It was now time to think about a future with the best of the island women. Question was, would she have me?

Of all the women that I had met on my Micronesian jaunt across the South Pacific, Winnie had the most welcoming sweet smile, and there it was, waiting for me. We hugged for the longest time, and then she blurted out that she wanted to come to Alaska with me. She had used her time away from me to think about what it would be like to be the wife of an Alaskan fisherman. Just a few minutes before, I was a wreck, and now I was the happiest dude in the South Pacific.

I made sure she knew that I wanted to marry her. She had contacted her family via her older sister in Manila, and she had their blessing. Only thing was that I was expected to go there and ask for her hand in marriage. Wow, I hadn't thought about that, but if I were the father, I would hope for the same respect.

We flew to Guam together and got to know each other better. We played like teenagers and just had a ton of fun. I had met a fellow on Palau that was the head chef at the most prominent restaurant in Guam. He really enjoyed hearing about Alaska, and he was fun to be around. "If you ever come to Guam," he quipped, "look me up and I'll make you a meal that you won't forget."

Unannounced, Winnie and I stopped by there one evening, and he was so happy to see me that he gave both of us a big hug. Then he announced to the customers that I was from Alaska. That guy was unreal, and a great cook. He presented us with steak and prawns that were out of this world, and then, after we finished the main course, he brought out a flambéed baked Alaska.

All too soon it was time for Winnie to go to the Philippines and for me to finish my itinerary to Saipan and Japan. Because we knew that we would be back together in the near future, our goodbye was not so bad. I still had an empty feeling as we parted, though.

I was glad that I went to Saipan, because it made me aware that there are islands and there are islands. Saipan sucked. It was 1978, and the place was overflowing with tourists, most of which were Japanese because of its proximity to Japan. I barely endured two days. Hey, what can I say? The other islands were utopia.

Japan was a culture shock. During my five-day stay (that was all I could handle), I found only two people that spoke English. It was a good thing that I know directions by the use of the sun; otherwise I would have been lost all the time instead of half the time. There were no names on the streets of Tokyo. A college woman that I met told me that the lack of street signs was deliberate to keep potential enemies from finding the Emperor.

During my pursuit of a market for Alaska shrimp, I was informed that I should forget that I mentioned it, because it was controlled by the Japanese mafia. I didn't have to be told twice. I was a bit ticked off that I had traveled halfway around the globe just to learn that I wasn't welcome. Nuts to them. I didn't enjoy having to search for my hotel every day anyhow. Adding insult to injury, it SNOWED four inches one day, and I froze my butt. I caught the next plane to Hawaii.

We need rain! It's been two weeks since Mount Redoubt spewed its ash all over Homer. Every time I go out to work on my boat or anything, the nasty grey stuff gets in my nose and eyes. Then I have to take off my shoes before entering the house or I make "ash tracks." I think it's time for a Blue-Eyed Eskimo dance to bring on some rain to settle the dust. Several times each winter, I do "forty-degree dances" that I hope will warm us up a smidgen. Hey, don't laugh, I'm good at it, so like Grandpa said, "Don't knock it till you've tried it three times!"

There should be a law that all Alaskans have to spend a month or more in Hawaii each winter. I kid you not; the place has the best weather in the world. It's 80° in the daytime, and 70° at night. A doctor could not have prescribed better therapy. After three days of basking in the sun on the warm sandy beach of Waikiki, the hole in my chest finally closed. The scar that it left would make an onlooker think that I had survived being shot. My soul always enjoys the smell and sight of the sea, and Hawaii gave me the very best. My bod was tanned to perfection as I lazily hung out, just soaking up the rays.

The view wasn't too shabby either. The definition of "Waikiki" must be "Bikini-ville." It takes a good eye to appreciate the perfect bikini, and I do believe that I would make a great judge at a contest. I had made a commitment to my "Filipino Baby," so I figured that I could look but not touch. I was getting restless anyhow, so the old saying "All good things must come to an end" was nagging at me.

Most people that visit Hawaii have vivid memories of the trip. I had the most enjoyable time of my life in Micronesia, so the time I spent in Hawaii was of little consequence, and it left me with very few memories to pass on. I do recall thinking that I would like to return some day and get another whiff of the tropical aromas, especially the Plumerias. They are the most fragrant of flowers.

I was experiencing repeated episodes of uncertainty as to whether Winnie would follow through with the plans that we had laid. It was as though melancholy was swooping down and tearing into my inner soul.

Before I left Hawaii, I called Kim and asked if she would mind picking me up at the Seattle airport the following day, which was a Saturday. She surprised me by getting several of my other friends to meet me too. Toot was in Seattle on business, so he was there for my homecoming. Jerry Thompson, another Alaskan fisherman friend was there too. It really cheered me up to see good friends again. Kim knew me too well, and immediately blurted, "You found a wife, didn't you?"

I told them straight out what had transpired and that I hoped it would all fall in place. We laughed and had the kind of visit that only good friends experience. They had had a few drinks before I got there, and then there were a few toasts, so our part of the bar became a tad noisy.

Kim asked if I would like to go to Tacoma and check on my new boat. Off we went like two little kids going to Disneyland. As I recall, she beat me by hitting fewer turtles than I did. I was out of practice. Strike that; she was just better at swerving than I was.

The boat builder had some questions for me, and I had one for him: "Is the boat going to be ready in March so I can do the herring fishery at Togiak?"

He assured me that it would be no problem. I was emphatic about being on time. I had ordered a new seine and the multitude of things that went along with the fishery, so it was imperative that the boat be in the water by the end of March. It was time for me to devote 100% of my time to my fishing business.

The woman that had been staying at my place while I was gone moved out a few days before I got back to Homer. After all the travel, things suddenly seemed awfully quiet, but I was almost too busy to let it bother me.

A few days elapsed and I hadn't heard from Winnie, so I tried to call her at her sister's place. The sister answered and didn't seem to understand who I was or what I wanted. I don't know if they'd ever talked to an American on the phone before, so I repeated Winnie's name. There was a long pause, but I could hear jabber in the background, so I knew she hadn't hung up. Then came that familiar sweet sound: "Jerre?" Again, the "r's" rolled, making my name sound quite seductive.

After a bit of small talk, Winnie asked me if I could come there to ask her father for her hand and then get married over there. I have to say that I was a little hesitant, but without thinking about the logistics, I said that I would be there as quickly as I could. The next day found me packing for a trip halfway around the world to the Philippines. In a way it seemed crazy, but I had enough "wild hairs" to go wherever necessary to get my woman.

It's a terrible long flight, but it gave me time to think about how to ask Mr. Nicomedez for his daughter's hand in marriage. According to Winnie, his English was limited and her mom spoke none. I knew that if I were he, I would expect politeness, respect, and a genuine smile. By the time I got to Manila, I had Super-Cub ass, which means that it had been too long in the saddle. It felt so good to get off the plane, but the heat hit me like a D-8 Cat. It was the hottest, most humid place that I'd ever been, but I forgot all about it when I saw the awaiting smile of my bronze maiden. Winnie and a few of her sisters were waving frantically. I lit up like a lightning bug.

People were pushing and shoving at the luggage terminal, making it difficult to be polite. All the Filipinos had humongous boxes, so the battlegrounds got more crowded and aggressive at the conveyor. Because I had some gifts for the relatives, I had brought more than usual. I finally did a little shoving and snagged my bags. We all piled into a Jeepney and off we went. The Jeepney is a fun innovation of the Filipinos. It is an extended WW2 Jeep that is mostly chrome. The breeze felt good but the black smoke from the zillions of buses and Jeepneys was almost unbearable. Winnie's hand in mine eased the pain, but I couldn't wait to head up to the province where Winnie's parents lived. I could tell that she had reservations about whether I could handle the simple life at her folks' place. Little did she know that I was a master of the simple life. I did realize, however, that I was out of my element and that the suffocating heat could be tough to handle.

Threading our way through the streets of Manila was a real blast. There are no lanes. All the vehicles, whether Jeepneys, buses, or tricycles, make their own lanes. There were inches between us and the millions of vehicles competing for a small space on the asphalt. Horns blared constantly. Even though we moved at a snail's pace, I laughed at the simplicity of it all.

As we neared the countryside, the scenery changed dramatically. Rice paddies were being worked with water buffalo called caribow. There was not a sign of wealth here. Animals and people did the work. During the 150-mile trip, I saw only a couple of tractors. These people were hard workers! Once in a while I would see other types of vegetables being grown, but the rice crops represented at least ninety percent of the fields. All the people, whether they were farmers or city folks, were immaculately clean. They were a proud people that didn't act "better than thou."

Winnie's family lived in a little village called Ataynan Bayambang. A river ran next to it, so all the huts were on stilts. It didn't take a detective to figure out that the river overflowed at times. Coconut trees adorned the village, and the homes were made of bamboo. Even the floors were made of split bamboo. I loved the setting.

Winnie's father led the procession to greet me. Following were her mama and brothers and sisters, and following them was the whole village of very curious onlookers. Most of them had not seen a white, blue-eyed American before. Some of the older men greeted me with "Hi, Joe," which was the greeting to GIs during WW2. The kids giggled about the hair on my legs and arms, and wanted to touch it. The women all gave flirty smiles, but weren't seriously flirting.

The dog under the hut wasn't nearly as pleasant. He was tethered by a small piece of rope tied to one of the bamboo posts. Stretching the rope to the limits, the medium-sized canine snarled and growled at me and made it obvious that he would love to chomp on my lily-white legs. I usually get along with dogs—try to never show any fear, but this critter didn't buy into it. Luckily, the rope held.

Most of the Philippine people are good-looking. The women are down-right beautiful. Neither men nor women have hair on their legs or arms. Also, they have practically zero fat. A good number of the female population are striking and have long, straight, black hair.

Winnie's father, Maximiano, spoke enough English for us to enjoy a limited conversation, but the mama, who was a queen, spoke none. She didn't need to speak English for me to realize that she was a gracious, loving person. I gave her a hug when Winnie introduced me to her. Smiling, she turned to Winnie and said something in Tagalog. Winnie told me that it was so nice of me to give her a hug. She then took my hand very gently and led me into their home. It was apparent that my hairy arms and legs were novel, because there was much staring, pointing, and stroking. The girls whispered and cooed about my blue eyes. I tried not to notice, but I was definitely humbled.

All the women and girls were summoned to the cooking area to prepare a meal. I asked if I could help, but was politely informed that I was a guest. Winnie said that it would be an appropriate time to talk to tatay (father). I casually ambled over to where he stood. His body was thin, but sinewy and muscular. His posture was perfectly straight. This man was obviously a hard, hard worker. With ten children, he had to be. Our eyes met, and his first question was blunt and to the point: "Why you like Winnie?"

Yikes, I thought, I'd better come up with a good response, and it better not have anything to do with her body or sexy eyes. I muttered something to the effect that I fell in love with her for the same reasons that he did when he fell in love with nanay (mother). I tried not to complicate the answer by lending too much detail, but did tell him that we had spent time in Palau and learned that we liked each other. He smiled as though he was okay with my reply, even though it seemed quite lame when I thought about it later. Now it was time for me to look confident and ask him the question of the day. I didn't know how else to say it, so I just blurted it out: "I'm asking you for permission to marry your daughter."

I was surprised that I got the whole sentence out before my tongue got tied in a knot. Everybody in the house heard me, and the place got silent. I couldn't help thinking, What if he says NO?

Then I noticed a slight grin, and he said, "Yes, okay."

It probably wasn't customary, but I grabbed his hand and shook it and then gave him a hug. I think that the whole household sensed my relief, because the chatter and laughter resumed. I think that my face returned to its normal color too.

From that moment on, Max and I were appreciative of each other. I would go to the fields with him and help all I could. It was a great experience to watch him plow fields with a cow pulling a single plow with an old weathered wooden handle that he held as he walked along guiding the blade. There were no tractors or machinery. Everything was done with a cow or water buffalo. We carried buckets of water from the river to irrigate the crops. I think that Max really appreciated my help with that chore because I could do that all day. I did have to take shelter under coconut trees once in a while though because it was so hot. Every day the temperature would hit ninety degrees or more, and it was very humid.

One day I expressed my desire for a coconut, but the trees were so tall that I thought getting one down would be just about impossible. I felt ashamed for mentioning it, because very soon a young man with a cloth tied to both ankles shinnied up one of the tallest trees. I would never have believed that a human could go straight up like he did. It seemed effortless. As soon as he reached the top, he took his machete out of the homemade scabbard and started hacking. Big green coconuts came slamming to the ground. This could be dangerous! I scurried back a few paces. Just about as quick as the proverbial wink, twenty or so big green coconuts lay on the ground. The guy came down with the same agility and speed with which he'd gone up. He casually picked up one of those huge morsels, hacked the end off, and presented it to me. Winnie nodded for me to drink the juice. My, it was so refreshing after a hot day's work. I thanked that guy many times, but I never knew if he understood English.

The longer I stayed, the more I realized that these were the hardest-working people on the planet, but at the same time the simple, stress-free lifestyle made me wonder if I would be doing the right thing by taking Winnie to my world. The extreme change could be too hard to handle. Even though I had explained to her what the climate was like in Alaska and how tough it can be fishing on the high seas, I wondered if she really understood.

Most Filipino people spend their whole lives within fifty miles of their homes. Jobs are almost impossible to come by. Winnie was definitely not your average Filipina. She had already shown that she was not content to spend the rest of her life as a farmer in a small village. Leaving the Philippines and going to Palau to work was like jumping off the edge of the earth. It was simply unheard of. Perhaps she was a wild-haired hybrid also. There seemed to be no second thoughts for her. She absolutely wanted to marry me and go to Alaska.

Getting permission and blessings from the parents was the easy part of the procedure. I was about to get an unwelcome education on how to get a woman from the Philippines to Alaska. We first had to go to Manila and stand in several different lines to prepare for a civil marriage and begin gathering all the necessary paperwork for Winnie to go to America. I almost passed out from the heat while in one of the lines. Finally, after a long tedious process, we found ourselves in front of a judge, being pronounced man and wife. At the time it seemed wonderful and relieving, but this was just the beginning. Now we had to prepare for a formal wedding—yes, a full-fledged church wedding with all the trimmings. This wedding would be just as extravagant as any American wedding. The reception was complete with a three-layer cake and a big full sized roast pig. Everybody from everywhere came. I did get a piece of the cake, but the pig was gone in a blink.

After a one-night honeymoon, we resumed standing in lines getting more paperwork. It was so frustrating for me. Nothing moves fast in Manila—not the taxis, the people, or the process. Being from Alaska where everything moves at a much faster pace, I imagined that people were trying their darnedest to stress me out. The heat added to the situation, which was becoming critical. Hardly ever was there a place to get a cold drink or to sit down. There were lines and more lines. People told us that we were in the wrong line after waiting for hours to get to an agent's desk. Here we were, a newly married couple that was supposed to be totally happy, and yet we were on the edge of hell!

I'm not sure how we made it, but finally we found ourselves in the line that I had been praying for, the line to get on the plane. Yahooooo! Even though I felt triumphant, it was so sad to leave Winnie's family. They were such gracious and loving people.

Our first stop on the trip was Hawaii. It provided an extension of a much-needed honeymoon. Then there was a stopover at Seattle. Once again I had called my friend Kim from Hawaii and asked her if she would meet me at the airport. When we arrived, she was there with a few of my Alaska fishing buddies. Even though I hadn't told them, they had figured out that I was bringing a bride home. After I introduced Winnie to my friends, Toot insisted we go into the bar and have a welcoming drink. We all had a good laugh when I told them how Winnie swept me off my feet. Toot stood up and gave a toast: "To the newlyweds. May you never come out from under the blankets for ten days!"

After checking the progress of my new boat, it was time to get on the plane to Anchorage. Winnie clung to my side as if she were attached. It was mid-March, so winter was still doing its thing. I told Winnie to wait in the terminal while I went to the parking place where I'd left my car. I had brought a coat for each of us. When I pulled up to the curb, she came out, and her slanted eyes got wide! The cold air took her breath away, and the sight of all the pure white snow was more than she could have imagined. Even though the car heater was putting out plenty of heat, she shivered uncontrollably. Within an hour, we were in Turnagain Pass, and the snow was ten feet deep. I turned into a pull-off and took a picture of my bride standing by a wall of snow that was twice as tall as she was.

When we got to the house that I had recently built on the shore of Kachemak Bay, we did like Toot had said. After a week or so, I suggested to Winnie that we have a reception at our house. She was for it, so I called friends and relatives and we had one of the wildest shindigs that can be imagined. So many people came that we were like fat sardines in a skinny

The Frances Lee, a crab boat breaks the way through the Bering Sea pack ice for us seiners.

can. Winnie showed us how to do a dance called Tinaclink. In the Philippines, they use two bamboo poles. I made some out of 2x2s. Just about everybody that tried the dance got their ankles bruised! We all laughed so hard that our stomachs hurt and happy tears rolled down our cheeks. People had brought enough beer and wine to make every adult in Alaska tipsy. The party was so joyous. It lasted into the wee hours. Last year's wild brown grass was still standing thick and tall. We didn't know it until the next afternoon, but lots of the guests slept in that grass. Every once in a while for several hours that day we saw bodies come crawling out of the grass.

Chapter 12

The Bering Sea

It was April and time for me to get with the program. My new 43-foot seine boat was being finished in Tacoma, and a net company was building a herring seine for me. Because it was a new venture, I had my work cut out for me. I had to put a team of seiners together and contract some crab boats to tender for us. Even with so much to do, I don't remember getting stressed much, and sure enough, it all came together.

When it was time to get the new boat, we flew to Tacoma, and Winnie christened the boat *Winter Wind*. She was a shallow draft twin screw (two engines and props) and fast compared to most seiners in those days. My oldest daughter, Cheryl, and another woman came along to help crew on the trip from Tacoma to Homer. None of us had traveled the Inside Passage, so the navigation would have to be meticulous. Parallel rule and calipers were necessary items, as was a good compass. I had all the charts for the whole trip. All went well, and we got to Homer just in time to load groceries and fishing gear in preparation for the 1000-mile trip to Togiak, which is at the northern part of the Bering Sea. We were about to try our luck at herring seining.

Prior to the maiden voyage of the *Winter Wind*, I had called John Slattebo, whom I had met at Majuro in the Marshall Islands. You might recall that I mentioned him earlier and said that he was a good pilot. I needed a spotter pilot for the herring fishery. I owned and flew a Piper PA-12, so I asked John if he would be interested in coming to Alaska and spotting for me and the other two seiners. He had always wanted to see

Alaska, so he jumped at the chance. Preparing for the herring fishery was like putting the pieces of a complex puzzle together, but now with John it was complete.

When John got to Homer, I showed him how to fly my plane. The kind of flying that John would be doing was totally different from what he had done in the past. His landings would be on soft, sloping sand beaches. I used the beach across the bay from our house to show him how to take off and land. I also taught him the art of slow flight. Small bush planes like mine will fly at 40 mph, but if flown much more slowly, they will stall out. This is especially true if the plane is making a turn. Because of John's flying background, he learned quickly.

I talked with Kenny Moore about the fishery, as he had fished there the year before. He was gracious enough to give me some helpful information about the trip over there and where to have my pilot go. Kenny had his spotter pilot operate out of Metervik Bay, so I told John that he should go there and set up camp. He wouldn't have to leave until several days after I left with the boat because, while it would take him only four hours to fly to Metervik, it would take me six to ten days to get there. John spent his extra week in Homer practicing on the local beaches.

To reach Togiak, we had to travel some of the most treacherous seas in the world. In order to get to the fishing area before the hordes of herring, we must depart in April, not the ideal month for seafarers because of the Vernal Equinox, which often brings strong wind and bad weather. There was no option, though; we had to go. One of the most important items that we would need was a good anchor. I decided to take three anchors to be safe, all of different designs because bottom conditions vary so much. They were all hefty and had plenty of chain. I had learned while long-lining for halibut that you can't be over-equipped with anchors. I've had them drag, bend, and break off completely. A spare anchor has to be kept in a accessible place because you might need it in a hurry.

Toot and Roy had agreed to co-op with me, and we would all travel together on the long voyage to Togiak. The weather was decent enough when we departed the Homer harbor, but the calm was short-lived. By the time we drew abreast of Dangerous Cape, the wind was out of the southeast at 25 knots. Shelikof Straights is seldom mellow, and on this day the sea was eight to ten feet. Toot owned the *Lucky Dove*, and Roy had the

Corina-Kay. They weren't as fast as my new boat, the *Winter Wind,* but all three of us had to throttle back to adjust to the sea conditions. When we reached Chignik, I told Toot and Roy to go on. I would catch up with them at False Pass. I needed to make some minor repairs that would require going on the grid. The natives at Chignik were friendly and helpful. Ernie Carlson introduced himself and proceeded to jump right into the work at hand. He was impressed with our new, fast, twin-screw boat. Soon afterward he became a high-liner at Chignik.

When the tide floated us off the grid the following morning, we pointed our nose south. The sea had moderated, so I got on step and made good time to False Pass. The marine forecast for the Bering Sea didn't sound too good, so we stayed at the pass with the rest of the fleet. The next morning the forecast had moderated from 45 knots to 25 N.W. It didn't sound as though the weather was going to get any better, so we all headed out the tricky channel and into the Bering Sea. Travel was slow, as the sea kept battering our port bow. Hourly the sea and wind grew. I kept close radio contact with the other guys. Kenny Moore said that he was going to go into Port Moller when he got abreast of it, and Roy, Toot, and I decided to do the same. By the time we dropped anchor, the wind had switched and was coming out of the northeast at forty knots. There was a low spit in front of us, which helped break the sea but did very little as far as stopping the wind. Before dark set in, Kushtaka was having fun, bringing the wind to 50 with gusts to 75. I put a second anchor out with plenty of scope on it. Now my anchors were in a Y configuration. There was no doubt that we were in for a vigilant anchor watch.

As darkness fell, the wind got much stronger. The other boats began dragging anchor, first Toot's and then the others'. Kenny's was the only boat equipped with an anemometer, so he kept us updated as to the wind speed. The noise was horrific as it screamed through the rigging. Even with two anchors out, I was dragging and had to jog on it. Kenny came on the radio and announced that his anemometer had pegged out at 100. There was just enough moonlight to see the deckhands on the other boats crawling on the decks to the anchor winches to retrieve their anchors, after which each boat would creep back toward the spit and set anchor again… and again. I insisted that the deckhands put their survival suits on when we had to reset our anchors so that if they got blown into the water, they might have a chance of surviving.

Kushtaka was enjoying himself so much that he kept snorting for three days and several times made winds that were more than 100 knots! On the third day, the wind subsided to sixty, and my crew begged me to let them go ashore. The anchors were holding, so I reluctantly gave in. My daughter Cheryl was with us and would be the observer in the spotter plane. She had the binoculars out and spotted some glass balls on the beach, so she and two of my crewmembers, Gene and Floyd, untied our ten-foot inflatable raft and managed to get it in the water. With the aid of the anchor line, they pulled themselves to the beach. I breathed a sigh of relief when they waded ashore. Cheryl had taken some garbage bags and a couple of burlap bags. When they came back an hour or two later, they had all the bags full of glass balls. There was barely enough room for all three of them in the raft. We put the bags of glass balls in the hold and padded them with buoys. After lashing the raft down, everyone had a good laugh about the trip to shore without any mishaps. It was a good cure for the anchor-dragging blues.

The next morning revealed clear skies, and the wind was now a day breeze, so it was time to head across the Bering Sea to our destination.

DAMNED THE DIURNAL TIDE!

The remainder of the trip across the Bering Sea was exceptionally pleasant. Our spirits lifted with the first sunshine we had seen in many days. Upon our arrival, Metervik Bay appeared to be a beautiful safe haven. The bay wasn't very big, but had plenty of room for ten or so boats. We dropped anchor near two other boats that got there ahead of us. After the long hard trip, it was so relaxing soaking up some of the afternoon sun. The lazy, luxurious feeling was short-lived, though, because Kenny Moore's skiff man, Jerry Clark, came over and asked me if I wanted to go ashore with him. He was taking their spotter pilot, Roger, and his observer to the beach where their plane was. My pilot was camped there too, and it would be good to talk with him, so I gladly accepted the invite. I jumped into the eighteen-foot aluminum seine skiff, and off we went.

It appeared to be low tide, because the tide flats came halfway out the bay. When the prop began to churn mud, we had to get out and walk the remaining 200 or so yards. Jerry didn't have an anchor for the skiff, so he would stay there and keep the boat in the shallow water until I came back. Roger's observer was a petite young woman that didn't have boots. Roger gallantly offered to piggyback the young maiden to the beach. The mud was only ankle deep, so Roger did fine for forty or fifty yards. He was totally spent, so I felt obligated to continue the piggyback express. By the time I got to the sandy part of the flats, the little 110-pound damsel had me sucking air too. It was a definite relief to put her down when we reached the sandy beach. She did smile and thank me though. She and Roger went to their plane and took off for Anchorage.

John greeted me and said that he had had a good sightseeing trip and that all had gone well. I had only been talking with him for a few minutes when I heard Jerry hollering, his voice barely audible across the distance. He said that the skiff was going dry and that he was having trouble pushing it out with the receding tide. I couldn't believe that the tide was still going out. I told John that I would talk with him some other time and that we would have radio contact. Jerry was still hollering at me as I trudged out to the skiff. As soon as I got there, we pushed the skiff together but didn't make much progress. The mud had enough sand in it that it hindered our efforts. We worked so hard that we were drenched with sweat. When we had exhausted our strength, we agreed that the tide would soon change and float the heavy seine skiff.

There are no seats in these workboats, so we sat on the gunnels and took our shirts off so we could cool down. Both of us were super thirsty, but we hadn't brought any water. Getting acquainted was pleasant. Jerry had some good Alaska experiences to share with me. In a short time we put our sweat-soaked shirts back on because a breeze was coming up. Our shirts only chilled us, so we donned our lightweight jackets, which were the only other clothing that we had with us.

Both of us had lots of experience with the humongous tides of Cook Inlet. The tides there can rise or fall nearly thirty feet within six hours. Six hours incoming, six hours outgoing; "The tide floodeth, and the tide ebbeth." It produces an extreme amount of current, so when we fished there, we attempted to adjust to the tide movement.

We were in a different world there at Metervik Bay. Not only were we at a place that was new to us, but capricious Mother Nature had a surprise in store for us. The sun that had been so welcome had succumbed to the

197

fast-moving stratus clouds. With the clouds came the all-too-familiar wind. We hunkered down in the bottom of the skiff as darkness approached. We talked about the possibilities of walking back to the beach, but decided it wouldn't be a good idea for a number of reasons. Surely the tide would turn soon, and we couldn't leave the skiff unattended because there was no anchor. Also, there would be no place to get out of the weather if we went ashore, because John had a very small tent and there were no trees or other cover in the area. So, there we were, two Jerry's shivering in the bottom of a cold metal skiff, waiting for an incoming tide that appeared to be late in arrival. Little did we know that we were experiencing our first *diurnal* tide. At the time neither of us had even heard of such a thing.

Our condition rapidly deteriorated, as did the weather. As our teeth began to chatter, we could see the seine boats in the distance lunging up and down with the building sea. Jerry and I huddled together, but the wind swooped down like a snowy owl trying to snatch a rabbit with its talons. Each hour that passed, we listened for the water to come in and float us. With our wet clothes, it wasn't long before we were victims of hypothermia. The teeth chatter was uncontrollable, and our bodies were shutting down. The cold wind had increased to forty knots or so. I had a brief thought of getting up and jumping around in an attempt to warm up, but realized that our best chance for survival was to stay huddled. And then it began to rain! Hypothermia prevented speech or any type of communication. I don't know how many hours passed, but I think we both died, because we stopped shivering and chattering. I can only say that God came along and brought us out of the grip of death, because after an eternity of time, we both suddenly realized that there was water lapping at the bow of the skiff. I don't know to this day how we started the outboard and lowered the prop into the shallow water, but we did. Within a few minutes of pounding into the raging sea, we pulled up to my boat, the *Winter Wind*. She was slamming up and down on the big breaking waves, which made it look impossible to get alongside and get on board. The crew had done a good job of putting several buoys out to keep us from smashing into the side of the boat, and Jerry did an excellent job of getting the skiff close enough for them to grab me and pull me aboard. I could never have gotten aboard by myself. I was totally helpless. For the rest of the night the crew had to reset the anchor many times, and it was late in the morning before I stopped shivering. The wind had blown our diesel cook stove out, so I had to drink lukewarm water to help cure my dehydration. My sleeping bag felt like heaven. I didn't even care that the boat was slamming up and down in the ten-foot, white-capped waves.

Our paths didn't cross for a long time afterward, but just a couple of years ago I ran into Jerry. He had been living in the South 48, but decided to come to Alaska for a visit. After a long hug and laughter, we recalled the death event. He reiterated that we were dead. He remembered the moment when we both stopped shivering. He said that it was like a dream and that God picked us up and brought us back to life.

Without knowing it at the time, we had experienced a diurnal tide. I won't attempt to explain how or why they come about, but they produce a low and a high tide every twelve hours rather than every six hours. It's complicated, but it has to do with the position of the moon and sun in relation to the earth, and the gravity of all three.

I've had more than my share of cold-weather experiences, so there was no excuse for the ignorance that I displayed at Metervik, but in my defense I will point out the frequency with which Alaskan commercial fishermen are lured into danger by the changeability of the weather. I should have taken a good winter coat when I jumped into that skiff, but still, I had no knowledge of a diurnal tide. Bad weather in Alaska is often preceded by the innocence of sun and calm. It was another of the never-ending lessons of survival. Ironically, Mother Nature has a way of using her magnetic lure and cause you drop your guard. If you survive her changing ways, you respect the sea to the point that you can't stay away from it.

The next day, when the weather got nice again, I put on some WARM clothing and took our own skiff to the beach to talk with John. This time I made sure that the tide was near high and that it wasn't going to run away from me. I had John move the plane and his camp a short distance to Nunavachak Bay. The water there was deeper, which would be better for anchoring, and the beach was longer for takeoffs and landings. As I headed down the beach, I turned and reminded John: "KEEP THE GREASY SIDE DOWN!" That is an old saying that pilots use when referring to the belly of the plane. In other words, don't let the plane get upside down!

I had made arrangements with a crabber that would be one of our tenders to bring several barrels of aviation gas. The boat was a LCM, which is a landing craft with a front ramp that can be lowered for loading or unloading. When he arrived, we had him nose up to the beach just before high tide, and we rolled the drums onto the beach.

We spent the next few days preparing the equipment and net. I flew with John a few times to see if the herring had showed. From the air, you can see the black balls of herring in the shallow water. On the third time out, John spotted a small school. It wasn't much, but it was a good sign.

In the meantime, the fleet had grown to a full-sized city of boats, seiners and tenders accompanied by more than thirty spotter planes, and with each plane was more tents and aviation gas. All of these planes would be using the same stretch of beach for takeoff and landing, which could lead to serious problems. The pilots got together and made an attempt to iron out some of the safety issues. It wouldn't be easy with that many planes, especially with all the tents to maneuver around. Safety would be of the greatest importance not only on the ground but also in the air. Would there be left hand turns or right? What elevation would each plane be flying? What radio frequency would be used? These and other questions would have to be addressed to keep planes from crashing and to keep everybody alive. The occupation of spotter is more dangerous than that of winter crab fisherman. All of these pilots knew the dangers, but the thought of getting rich seemed to be the bottom line. Being a pilot myself, I could relate to their love of such a venture. Most of these guys would spot for three or more boats, and would receive as much as ten percent of the profits. If they set their boats on large schools of herring, they could make more money in one hour than they could all year at anything else.

The tension and excitement grew by the hour. The search was on, making for more and more air traffic. When a boat pulled anchor, it got everyone's attention because it might mean that its pilot had seen a big school of herring. Boats would idle out so as not to attract attention. For the most part, I would pull anchor before daylight and just drift, totally ready to move. Most of the boats had radios with scrambled frequencies so that nobody knew what they were up to. The boats that didn't have scramblers used codes and tricks to screw the others up. They might send one of their co-op boats roaring out the bay to lure us in the wrong direction. Being new at the game, I fell for a couple of those tricks. After a short while I figured that the best tactic was to keep John in the air as much as possible.

Roy did his share of running around too, but Toot remained calm and stayed anchored most of the time. I didn't realize it at the time, but he and his crew smoked lots of wacky tobacky. Shortly after we arrived at the herring grounds, Toot said that he was going to have our pilot fly him to Kenai for the day. When I questioned him about why he wanted to go to Kenai, his response was that I had Winnie with me, and that I had my hand on it every night. What could I say? He definitely needed to get together with his wife. There is an old saying: "When a fisherman runs out of bread, he has to go home and get bred."

When it comes to spotter pilots, there are lots of also-rans, and then there are a few high-liners, just like fishermen. I knew which pilots were renowned for being the best, so had John keep close tabs on them. I was proud of the way John had gotten so proficient in such a short time. When the herring showed up, he promptly set me on a decent school, and then set Roy. I had never experienced anything, I mean nothing on the planet that was anywhere near as exciting! The whole scene was surreal. Several other seiners were vying for the same school of fish that John was setting me on. When I glanced up at the planes, it looked like a collision could happen at any moment. John's voice rang with excitement as he gave me orders to turn one way or another and to punch the throttles to get ahead of other boats. Some of the experienced seiners tried to intimidate me by nudging the side of my boat. I just did what I had to and obeyed John's instructions. We started our set just before the boat next to me, so he went after another school of fish. Our set went off without any problems and John said that it looked good. My set had enough fish that I had my skiff man snap some large buoys on the cork line. It was a good decision because after we had the seine pursed up, the fish sounded and pulled the corks down. We almost screwed up by drying up the net too much, and tons of fish nearly turned our boat over! Our starboard rail was almost in the water. The tender that came to suck the fish out of our net did a super job of saving us and the fish. Fred, on the *Alaska Adventure*, came alongside our net, and he literally hung over the side of his boat and reached underwater to pull our cork line up. He was the greatest. He definitely knew what he was doing. We put nearly 100 tons on his crab boat. Roy's set didn't produce as much, but we were enjoying a good start.

All of the fish caught in the Togiak fishery would be sold to the Japanese who would use them for their roe. It is a delicacy in Japan, a very expensive delicacy. We tried cooking some in various ways. Our favorite was to scramble them with eggs, but we didn't go gaga over them.

The eggs and scales of herring are like glue. They stick to anything that comes in contact with them. Sometimes, after taking several showers, we would still find scales stuck to our fingernails. It was almost impossible to clean them off the boat. I've always contended that the more fish gurry, slime, and scales that you have on your boat, the better you are doing. Unlike salmon and halibut, these little buggers don't have to be put aboard. The tenders are all equipped with a huge suction hose that sucks the herring out of the net and into the tender.

The price that was paid by some of the participants, their boats, and their planes was heartbreaking. Several planes were wrecked on the beach, a boat totally burned, and there were two deaths. Our operation of three boats, a plane, and three tenders was spared from any disasters. We fished until there were no more fish with roe. The Japanese paid an all-time high price that year, so we shared the profits with our tenders.

During the first couple of years of herring fishing at Togiak, the openings and closures were determined by the fishermen. Later the department of Fish and Game would make announcements when we were to fish, and when to end the season.

On the return trip, all was going well until we got to Shelikof Straights. The following sea was twelve to fourteen feet, but we were able to chug along at half throttle. Then, when we were halfway across the Straights, my starboard engine began slowing. The constant pounding had caused the filters to plug. I was the only one on board that was familiar with the system, so I had to go down into the engine room to clear the filters. Not fun! My head was continually hitting the floor stringers, and diesel fuel was splashing everywhere when I took each filter off. For the first time ever I was feeling nauseated. As soon as I completed the task, I clambered back up to the cabin and started the engine. It ran well, so I had one of the deckhands take the wheel while I got prone at the dinette. The nausea soon went away, so I can still say I never puked at sea.

Now that we had a boat capable of seining, our season was extended and the work became harder. There would be no time to relax and savor the fruits of the herring season, because we had lots of work to do to get ready for halibut long-lining. All of the seine equipment had to be taken off, the halibut gear put on, thousands of hooks baited, and the hold filled with ice. The halibut fishery in those days would go on for fourteen consecutive days, a real marathon. I fish ed near the banks east of Kodiak. The water is seldom calm there, but it often produces good catches. When the gear is being picked, all of the fish have to be gutted, gilled, and iced in the fish hold.

Billy Pepper was one of my deckhands. He kept monotony to a minimum because he was always telling stories or singing (even though he couldn't carry a tune if he had a spare pocket).

For the first few days and nights, non-stop winds produced seas to fifteen feet. Daytime wasn't so bad because you could see the line and hooks as you were pulling gear. Nighttime was a different story. Every wave slammed against the boat, and the long line got as taut as stretch pants on a fat lady. Neither the crew nor I could relax for a second. It was important to gaff a fish at the instant that it broke the surface, but it was nearly impossible to see the fish until the head came out and the fish started thrashing around. Each hook had to be unsnapped precisely when it came out of the water; otherwise it would get wrapped in the block. Also, a hook swinging about could tear into a deckhand's skin and cause some damage. I know of three fishermen that were pulled overboard by halibut hooks in the hand. All three were fortunate enough to make it back to the boat, but then had to go through the hook removal procedure.

When the conditions are nasty, it saps everybody's energy. It becomes hard to keep your eyes open, and yet we all know that we have to be alert. Every time one of us gaffed a fish and threw it into the boat, the wave action made the fish slide from one side of the deck to the other. A big one could break your leg if you didn't have your act together.

One day the sea was too rough to pick gear, so we went into a small bay on Afognak Island. I needed to make some adjustments on the boat anyhow, so it was good to drop the pick (anchor) in a protected bay. Even though the bay was fairly calm, the heavy rollers were crashing on the beach. Billy started in on me to let him and his buddy, Bilbo, go to the beach. I told him that the surf was too big and they didn't have the experience necessary to get to the beach without a catastrophe. Persistent bugger that he was, he insisted that they had lots of experience, and it would be a piece of cake. I knew better, but I had glassed the beach and could see that there were twenty or more crab buoys washed up on the high water line. So I told them that they could go, but with two stipulations: first, they would have to listen carefully to my instructions on how to beach the inflatable raft without a mishap, and secondly they would have to bring all the crab buoys back. "No problem" was the response. I proceeded to tell them that when they got close to where the waves were starting to break, they would turn the raft so the bow was pointing out to sea. Then they would watch the waves, which were breaking in a series of five. After the fifth wave there would be a short lull and that would be the time to row backwards quickly. As soon as the raft hit the beach, they were to jump out. They again assured me that it would be "no sweat."

I got the video camera out and bade them good sailing. Billy rowed and Bilbo sat in the stern. He rowed like he actually had done it before, but when they were supposed to turn, they went in too close, and the surf promptly flipped them upside down. There was nothing that I could do to save them, so I continued taking videos. I watched through the tele-photo lens to see two soaked rats come popping up from under the raft. They grabbed the bowline and pulled the raft up on the beach. They were fortunate not to have drowned. I was surprised again when I saw them gathering buoys and hauling them to the calmest end of the bay. They tied all of them to the raft and pushed off successfully. When they were almost back to the *Winter Wind*, Billy hollered out, "I told you it would be a piece of cake!"

Twenty-five years later Billy continued the mariner lifestyle and began skippering a big research boat, the *Tiglax*. He was dating Liz, who patiently waited for Billy to wise up to the fact that she wanted to be married. He finally got the picture, and today they are a happy married couple, fun to be around.

When we went out to sea the following day, it was flat calm. As we picked our gear, the beautiful shearwaters gathered. They are the most graceful of sea birds. When they landed close to the boat, we could hear them clucking like chickens. Their manners resembled Emily Post. They don't gobble their food like seagulls. The shearwaters were a joy to watch as we picked our gear.

We didn't do great that trip, but the guys had a good Alaskan survival story to tell. When we got back to Homer and delivered the fish, it was time again to prepare for another fishery: salmon in Cook Inlet again. So the chore of taking off all the halibut gear and replacing it with a gillnet and all the other paraphernalia for salmon fishing was at hand.

Winnie would join me again and we would do a mom and pop operation. I loved not having to hire a crew for this fishery, and Winnie enjoyed salmon fishing, especially when it was not rough. She didn't have an iron stomach like me. After fishing for many years by myself, it was wonderful to have her help and to share her companionship. My little Filipino wife caught on quickly and adapted to Alaska living much faster than I expected. As a matter of fact, she was getting hooked on Alaska like I was. The non-stop adventure was contagious.

When we were at home, Winnie would let her long, flowing, black hair down, and I loved it. It was so complementary to her beautiful bronze skin. Waking up beside her each morning was a privilege, and I never took it for granted. If we worked in the garden or pounded nails at our new house, she would twirl the mass of hair into a bun and stick a thing like a chopstick in it. No matter what we did, she adapted to our Alaska lifestyle. I knew how hard it must have been. The changes were extreme. The weather, the people, and the way of life had to be tough to get used to. I tried my best to help her with the adjustment, and to remind her often that I loved her. All of her loved ones were halfway around the world, and the only way to communicate with them was by letter. There were no phones where her relatives lived. We were too busy for her to get melancholy from missing her family, but once in a great while I would notice the sadness in her eyes. During those times I would buy her some new clothes or some flowers, or give her some extra hugs.

Changing from one fishery to another is almost like moving. You pack up a ton of stuff, bring it home, and then take a ton of different stuff back to the boat. You learn to mark all the boxes and bags so that you can identify everything the next time you switch back to the fishery that it pertains to. Because of her size, living on the *Winter Wind* was much more pleasant and luxurious, but doing a changeover with my new boat was quite a chore compared to the smaller boats that I owned in the past.

The following year the procedures were nearly the same, except that we didn't have to buy new equipment. We would start the spring season with herring in Togiak. All three of the crewmembers that we had on the previous season had other commitments, as did our spotter pilot, John. It wasn't too difficult finding a crew, but it took a while to locate a good pilot. We really got lucky. A friend of ours told us about Ray Steele. Ray had been flying for Homer Air taxi, but was anxious to do some spotting for a group of boats if he could find some good fishermen. He had spotted for herring seiners in Prince William Sound before, but it would be his first shot at doing the same at Togiak. As it turned out, Ray not only proved his ability as a very good spotter, but he was a joy to work with. He and his wife, Sally, have been friends ever since.

The crew was a Duke's mixture. Mike Bly would be the skiff man, and one of the other two should have taken a job elsewhere. I didn't know it at the time, but one of the guys was coming off a drug habit. He appeared spaced out all the time and did nothing while the others worked diligently. I had to let him go before we reached the herring grounds. The third deckhand did most things backwards even though I patiently coached him over and over.

I made arrangements for Winnie to fly over to Togiak with one of the pilots. The boat ride would be too tough of a trip for her. She was super happy when I told her.

Poor Mike Bly. We weren't fifty miles out of Homer when he started barfing. He was a tall, lean, in-shape blond dude that didn't have an ounce to spare. He went into the head, closed the door, and kept calling ralff. He never came out! I had to check on him every hour or so to see if he was still alive. His face was as white as any I had ever seen. The weather was plenty snotty, so the boat was constantly plunging up and down. I felt sorry for Mike, but I had my hands full with the weather. The wind was out of the south, so was pretty much in our face, but the sea was only about ten feet. Other than Mike being sick, we were doing all right at half throttle. I was hoping that the weather would be better towards the west side of the Straights, so I angled toward the Alaska Peninsula.

After six hours of banging in the heavy slop, the weather hadn't changed. I checked the updated forecast on my vhf radio. According to Peggy, we were to expect more of the same. Sometimes, more of the same is good. At least we were making progress, even if it was slow and uncomfortable. My radar would show any obstacles or other boats in our path, and the windshield wipers gave me some visibility. The non-ending spray did make for limited vision, but my head wasn't hitting the ceiling, so I was okay with the conditions.

The other two crewmembers were down in the fo'c'sle in their bunks, and Mike was still in the head. I was hanging onto the armrest with my left arm to help absorb the pounding. Everything seemed fine. Then, without notice, all hell broke loose and life at sea changed dramatically. A monster rogue wave hit us like an 800-pound ape. Had I seen the wave coming, I might have eased the impact by bringing the boat about, and throttling back, but I was totally blindsided. The window in front of my face imploded, and hundreds of gallons of green salt water gushed in. It knocked me down into the fo'c'sle, which was now a very cold swimming pool. Glass from the window had speared into the opposite wall, but had miraculously missed me. If just one of those shards of glass had pierced my head or neck, I could easily have been in the hands of the grim reaper. As I scrambled back up to the cabin, I was unsure what had happened. The engines were protected, so they were still running. I grabbed the throttles and slowed our forward progress. Then I quickly changed course to the west. I had to respond quickly and assess the damages.

All three crewmembers immediately joined me, all of us wondering what exactly had just happened. We had all heard of the legendary rogue waves, but never in our wildest of dreams had we thought that we would be the victims of one. The big ships call such a wave a freak wave or extreme wave. The Germans have an impressive name; they call it "monsterwellen."

We were lucky to have survived. Every year there are ships sunk by the nasty critters, which are usually born of three waves coming together from different directions, thence making one humongous wave, which then travels in whatever direction it chooses. The one that hit us came so fast and from a different direction than the waves that continuously pounded us all day, so I didn't even see it coming.

All of us except Mike were soaking wet. The wave had sent water over the bridge and into the chimney of our cook stove, which runs continuously, but had been snuffed out. I instructed Mike to get the water out of the stove and restart it. Otherwise, we were going to shiver to death. With no window, the cabin temperature was the same as outside, which was near freezing. I told the other guys to find some buckets and start bailing the water out of the fo'c'sle. The pump wasn't designed to remove water from the fo'c'sle, so this had to be done by a bucket brigade. We were quite bow heavy, but the crew responded like true mariners and we were soon rid of the massive amount of water that Ms. Rogue had deposited.

After examining our drenched chart, I determined that we were abreast of Kuliak Bay. We could find shelter there from the south wind and better assess our situation, so that was where I headed. With the exception of the vhf radio, all of our electronics were dead. The radar, depth sounder, and autopilot were useless. As we neared the bay, I had one of the deckhands take soundings with a weight on a small line. When we sounded four fathoms (24 feet), I dropped the anchor. It was a great relief to be in the refuge of Kuliak. We could actually feel the heat coming from the diesel stove, even though most of it was going out the nonexistent window. We took one of the plywood galley seats and screwed it onto the outside of the missing window, and things started getting more comfortable. The guys took their heavily drenched sleeping bags outside and hung them in the rigging. Then they bailed the remaining water out of their sleeping quarters.

While we were working, I heard a voice on the vhf radio. Two seiners were near enough for us to overhear them conversing. I could barely hear one of them, but judging by the way the other ones voice boomed in, he had to be close. I recognized the faint one to be Harold Engebretsen, but didn't know the guy that was closer. I called Harold and he responded immediately. I told him about our encounter with the rogue wave, explained that we didn't have any electronics to navigate with, and asked him if it would be possible to travel with him. He responded that his position was nearly forty miles south of me, but that his friend was close to me. He told me the guy's name, and I called him and asked if he would mind if we traveled with him because with the weather as it was, we wouldn't be able to see landmarks. Without any electronics, navigation would be very difficult for us.

He responded by telling me that my boat would be too slow to keep up with him. "Sorry, Cap, I can't slow down for you," was his reply.

I couldn't believe what I was hearing. My plea for help was declined and that was his last word to me. Harold was too far south to expect him to wait for us to catch up, but the other guy was within a few miles of our position. Oh well, we would just have to wait for better weather.

Sleeping in damp sleeping bags and clothing was a bit uncomfortable, but the stove made it tolerable. Morning so often opens the door to a better day, and I'm happy to say that it did for us. Rays of sun dominated the partly cloudy sky, and the wind had subsided to twenty knots. We pulled anchor and departed early so that we might reach Sand Point by evening. Navigation was of necessity by visual means, so I had to pay attention to landmarks in relation to my speed. All went well as we cruised down Shelikof. When we eased into the small boat harbor in Sand Point, I contacted the harbormaster to find out where he would like us to moor. I later found out that the Scandinavian accent I heard in reply was that of Mr. Hansen, who was seventy years of age and ran the harbor by himself. He cheerfully told me to park wherever I wanted. When we got tied up, he came down and told us all there was to know about Sand Point, including the location of the bar. I'm a one-beer kind of a guy, but the crew indicated that the bar sounded inviting.

Remote bars in Alaska have the potential for rowdiness, but chances are that anyone who spends any time in one will make new friends there. Upon taking my seat at the bar, I couldn't help but notice the arms on the barmaid. Either she'd worked as a lumberjack in the past (there were no trees in Sand Point), or she arm-wrestled to make extra money. The two gents next to me were in the midst of a heated argument, so I had to giggle to myself as I ordered my beer. The fellow two seats over made a nasty remark to the one sitting next to me. It was something to do with "asshole." Both of them had obviously been drinking for some time, because their words were slurred. I felt like having some fun, so I nudged the gent next to me and told him not to take that kind of talk from Mr. Badmouth. My deckhand, Lee Martin, was sitting on the other side of me, and he goaded them on too. The guy took our advice and hollered some obscenities back to Badmouth. The barmaid was as quick as she was strong. She whipped out a baseball bat from under the counter and held it close to their noses while she screamed at them in a husky voice that they'd better settle down pronto or she would ban them from the bar for a month. YIKES! The whole bar went so quiet that I could hear Mike breathing, and he was three seats away. It was the only bar for hundreds of miles, so these local boys mellowed right out.

The next morning I was able to locate a piece of Lexan (plastic) to replace the plywood covering the window on the boat. Lee took care of the window while I studied the charts. Without electronics it would be crucial to know distances and landmarks. How nice! Now I could sit in the captains' chair and see without standing off to the side of the steering wheel.

After thanking Mr. Hansen for all his help, we set out for False Pass where the Alaska Peninsula ends and the Aleutian Islands begin. The passage is tricky to get through and should only be attempted when the tide is flooding. When we arrived, the fleet was stacked up, waiting for better weather. The Bering Sea had been fairly ragged for the past several days. The conditions were supposed to moderate the following morning, so everyone was ready to journey north. With decent conditions, it would take two days and a night to get across the Bering Sea.

Neither time, nor tide, nor fish wait for any man, so it was time to point our bows into the northwesterly winds of the Bering Sea. After winding our way through the channel of the Pass, we entered the vast sea, which was named after the explorer Vitus Bering. Perhaps a better name for this charming body of water should have been the Daring Sea. The wind was to have come down from gale force to small craft warning. Sure enough, it was blowing only 25, with seven-foot capping seas. Even though my boat was faster than the larger crab boats, I thought it would be better to travel with them. As the day went on, I was thankful that I made that decision.

The Bering Sea is big and yet fairly shallow for its size. When high wind enters the equation, the combination of big and shallow presents huge waves that are close together. We had done the Bering Sea the previous year, so we were hoping for a smoother trip this time. Twenty-five knot winds are generally tolerable, and in Alaska, especially near the equinox, are a fairly common occurrence. Before we reached Amak Island, which is a short distance north of False Pass, the wind began to pick up and came out of the northwest. I fell in line with the processor ship *Marin 1*, which was being towed by a crab boat, the *Nuka Island*. By staying a short distance to the quarter stern of the *Marin 1*, I was able to take advantage of the sea being broken down some. The wind increased to forty, then to fifty, and the darkness of an angry night fell upon us. The complexion of the sea changed dramatically when it got dark. The constant pounding of the waves against the hull and the howling noise of the wind going through the rigging made me feel like I was preparing for battle. Obviously vision was limited. The windshield wipers were in overdrive, but it didn't make much difference as the green waves constantly slammed the windows. The primal forces of the wind and sea were at work, and I had to be prepared for whatever they had in store for us.

I knew my own abilities but not those of my crew, so I was resigned to run the boat myself. It was my responsibility. I have stayed awake day and night many times while fishing in the past and knew I could do it this time and maintain the necessary degree of alertness. Also, I had a feel for the *Winter Wind*. I knew when I needed more throttle or less. Some finesse was required with the controls in that type of sea. There was absolutely no room for the least bit of error.

During situations like this, I wish that I had had the presence of mind to snatch up my Nikon and trip the shutter a few times. In the past, I took my camera everywhere and was quite good about taking photos. I have thousands of pictures of Alaska and the people and animals that reside here. But when survival is at stake, I seem to forget the camera. Although this trip and many others are etched in my mind, I regret that I don't have pictures to show how outrageous and exciting the sea can be.

As the night went by, the wind got stronger. The crabbers had to throttle back because of the increased size of the waves. Every hour or so one of the big boat captains would call me and ask how I was doing. With forty-foot seas, they couldn't see my boat most of the time. Each wave required me to give lots of throttle to get over the top and then throttle totally back when going down the other side. The importance of staying just the right distance from the *Marin's* stern was crucial. The crew were in their cozy bunks down in the fo'c'sle, but there was no way they could be sleeping. They had to hold on to keep their heads from hitting the ceiling each time the boat slammed down in the trough of a wave. Sometime around 4:00 a.m. my eyes didn't want to obey me any longer. The strain of the night and the attention that I had to give it had taken its toll. Bob had gotten up and was sitting expressionless at the galley table. I asked him if he thought he could take the wheel for a short time. He assured me that he would be fine with it, so after briefing him as to what our position needed to be in relation to the *Marin I* and the constant throttling it would require, I switched places with him. I apprehensively watched him and quickly noticed a mesmerized look on his face. Apparently the immensity of the sea put him into shock. The distance between us and the *Marin I* was closing by the second. I told him to throttle back, but there was zero response. I hollered at him again, but still nothing. I jumped out of my galley seat and grabbed the throttles and shifter. I threw it into full reverse and avoided a collision by inches. I still had to get on the controls so I could keep our position, or the sea would swallow us in an instant. I don't remember for sure, but I think I threw Bob on the floor so I could get into the captain's seat. My eyes got the message and opened up as wide as ever.

Shortly after I resumed wheel watch, a mayday came on the vhf. The *Vonnie Marie*, a ninety-foot crabber being skippered by Wes Humbyrd, was heeled over, and Wes thought they were going down. He was much closer to the shoreline than the rest of us, so it would take quite a while for anyone to reach him. Maydays always gave me a weak feeling, especially if I wasn't close enough to help the boat in distress. Everyone gave a sigh of relief when Wes came back on the radio and said that the boat had righted. I recently saw Wes and I asked him what his thoughts were during that trip. He said, "He was damned scared."

If any of my readers have watched *The Deadliest Catch* and have been the least bit skeptical about the danger involved, or whether the crews of the crab boats are presenting a fake smile for the cameras when green waves are trying their best to wash them off the deck, I will tell you right now that the Bering Sea is every bit as challenging as it appears. There is no trick photography! The cameramen surely must wish that they hadn't signed for such miserable duty, but the skippers and the crewmembers are like me. They are doing their job and at times doing everything possible to survive. Death is not a sliver of a thought.

As the night turned to dawn, the sea hadn't relented in the slightest. One of the crabbers said that our speed through the night was minus two knots. Oh, how wonderful, we went backwards. Daylight helped, but the weather continued to pound the dickens out of us. I still had to work the controls like I was in a yo-yo contest. Dawn is always a rejuvenator when I have had to stay up all night. Night is for romance and thieves. There is nothing fun about the darkness of night when you are battling forty-foot seas.

At midday one of the big boats that had a single-side-band radio came on and announced that the weather forecast was for more of the same. Gale force winds were the menu for at least the next day or two. Upon hearing this, I knew that I had to go to plan B. I figured that we must not be more than ten or fifteen miles west of Port Moller, so I called Bob Tremaine, whom I'd known for many years and who was traveling with our group. He owned the 95-foot *Kamishak Queen*. I informed him that I didn't want to do another night like the previous one and that I was going to try to make it to Port Moller to wait for the sea to mellow out. He knew that I didn't have any electronics to navigate with, so he said that he would lead me over there. I contended that if I could get a bearing he wouldn't have to go out of his way. He insisted on leading me, and I was glad he did, because the wind kept pushing us south. I probably wouldn't have found the entrance to the bay without him. Also, I was able to stay in the lee of his boat and it broke the sea enough that I had a much smoother ride.

When I could see the entrance buoy, I told Bob to go on his way, and bade him "good traveling." I was ecstatic when we rounded the point and got out of that miserable rough sea. I had no more than dropped anchor when Bob came on the radio. "Mayday, mayday! Jerre, we're sinking!"

I couldn't believe my ears, but I grabbed the mike and told him that I would pull my anchor and be right out there. He should be easy to find. I knew he wasn't far. I had let out lots of anchor line, so it took a while to bring the anchor in. Black smoke shot out of my exhaust as I blasted out full bore. I was the only one that could save Bob and his crew.

Within a few minutes, Bob came on the radio again. He had lucked out and his boat had righted itself. He was deck-loaded with two thirty-foot aluminum boats that were chained to the deck, which made the *Kamishak Queen* top heavy. A herky-sized wave had caught him and put the boat on its side. The engineer thought they had split a seam, because water was flooding the engine room. Actually, the water was coming from the large air vent on the side of the boat, and when the water settled to the bottom, it acted like ballast and brought the boat back to its upright position. After I was sure that Bob was all right, I turned the *Winter Wind* and eased back to the calm water of Port Moller. Suddenly I was over-whelmed by the urge to cry. The past two days were nonstop near-death events for all of us that traveled the dark side of the Bering Sea. All of us that survived that trip were a little ragged around the edges, but extremely thankful that we made it.

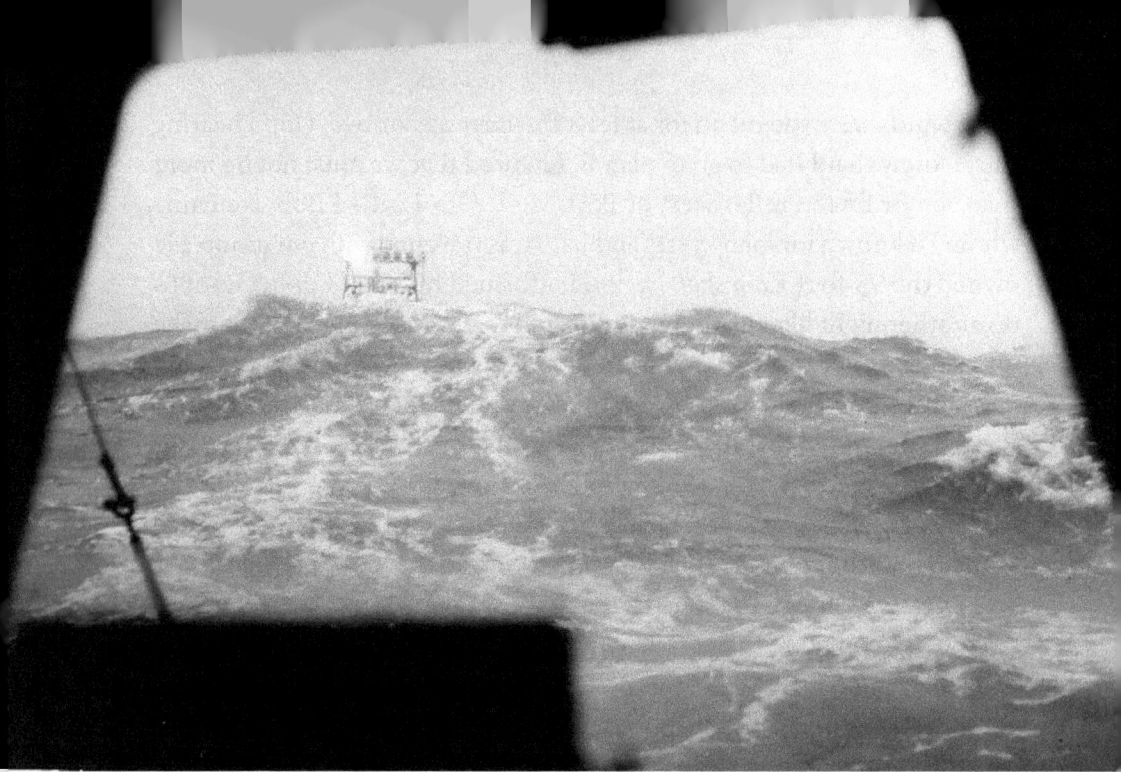

I barely had time to snap this picture while crossing the Bering Sea.

Two boats, the *Vonnie Marie* and the *Kamishak Queen*, had almost gone to Davy Jones's locker. My boat, the *Winter Wind*, could not have survived if I hadn't had the big boats to break the sea for me. We were humbled and brought to our knees. God was with us and had given us the strength to endure. All of us realized that the outcome could have been catastrophic.

Times like the one that I just described make me realize that most mariners are special people. And it actually seems that it is times like this that draws us closer to the sea. I've shared that thought with other mariners that have spent lots of time at sea, and they concur. Many of my friends that have gone down at sea leave me thinking that it's probably not so bad to die while doing what you love. I don't want to sound like a martyr, so I'll leave it at that.

It always amazes me how the sea conditions can change from terribly nasty to mirror calm within hours. The following morning was so still that it brought me out of my bunk, thinking that something was wrong, but after rubbing the sleep out of my eyes and peering out the window, I realized that it was just nice and calm. There was no red sky, so I didn't feel any need to check the forecast. It isn't always easy for a meteorologist to predict Alaska's weather, so when we entered the Bering Sea, we thought the conditions would be moderate. I wasn't troubled by thoughts that I had made the wrong decision, but I also knew that I couldn't have made it without help. I was at peace as I put the coffee on, fired up the engines, and got underway. What a pleasure it was to sit up on the flying bridge with a cup of strong black coffee and travel at cruise speed. Yes, life was good.

Before the fishing started, we watched a couple of plane crashes on the beach at Nunavachak Bay. Nobody got killed, but some pilots lost their livelihood. We had no problem whiling our time away. We cruised over to Walrus Island and got within a few feet of several hundred walruses. They sure do stink! They don't show any respect for each other either. Half of them had blood oozing out of the places that their neighbors' tusks had jabbed. Maybe if I weighed 3000 pounds, I would be unruly and stinky too.

We also went to some of the beaches and found some artifacts. Robby Hoedel brought his boat, the *Windigo*, to the same beach that we were searching for some of the 2000-year-old ivory artifacts. He and I had been friends for a long while, so we were side by side when we caught a glimpse of something protruding from the sand. Both of us had a screwdriver for such an occasion, so we started digging. It didn't take long before we were staring at the most beautiful human skull and it was a magnificent bronze color. It had apparently been frozen in the ground for thousands of years. For a fleeting moment, it seemed to be a prize to behold. Robby and I both knew that natives believe that the worst luck will be cast upon anyone that removes and keeps a skull. I had heard a story of a fisherman that found one and put it on his boat, and the boat sank. We briefly discussed the matter and agreed that no matter how good it might look on the mantle, it would be best left where we found it.

Most fishermen have great respect for tradition and superstition. The old-school mariners were scrupulous on such things. Joe Litchfield, a mariner-fisherman friend of mine, who knows more about the sea than I could learn if I lived to be 150, staunchly adheres to all the superstitions: "Don't put a hatch cover upside down. Don't leave port on a Friday. Don't whistle in the wheelhouse, and if it's up to me, I won't take a woman or a banana aboard!" Joe can rattle off superstitions for hours.

Actually, for every mariner superstition that man has come up with, there is a way to ward it off. So if you are concerned that you might have violated one of Mr. Scratch's (the devil's) hardcore rules, you can get around it by trusting that "for every action, there is an equal and opposite reaction." As an example, if you were at sea and realized that some jerk had brought a banana aboard, you would make sure that the banana was totally eaten and then stand on your right foot and simply throw the peel in the water.

Robby was always a kick to be around. Sometimes his and a couple of other boats would tie up to ours when it was calm, and the musicians would gather on our boat. The talent was unbelievably professional. There were violins, guitars, harmonicas, and a banjo. A couple of the guys sang as well as John Denver or Johnny Cash. The music saturated my mind, and the lingering thoughts of wild seas and plane crashes subsided. Yes, "Sunshine on My Shoulder" always makes me happy.

At night-fall, the wind came up and changed the mood once again. Our boat was fairly close to shore and a bluff that blocked some of the 25 to 30 knot wind. The problem was that the bluff was causing williwaw conditions. It would blow us one way for a short while and stretch our anchor line to the max. Then it would go slack and the boat would go in the opposite direction and stretch the anchor-line again. This went on all night. We didn't drag anchor much, but lots of the boats with deck lights showed them scurrying with anchor drills.

That year Fish and Game said that they would announce the openings. They needed to regulate the biomass, and to do so they would allow us a set percentage of it. They said that they would try to give us a twelve-hour advance notice. One good thing about that was that we fishermen could remain on anchor until their announcement came. Fish and Game would take samples from schools of herring and check the percentage of roe content. By doing that, they would know the precise time to start the fishing. There was some concern that it would cause chaos because many boats would be vying for the same school of fish. For me, it is the chaos and the resulting excitement that turn my crank.

On the morning that we were supposed to start fishing, every engine was churning. All of the seiners, tenders, and planes were on the move. It was a surreal sight. Minute by minute, the excitement escalated. All of the skippers knew where they wanted to make their set. The spotters were swarming above and giving their boats orders as to where they should be when the time came to fish. There were way too many planes in one small bit of airspace, but I couldn't be concerned with that, because I was bumping and grinding with lots of other hungry seiners. Ray Steele was our spotter and I listened to him intently. He was giving me instructions on the radio: "Turn right ten degrees; speed it up a little; don't let that boat get ahead of you; now turn twenty degrees left, etc., etc."

The sky overhead was cluttered with planes, but they looked more like a swarm of bees. The pilots had their work cut out for them. They had to watch out for the swarm, plus watch the movement of the herring and the boats. They needed three sets of eyes to do their job without a mishap.

I thoroughly enjoyed the frantic excitement. There is no event at sea that could come close to matching what I was experiencing. It was so intense, yet profound. My inner being was tested to the limits, and I loved every second. In many ways it was a repeat of previous years, but there was always happenings that occurred that made each herring season stand out in its own way. The intensity of excitement never lessened.

Mike was in the seine skiff with the engine running and ready. The skiff was tight to our stern with a quick release. The pushing, shoving, and bumping were almost too much, but I was doing my best to adhere to our pilot's instructions. It was his show. The school of herring that we were battling for was big—really big. Still, there would be boats that would get nothing. I again refused to be one of the unfortunate. If we must bump, I was happy to accommodate. To my aft and starboard, my eye caught the corks flying out the stern of a big, white seine boat. Uh oh, there went another one at ten o'clock. My exhaust bellowed black smoke as I headed off the guy next to me. The pilot screamed to pull the pin, meaning to release the seine skiff and start the set. Mike and the skiff made an abrupt 180 and the net whipped out the stern. I made an oval that ended close to the skiff. All of the other boats were setting too, each one hoping to get a piece of the huge school. Ray gave me instructions to close my set; then he gained altitude to get out of the menagerie of planes. One of the deckhands was on the bow. He took a line from Mike and tied it to a cleat at mid-ship. Mike then took the skiff outside the net and watched for places that the little silver fish were trying to escape. He went back and forth to keep them from boiling over the cork line. If the fish persisted, he would have to snap large buoys to the cork line. All the crew knew their job. I ran the hydraulics and barked orders. I'd like to say that I gave orders softly, but the excitement caused me to be a tad boisterous, and I wanted to be sure that the crew knew what I wanted them to do.

Putting a net around the fish was a small part of the actual containment. I took the purse line and made three wraps on the niggerhead winch (I don't know why it's called that, but it is). Taking in the purse line gathers the lead line and the rings, which prevents the fish from getting out the bottom. I glanced up and noticed that the herring were pulling the net down in another spot and boiling over the cork line. Herring are small fish, but in multitudes their strength is awesome. I hollered to Mike and pointed to the spot. He got there quickly, but the cork line was already down. Mike leaned over the side of the skiff, submerging his lean upper body and strong arms. Twenty seconds went by before he came up with the cork line in his mighty grip. There was no way that Mike would have let that cork line go. Yes, folks, that act was above and beyond duty, and it saved the day. We continued to dry up the net until we dared not bring in any more. The procedure was complete and we had captured the little buggers. I could tell that the net contained 150 tons or more. Three cheers!

I called the processor on the vhf and told him to send a tender over to suck the fish out of our net. He told me to stand by. The crew was jubilant and giving high fives. Ray called and congratulated us. An hour passed and we were still waiting for a tender. I called the processor again, and he informed me that he had to use all of the tenders for a huge set that Kenny Jones had landed. He said that I should hang on because there were more tenders coming.

Waiting is not one of my favorite pastimes, whether it is in the post office, store, or in Nunavachak Bay. It was out of my hands, though, so I had to contain my thoughts and remain calm. I had the crew let out some of the net so the herring wouldn't be so crowded that they would start spawning in it, but an hour or so later I could see clouds of milky water from the milt of the male fish. They didn't care what they spawned on, so even though they lacked kelp or rocks, they did their thing in 100 fathoms of Jerre's net. The tide was rising and the current was starting to move us towards some rocks. A few more hours passed before I could make contact with the processor, and he informed me that there would be no tenders available.

I didn't have to pass the message on to my crew. They could tell by the disappointed look on my face that we had to turn the set loose. I can't put into words how I felt at that moment. The day had started with the greatest excitement, the highest of highs, then suddenly plunged to rock bottom. A mariner knows that he has no say in what Mother Nature dishes out, but when someone you're counting on lets you down and determines your fate, it sucks totally. After releasing the massive school of fish, there was nothing to do but go back to our anchorage and lick the terrible wound.

As fatigued as we were, none of us slept that night. Early the next morning I pulled anchor and cruised over to the processor ship. I met with the superintendent, and he assured me that he would have a tender for me on the next opening. This was a small consolation after having dumped a set with many thousands of dollars worth of fish. The season went on, and we made enough landings to make an okay season, but it was still sickening to think about the mother lode that we had to turn loose.

The 1000-mile trip back was quiet and uneventful. I had plenty of time to reflect on the season. It was tough. I had no problem taking responsibility for both successes and failures brought about by my own actions, but it was hard to accept that my season had been diminished by someone else. Before we reached the safe haven of the Homer harbor, I had decided to stop sniveling and to go on to be stronger and better. There are times in everybody's lives that they would give anything to change history, but it can't be done. The good news was that we survived some of the most outrageously awesome seas and succeeded in navigating like days of old without the aid of electronics. "When the going gets tough, the tough get tougher!"

Beaver Nelson told me about a time when he had made a super big herring set. "The whole net was full! We were millionaires," he quipped with excitement that was portrayed by the look on his face and the sound of his voice. "But then we noticed that the mass of fish was getting smaller. Darn, we'd snagged a rock and ripped a hole in the net. Just as quick as we thought we were rich, we were as poor as when we started."

Winnie had flown back to Homer with Ray, so she was there to greet me when I pulled into our slip at the harbor. She was not only my mate, but also my first mate on the boat. We were back on terra firma, so for the next few days we were nothing if not the best of mates.

Last night, as Winnie and I were enjoying the comforts of our cozy home, the wind came up and was trying its darnedest to make life miserable. Winnie went into the bathroom, lifted the toilet seat, and announced that there were whitecaps in the toilet. It was often that way when we were on the boat, but not at home. We laughed and laughed at such a humorous remark.

Soon we would have to prepare for halibut long-lining, but I wanted to get my legs in shape so that I could compete in the Mount Marathon race again. One day when I was lacing up my running shoes, I asked my non-running wife if she would like to go along. She hadn't shown any interest before, but she surprised me by saying yes.

She also surprised me by running like she had been doing it for a long time. Having Winnie run with me brought smiles to her face and mine. The more time we spent together, the more we bonded, and the closer we became. Until that time, I had always run by myself. Now I had more incentive to improve.

Each year toward the later part of winter I would have to commit to some races; otherwise I would procrastinate on my training. I don't like to see others procrastinate, so I wouldn't allow myself to skip training sessions. Knowing that signing up for races was the carrot that spurred me on, I got Winnie to agree to some 5k and 10k races. Right from the start, she was winning ribbons. Medals and ribbons served as bigger carrots, inspiring both of us to train harder and get stronger and faster. So, when we weren't fishing, we ran together.

The following spring's halibut season wasn't much different from the others except that I took Galen and Buck, both seasoned fishermen. When we got out to the Banks and I looked through my binoculars, I saw more boats in the area than I had ever seen in previous years. The International Halibut Commission had put stricter regulations in place. Fishing would be done in 24-hour openings, so once I had committed to an area to set my gear for any given opening, I had to make the best of it. There wasn't enough time to travel to another location.

I watched the closest boats and tried not to set near their lines. Even so, when it was time to pick up gear, it was not good. All of my strings of gear had other lines strung on top of them. Every time a line crossed ours, it put a terrible strain on our set. We would have to cut the other line and tie it back together under ours. Most of the time when this happened, there were also gobs of hooks tangled. It was an ugly sight, and hard to straighten out.

Then the ornery sea lions came to pay us a visit. They would follow the hooked halibut and rip them off the hooks. It's against the law to shoot these monstrous animals, and they seem to know it. They would come up and tug at a hooked halibut right next to the boat, and all we could do was holler at them. There is a rookery at Marmot Island, which wasn't far from the Banks, so through the years they had gotten wise enough to know that they could steal from us with no consequences.

For some reason, the fish were smaller that year. The few fish that we did land were thirty pounds or less. I felt bad for Galen and Buck, and they probably thought that, like Billy on the *Andrea Gail* in the movie *The Perfect Storm*, I was incapable of catching a fish. We barely made expenses. Usually there's plenty of work to do while running back to port. The fish have to be gutted and iced, which is a tough job when you have lots of fish, but that time it was a quiet ride home. The only good things about the trip were that it was calm and that we had enough beer for Buck.

After two or three drift gillnet Cook Inlet seasons, Winnie had become the best deckhand ever. She did everything that I didn't have time to do, and more. There weren't many boats that out-fished us.

Chapter 13

A Gentleman's Game

The importance of taking time to play can't be overemphasized. Play is a deterrent of stress and is just a good thing to incorporate into one's life.

I enjoy looking at the local bulletin boards in town, and one day I saw a notice that caught my eye. It was like the one that says, "We're looking for a few Good Men!" The bulletin that I was mesmerized by said a rugby team was being formed and that anybody interested should show up at the junior high football field on a certain date. I had never seen a rugby game, but I knew that it was a contact sport. That was definitely something I had to check out. I think I had it in my mind that it must be like football. Actually the only similarity is that the ball is shaped the same (but slightly bigger). Other than that, the game is so different from American football that it is quite hard to learn the rules. You can't forward pass, can't block, can't wear any protective gear, but you must be a gentleman before and after a game.

I became one of the first members of Homer's Irish Lords rugby team. Barry Reese and Bob Evans had played the game in college, so they automatically were the coaches and instructors. A few of the other guys that showed up had played the game before too, which meant I had more guys to learn from. A rugby team consists of fifteen players. In a small town like Homer (at that time 3000 at the most), it wasn't easy to come up with that many gents that enjoyed getting smashed and bloodied, but good fortune happened at the dock by the boat harbor. We had a Coast Guard ship stationed here, so we were able to coax a few Coasties to join us. Eventually we ended up with eighteen or nineteen guys, all obviously burdened by low IQs.

After trying a couple of different positions, I found my niche. My position was right in the middle of the scrum. I was the best hooker in Homer! When the ball was thrown into the center of a scrum, I would hook the ball back to my teammates. Of course my opposition was trying to do the same for his team, so my shins took a beating in every game. Barry was insistent that we had to be in shape because all of the teams that we were to play were bigger than we were. We had to be fearless and fast. Our opponents were from bigger towns like Kenai, Anchorage, and Fairbanks where there were more big guys to choose from. One of the teams from Anchorage was made up of a couple of medium-sized "whities" and twenty super-sized Samoans. I was lucky because I was midway through my running season, so I was used to doing three sets of forty pushups and many sprints up and down the field. Before we had our first game, we all saw our fat turning to muscle and the muscle acquiring more definition. We were hyped to the hilt and confident that we could beat any team.

Our first game was at home against the Barbos. Both teams formed a line in the middle of the field, and we shook each other's hands and wished our opponents "Good luck, laddie." Then we proceeded to put the hurt on each other and draw as much blood as a good vampire would. It's a lovely game. There was one pretty boy that thought he wanted to be a rugby player, but he never tackled anyone, and he didn't want the ball for fear of messing up his wavy hair. He was the only one of our team that didn't have blood and mud on his uniform. We won our first game by a "tri," so we knew that we were an authentic team. At the end of the game as in the beginning, we lined up and congratulated each other with a "Well done, laddie."

I was a lightweight both when it came to the consumption of alcoholic beverages and the misuse—or should I say abuse—of the English language. Real rugby players are just the opposite. They don't swear, exactly; they just cuss a bit while happy and smiley. A lot of the cussing is incorporated into their songs. I seemed to be the only one that didn't know the lyrics to any of the chants or songs, but I felt obligated to pretend. There was the "gang-bang" song: "When I was younger and in my prime, I used to gang-bang all the time. Now I'm older and turning grey, so I only gang-bang once a day." Sometimes an unsuspecting woman would be lifted up on the bar and everybody would sing a version of "Alouette" to her. Then there was the canoe race. It didn't have anything to do with canoes, but more to do with double shots of Jameson Irish Whiskey. It was all in fun, and no one seemed offended or hurt. The rugby parties created the kind of laughter that makes happy tears and stomachs hurt.

I do remember one party that wasn't totally fun though. We treated the Dragons to a barbeque at the Waterfront Bar. The Dragons got a bit rowdy and spilled a fair amount of beer on the floor, and some of the players intercepted a young couple that happened in. The guys handcuffed the couple together, and then one of the fellas swallowed the key. I have to say that some things got a tad out of hand and the bar owner kicked us out and barred us from coming there again. I can't say that I blamed him. Sometime after that, Chip, who was one of our players, bought the Waterfront and changed the name to Duggan's, so we aren't barred from there anymore.

Even though Anchorage had four teams, their parties were a two or three on the one-to-ten scale. The Fairbanks Sundogs, on the other hand, knew how to throw a descent shindig. From Homer, the drive is more than 500 miles, which meant sitting in the saddle for about twelve hours. After we played a couple of games, we were ready to relax and eat some meat and drink something cold. The Sundogs are real Alaskans and treated us like royalty. We all pointed our noses toward the northeast and gathered at Chena Hot Springs. The Sundogs served us the best barbeque steaks and all the trimmings. There was an abundance of ice-cold beer and soft drinks, which we consumed while soaking in the hot springs. There aren't many things that feel better than this combination. To top off the eating, drinking, and soaking, we bedded down in the loft of a large building that was reserved for us Homer boys and our families.

The after-game parties at Homer weren't always at bars. Quite often we would take the visiting team to a secluded beach on Kachemak Bay. The Samoans loved us for doing this, because they knew that they would have barbequed fish and beer until it came out their ears. I don't know if there is such a thing as a small or medium-sized Samoan. All of the guys that played rugby were big—*really* big. They could put away lots of fish and beer. One of their claims to greatness was their non-ending, contagious giggling.

During one of those beach parties, a large number of players from both teams surrounded the bonfire. One keg of beer had already been devoured when someone threw a pebble into Mark's plastic cup of beer. Mark was one of our biggest teammates. He has the space in his large frame for several gallons of beer. The guy that threw the pebble told Mark that if someone throws a pebble in your glass you have to chug your beer. Oh yes, let the party begin! Now everyone was throwing pebbles into anyone's beer that they could. For some reason several of the participants zeroed in on Mark. Between glasses of beer, Mark showed off by chugging a cube of butter, or downing a bottle of catsup or anything within arm's reach. The more we laughed, the more stuff Mark chugged. Then, without saying anything, he put his empty cup down, raised his arms up, pointed to the sky, and jutted his jaw forward. Suddenly, a four-inch gusher of stomach content arched like a giant rainbow toward the fire. It was a Boone and Crockett barf! This was not only a reMARKable regurgitation, but it beat any that I had seen at sea. Mark grinned from ear to ear when everyone applauded. Then he put his arms up again, pointed to the sky, and repeated the act. The second regurgitation was as spectacular as the first!

During the seven years that our team, the Irish Lords, existed, we were Alaska State champions twice. Every game we played was a thrill of a lifetime for me. As might be expected, there were a few injuries. Dr. Dan lost his spleen, and an air force guy got the worst leg break that I've ever seen. The lower bone was sticking out of a bloody hole. I was the recipient of a broken ligament. It was the big one just below the kneecap. We were in a big ruck, and some guy came flying into the pile. You could hear the ligament pop from the sidelines. I couldn't do much for three months. I didn't go to the doctor with it, so it's still a little weak. Every year before my mountain running gets underway, I do lots of weightlifting so that the muscles are strong enough to support it.

Like the old saying goes, "All good things must come to an end." One of the guys caught an Irish Lord fish, and we gathered at his house and had an official burial of the Irish Lords. We made it look and sound like fun, but it was a sad affair to me. It had to be done because it was getting harder and harder to keep enough people to do the organizing and playing. I'm extremely appreciative of all of the members of the team. It was an honor

to play and to share the great camaraderie. I never learned the words to the numerous "cute" songs that all the other guys sang in jovial unison. "Rump-tittie, rump-tittie, rump-tittie tittie."

Chapter 14

Park People

Through the years that I hunted, guided, and trapped at Twin Lakes, I used two log cabins that I built and three others that I bought from squeaky, skinny old Frank Bell, who sold them to me because he was getting to the age where his body was getting tired. I was hunting by myself near the small creek at the junction of the upper and lower Twin Lakes when I first met Frank. Other than Dick Proeneke, who was my only neighbor across the lake, I hardly ever saw another human, so I was startled when seemingly out of nowhere a shrill voice sounded, saying, "Hey, there." It came from a skinny guy with a short, grey, stubbly face, paddling the crudest-looking kayak that I had ever laid eyes on. The ancient, dark green canvas that covered the broken wooden frame was patched with gobs of spruce pitch, but there were still lots of holes above water level. "How you doing there, sonny?" the cheery old guy quipped.

He introduced himself and made sure that he had my name correct. Then he rattled on like the proverbial magpie. He went on and on nonstop. He told me that his Indian friend was up the valley, looking for the caribou that had left a single track by the lake. He said that the Indian without a doubt would kill the caribou. Within fifteen minutes he had given me a short version of his life and, without taking a breath, asked me if I wanted to buy his three cabins. I had seen all of them in my travels and wondered who built them.

Frank wiggled his way out of the dilapidated kayak. I couldn't believe that a body could be so skinny and still be alive. It was a good thing that he had on a sturdy leather belt; otherwise there was nothing to hold his holey pants on. He stretched a bit and took a leak, all the while yakking. When I indicated that I would be interested in his cabins, he told me that he wintered in North Kenai and that he was in the phone book. "Give me a call in October and I'll make a deal with you," he suggested.

About that time we heard a shot up the valley, then six or eight more. Frank grinned and said that the Indian wasn't a good shot, but somehow he always got the animal. He was right. The Indian had shot a bull caribou that had the biggest, thickest horns I had ever seen. I didn't hang around to see how they got the meat back to their cabin with that raggedy, moth-bitten kayak. I had some hunting of my own to do.

After the fall hunting season, I looked up Frank's number and gave him a call. His memory was as sharp as a twenty-year-old. He not only remembered me, but was confident that I would call and purchase his cabins. For $800 I could buy all three, and he even declared that he had applied for patent for the land by the cabin at Snipe Lake, and that when he got patent he would transfer it to me.

Frank Bell sounded like an honorable man, so I sent him a check. In return he sent me a receipt for "payment in full."

The cabin that was near the first bend of the Chilakadrotna River was leaning a bit, and the logs were not peeled. Number two cabin was on the upper lake a couple of miles east of my cabins and was in good shape. I spent quite a bit of time the following spring rejuvenating number two cabin and Snipe Lake cabin. These two were located ideally for trapping and hunting.

In the meantime, I followed up on the patent that Frank had applied for. Frank died while we were waiting for that precious little piece of paper. It wasn't long after that I received a letter informing me that Frank hadn't given adequate description of the parcel, so they would not issue a patent. I called them and told them that the area wasn't surveyed, so it would have been difficult to give any better description than Frank did. Of course my effort was to no avail because they had their minds made up. I had no experience with matters that dealt with law. I just used my cabins and dropped the subject.

Then came Jimmy Carter. Darned that president! He was like a cat in the night. With one swift stroke of the pen, he turned the whole area into a national park. Even though I owned one of the only two patented parcels in the vast area, he didn't bother asking me what I thought about turning my hunting grounds into a park. I'm sure that my feelings were pretty much like those of the American Indians in the 1800s. Our government has a consistent record for taking land from people without discussing the matter with "the people."

I honestly didn't put a whole lot of importance on it when I heard about it, but a short time later I began to realize the ugly scope of the matter. Winnie and I continued to use the area the same as usual. We trapped in the winter and hunted in the fall. I had quit guiding because I was commercial fishing enough that it left little time for babysitting hunters. Also, I was enjoying the time with Winnie, so I wasn't about to leave her home by herself, even though I had had good times guiding.

Then the park service began their push and shove mentality, and made itself known. We had taken our little skiff toward the east end of the lake in search of a moose. Both of us have good eyes for spotting game, so it wasn't long before I saw the shiny, light-colored horn of a bull moose. He was a big guy, so it would have been near to impossible to hide those huge antlers. We parked the skiff and climbed to a spot that would take us slightly downwind of the bull. It was an easy stalk, and I downed him with a single shot through the neck. No meat is wasted with that kind of bullet placement. When I started the gutting process, both of us were delighted to see the globs of fat, which meant that the bull was not in rut.

Mature bull caribou often produce three to four hundred pounds of the best kind of meat. Prior to the rut, they have as much fat as moose, but after they start the rut, which occurs around the third week in September, the meat turns so rank that nobody would dare kill one, because even dogs won't eat it. It would gag a maggot!

We had been working on the animal twenty minutes or so when I heard the drone of a plane approaching. Sure enough, a 185 on floats was headed right toward our skiff. It taxied to shore and three guys piled out in a hurried fashion. I put my scope on them to see if it was someone I knew. They made a beeline straight toward us. I was puzzled as to how anyone would know that we were up on this brushy mountainside. The only other person within fifty miles was our neighbor across the lake, Dick Proeneke.

I continued the gutting process as the three men trudged directly toward us. As they neared, I could see that they had rifles on their shoulders and holstered handguns. They seemed to know who I was, because they didn't ask my name when they identified themselves as park rangers. One of them began taking pictures, so I told Winnie to stand back and let the people take pictures of the dead moose. The guy that appeared to be in charge asked me if we were sport hunting. Duh, what an idiot. I didn't have to be Sherlock Holmes to know that I couldn't hunt in the park in any other fashion than for our personal use, and that was what I was doing. I simply replied that we liked moose meat. Then I told them that I had to get to work cutting up the moose. They stammered around like they didn't know what their purpose in life was, and I ignored their lingering presence. They mumbled amongst themselves as they began their descent to the plane.

Winnie asked me what that was all about, and being the honest person that I am, I replied that I had no idea. The plane departed and headed toward Lake Clark, which is where the park service headquarters was located.

I couldn't help thinking about our visit and how those rangers knew our exact location and that we had killed a moose. There was only one answer: our good old-time friend Dick must have been coerced into being a spy for them. Obviously they equipped him with a radio so he could contact them when he thought someone might be violating their newly established park. There was no other explanation, and it made me sad to think that Dick would do such a thing. During the mid-sixties when my family and I were building our log cabin, we could hear Dick across the lake doing the same. We became good friends and throughout the years had many great visits. Most times when we came over from our homestead in Kasilof, we would bring him baked goods and fresh produce. We shared meat with him whenever we got a moose, caribou, or sheep. He even paid us a visit or two at our homestead and showed us movies that he had taken at the lakes.

I believe that when Dick was fairly young he got his heart broken and never took a chance at love again. If a moose happened his way, and it was cold enough to keep the meat, Dick would shoot it. Later on he stopped hunting because he found that he could get all the meat he needed from me or his friends at Lake Clark, the Alsworths. Dick wrote a book called

One Man's Wilderness, which seemed like an inappropriate title to me, because my family and I were at Twin Lakes before Dick. Other than the name, the book is nicely done.

I was saddened to think that he had called the rangers and told them exactly where to find me with my dead moose. I found myself getting furious. He never once talked to me about the matter. Perhaps if he had taken the time and respected me as much as I did him, he might have acted differently. I had hunted there for several years before he came. Also I had received patent on my Trade and Manufacturing site after building the cabins, whereas Dick was squatting. (Later on, his friends Babe and Mary Alsworth acquired the land that Dick was squatting on. Mary was native, so she was able to obtain native land. I think they gave the land to Dick.)

The following year after salmon season, we went back to the lakes. We had the usual battle with the porcupines. They didn't seem to want any part of coexistence. Almost every night they would pay us a visit and start munching on the cabin. They weren't fussy; they would chew on the logs or the roof. The cabin always had holes despite our continual repairs. When they came at night, I would have to go out and thump them with an axe handle. There must have been more porkies (I called them the devil) per square mile than any other species of animal, and that includes voles and shrews. Most of the cottonwood trees in the area had lots of the bark chewed off too. There were way too many of these yellow-toothed wood-eating vampires. I couldn't help wondering if these prickly-backed vandals were park rangers incognito.

Anyhow, we were on our annual meat hunt. There was freshness in the air, reminding us that winter was around the corner. The leaves had begun to fall, which meant that the caribou would be starting to come down off the mountains. Soon the bulls would be gathering with cows and they would begin their fall migration. I had seen fresh caribou tracks near the same place Frank's Indian friend had gotten that big one. I told Winnie that it was time to put the hammers and nails down.

It was midday before we paddled down the lake to the junction creek. We watched grayling and trout breaking the surface of the calm lake while we ate lunch. The weather was as nice as it gets. It would have been a treat to lie on the beach or the nearby moss and let the sun soak into our souls, but survival instincts were prevailing, and I was answering the call. We paralleled the dry creek bottom, staying on the softness of the tundra, which gave us stealth. I'm pretty good at spotting game, but sometimes I'd be looking in the distance and miss critters that were close by. Winnie tugged on my shirttail and slowly pointed to something ahead and to our left. It was a bull caribou with its head down, feeding. The willows still had some of their leaves, so it was hard to detect him when he wasn't moving. I eased my 7mm magnum to my shoulder, and in a split second the bull became our winter meat. No matter how many times I stalk and kill an animal for my family and me, it is a jubilant experience.

Our bull was taken at the perfect time. It was fat as a butterball. We put the quarters in cotton bags, which we lashed to the army pack boards that both Winnie and I had. Winnie helped by carrying the back straps, neck, and rib meat. When we got to the skiff, we put the bags in the shade, and I left my rifle so I didn't have the extra weight to carry as we headed back for another load. There aren't many bears around the Twin Lakes area, so I wasn't too concerned about a bear encounter. It was only about a half mile back to the kill, so in a short time we were cutting more meat off. There was so much fat that we had to discard some of it. We stopped for an instant because we heard the distinctive sound of an airplane, but in a minute the sound went away. Winnie likes to cook the meaty bones for soup, so we were sawing the backbone when two guys burst out of the brush with sawed-off shotguns pointed at us. They definitely startled us, but then I quickly noticed that they were wearing the telltale park ranger garb. They weren't the same guys that approached us the year before, but they asked the same question: "Are you sport hunting?"

I kept on sawing bones and just gave them a simple no.

The lead guy was unhappy. He proceeded to tell us that he was recruited from the Lower 48 to come to Alaska and set people straight about the national parks. I asked him what the sawed-off shotguns were for. He gave me the lame answer that it was bear country. Then he attempted to intimidate us by telling us that he issued the first citations in Alaska parks and that he made a couple of old sourdoughs leave because they were trespassing. You can't fool a "foo foo fly"; I knew where this jerk was coming from. The other ranger had been quiet until the lead guy took a breath to lay some more B.S. on deaf ears. The number two man held out his hand and said, "Here is the ammunition that we took out of your gun back at your skiff."

I was in total disbelief. These two dunces took the ammunition out of my gun. Nobody, but nobody had ever touched my gun without my consent! I felt my face getting flushed to the point that I had to calm myself. Winnie feared that I was about to commit an unkind act, and she put her arm around me to bring me back to reality. I grabbed my ammunition from the guy and told him never to do that again. At that point I decided that I had had enough of those two and that I would not say one more word to them. We put our packs on and left them standing there with Mr. Jerk still yakking away.

During the years that the park rangers were harassing us, they were doing the same to the poor subsistence people along the Yukon River. Folks that had built nice log cabins and lived a tranquil subsistence lifestyle, gardening, fishing, and hunting were served notice to leave. Their cabins were burned, their lives destroyed. The park service was on a mission to get rid of any humanity that resided within the boundaries of THEIR parks.

When we got back to the cabin and hung the meat, neither of us spoke much. Then Winnie looked at me with a tear in her eye and said something that I've never forgotten. She said, "They make me feel like a criminal."

I could understand her thoughts, but I assured her that if we had done anything wrong they would have given us a citation. We did nothing against the law. They were just making a half-assed attempt to scare us. I'm not scared of anything except big sharks when they circle me in the water. But I had two of us to consider, and Winnie was scared.

The next day we tidied up our wonderful home away from home and nailed the shutters over the two small windows. I had to hold back my own tears as we loaded the plane. It was the same feelings that I had when I left my homestead. Twin Lakes held some of the fondest memories that I've ever had. Just the serene beauty of the turquoise lakes and the mountains takes your breath away. The mountains on this side of the Alaska Range have a multitude of light brown colors compared to many of the mountainous areas in Alaska, which are darker shades of green and black. The change in appearance compared to the east side of this long stretch of mountains makes you wonder how they could be of the same range. Like several other places in Alaska, I had become a part of it. I've been on the top of almost every mountain within twenty miles in all directions.

The day was clear and calm, so I gained altitude and flew over the top. Without speaking, I knew that Winnie and I shared the same feelings.

We flew by the 10,000-foot snow-capped peak of Mount Redoubt and took in her majestic beauty, and still, neither of us spoke. When we were almost across Cook Inlet, I looked back at Winnie and told her how beautiful she was. It was the truth, but I was also trying to get her to forget the park people.

When I got back to Homer, I decided that I had an obligation to find out what the park service head office had to say about the treatment that we were getting. I drove to Anchorage, a five-hour drive, and went to the park headquarters office unannounced. I knew who the head man was, so I ignored the receptionist and opened the door that had his name on it. I informed him who I was and why I was there. I asked him why his troops were harassing us, and he said that he had no knowledge of any of his rangers visiting us at Twin Lakes.

Wow, I thought, either I'm dealing with a liar, or he just had a brain fart. I could tell that he had no intention of lending an ear to my cause. I told him to call off the troops, especially the ones with sawed-off shotguns. He seemingly didn't know how to respond to me because he just stood there staring at me. I just turned and walked out.

They didn't deserve any more of our thoughts or time. For them I have a saying: "Life is tough, but it's tougher when you're stupid."

My mind was devising ways to make these people pay for the suffering they were causing us. I was barely able to control my thoughts, and this was beginning to worry me. There had been one other time in my life when I wanted to get even with someone, but I didn't allow evil to win. I left it in God's hands. I knew that would be the best course this time too, and yet thoughts of revenge nagged at me. When people like these try to intimidate you with their power trip and their sawed-off shotguns, you feel honor-bound to take a stand. There were times that I could have easily thrown them off my trail and then circled back and sunk their float plane, but I knew who my enemy was, and they weren't worth the battle. It would have been like trapping shrews. No matter how many you get rid of, there are always that many more to plague you. It seems that in this rapid world of change there is always someone gnawing at your ankles. I can't help thinking of a comment that a supreme justice once made. With great wisdom he said, "The right most valued by all civilized men is the right to be LEFT ALONE."

November is the month that we start gathering our trapping supplies. We don't dare start piling the stuff any earlier, or the heap would grow so big that we wouldn't get it in a 747. It was going to require more than two trips because we had acquired a third member to our household. Early in the spring we made a trip to Anchorage and took our pick of a litter of Malamutes. We decided on the biggest male because he was the cutest. Yes, I know that sounds sissified, but I can't think of any other reason that we chose him. When it was time to go back to Twin Lakes to trap, the puppy was the size of a Mack truck, and he was only half grown. We named him Truk because of the Trukese people, who are extra large. At a young age the dog was already showing signs of great intelligence, but also of possessing a mind of his own. It seemed that if he got more than 62½ feet away from us, he pretended not to hear us. The first time he pulled his deaf trick on us, he just kept trotting up the road despite all of my hollering, never once looking back. Ten minutes later I could faintly hear Bruce Willard screaming obscenities. Bruce had a herd of cattle, so I didn't have to ponder what the problem was. I started running up the hill, hoping that I would catch Truk before the buckshot did. Lucky for that Malamute, I was a good runner, because Bruce would have put some lead in that dog and I wouldn't have blamed him.

Truk was growing up to be one BIG dog, and not only that, he was smart—too smart for his own good sometimes. He would get into mischief, and he could be headstrong. Unfortunately, the usual disciplinary measures didn't work with Truk. Scolding, rolled up newspapers—Truk couldn't have cared less. Stronger measures were called for if the dog was to be a good canine citizen. Luckily, when they were applied, Truk learned more quickly than any dog I've been around. We were down at the boat harbor one time talking with a fishing buddy. I turned just in time to see Truk taking a dump on the dock. This was bad for a couple of reasons: firstly, if a dog poops on the docks, the owner has to clean it up; secondly, the owner has to clean it up. It's right up there on the list of my least favorite chores in life. It's real close to changing a diaper. I'm sorry to admit that my reflexes kicked in, and I hit Truk with my fist right between the eyes. He let out a yelp, and I grabbed him by the nape of his neck and the hair on his back and pulled him over to the edge of the float. I pushed his butt to where it was hanging over the water and told him in a very harsh voice that if he had to poop, do it over the water! The next time we went down to the floats, he did just that. No kidding. I petted him and gave him a hug. He licked my face and smiled at me.

It was nearly midwinter before the big lakes froze thick enough to land on with skis. I think it did require three trips to haul all our gear and supplies, but we finally settled in to our cozy cabin. When we started setting traps, I took a small #1 trap and opened the jaws just enough to go over Truk's paw. It didn't hurt much at all, but he got the picture and never got near any of our sets.

I was going to start building another small cabin for a banya (sauna). We had a big homemade sled that we used for hauling wood, and there was a stand of timber not far away that had nice straight spruce that would be perfect for the structure. I would go to where the trees were and cut six or eight logs, load the sled, and tell Truk to take it to Winnie. I had to teach him to jerk the sled sideways to break the runners loose. Then he would dig in with his big paws and pull until his chest was almost on the snow-covered ice. He would take the load nearly half a mile to Winnie, and she would release the logs and send Truk back to me. He almost looked like he was enjoying his newly-learned duty.

Even on days that Truk didn't have to work, he had a voracious appetite. For the most part, he ate the same food that we did. There was no way that we could have brought hundreds of pounds of dog food in our small airplane, so he got to eat like a people. There was one exception. When we snared snowshoe rabbits, we ate the fleshy parts, and Truk got the leftovers. I happened to catch him snitching some lower leg bones with the furry feet attached that I had temporarily left outside the door. When I caught him in the act, he was swallowing one of the leg-bones, including the big furry foot. Yep, he devoured it without chewing the morsel. Winnie came out to see what I was laughing so hard about. I told her to watch Truk. There was one furry foot left. I told Truk that it was okay, so he gulped that one down like he hadn't eaten in a month. You could see the foot slide down his big throat in one piece. We laughed so hard that Truk started running circles around us, as if he were laughing too.

Our Malamute's fur got woollier as the winter progressed, so he appeared to have doubled his size. He became a loving buddy of both of us. With his youth came friskiness, which the majority of the time was fun to watch.

Truk and Winnie at our trapping cabin

One day we were walking down the lake towards the west end of our trap line. Truk was pulling the sled with our traps and supplies as usual. Suddenly his sharp eyes spotted a small herd of caribou across the lake. His wolf nature kicked in, and he took off in high gear and never looked back. Of course both of us were yelling at him to come back, but we knew that all our shouting was in vain. We could see the contents of the sled flying out helter-skelter. He went out of view when he got a mile and a half across the lake. The caribou were in no danger because there wasn't much snow. I was fuming, but there was nothing I could do. We just trudged back to the cabin and wrote the day off.

It was getting dark when the caribou hunter timidly came back. He knew he was in trouble, and lowered his head in shame. I was still fuming, so for the second time I hit him in the snout with my fist. He knew it was coming, and didn't make any attempt to avoid the punishment. A mere yelp, but very submissive. Again, it only took one little punch in the nose and he never again chased caribou. Thank goodness, Truk obeyed consistently after that, and I never had to lay a hand on him again.

Winnie was getting a bit fearful of his playful manner. He could easily knock her down when he got frisky. Once in a while he would stand on his rear feet and put his front feet on her shoulders so he could give her a dog "tongue kiss." He was just being loving, but Winnie didn't appreciate the slobber. Neither of us could keep from loving him to pieces because he had so many great qualities and he did so much work for us.

Our old Élan snow machine had not been used for a long time because the tracks were sagging. I didn't want to get out in the pucker-brush and have the track come off. The adjustment bolt was broken, so I was unable to stretch the track. After examining the derelict and giving the matter some thought, I figured that maybe I could stretch the old track if I improvised a homemade turnbuckle. I twisted several strands of trapping wire together and then stuck a two-inch spruce pole in the center. I duplicated the Jerre-rigged turnbuckle for the other side. Then I merely had to twist the poles to take the sag out of the track. Good thinking, huh? When I got one side stretched, I had Winnie hold the pole and warned her not to let it go. I then twisted the other pole to take up the other side. It was getting a good strain on it when it slipped out of my wet hands. It hit me in the face and knocked me unconscious. It released the strain on Winnie's side, so she ran around to help me. When I came to a few seconds later, Winnie was crying and screaming for me to wake up. There was blood all over the surrounding snow. My lip and the inside of my mouth were split, and my cheek had a big, deep gash in it. With Winnie's help, I staggered into the cabin. I stopped most of the bleeding by holding snow on the wounds. We didn't have a great deal of first aid equipment, but the strangest thing had happened during our fall hunting. We were on a game trail near the upper end of the lake when Winnie bent down and picked something up. As weird as it sounds, it was a suture that was still in the package! At the time, we had no idea what we could possibly use it for, but my wife put it in our first aid kit. When I told her that the gaping wound in my cheek was going to have to be sewed up, she remembered that suture and where she had put it.

When I broke the news to her that she was to be the seamstress, she cried and claimed that she couldn't do it. I assured her that it would be all right and that I would show her how to do a baseball stitch. It took a while for her to accept the thought, so in the meantime I put more snow on my wounds to help numb them and to keep them from swelling. When she stuck the curved needle into the thick cheek skin, she burst out with more tears. It was hurting her more emotionally than it was me physically. Again, I had to calm her. I told her to make the stitches about a quarter of an inch apart. Each time she made a stitch, she whimpered. I tried to be a good patient and not move, but it did make me flinch a bit. The wound had gone through my mouth, but we only sewed the skin. My lip was split but I just put a band-aid on it to hold it in place until it healed itself. It took only eight or ten stitches, and my little seamstress did an excellent job. After a year or so you couldn't even tell that I had dumbed out and let a turnbuckle get the best of me.

I made a simple NO TRESPASSING sign soon after we flew into our place at Twin Lakes. I thought that if the park service people paid us a visit, I would let them know that they were not welcome. I nailed a stake to it so that it could be stuck in the snow by the edge of the lake. The day came when I was to enjoy the pleasure of using that sign. It was a bitter, cold, windy day with the snow blowing sideways. The wind chill must have been -50° —frostbite weather—so we stayed inside. We used it as an opportunity to clean house and do some baking. We used sourdough daily for hotcakes and bread, but it was time for a chocolate sourdough cake.

Suddenly there was the unmistakable sound of a nearby airplane. I rubbed the frosted window just in time to see a Cessna 185 on skis landing by the point by our cabin. It taxied out of sight to turn around. I knew that it had to be a ranger, so I grabbed my sign, ran out to the edge of the lake, stuck it in the snow next to the trail, and went back inside. As the guy parked the plane and put a cowl cover on, I wondered why anyone would fly in that kind of weather. The snow was blowing so hard that he didn't even see my sign.

I slung the door open and hollered out, "Hey! Didn't you see my sign?"

The guy was so startled that he almost tripped over himself trying to step backwards to get a look at the sign. He started stammering that he was sorry, but I told him to get off my property. He was shaking as he tried to explain that he was new to the park service and that he was a local man from Takotna. The soft side of me gave in, and I told him to come up for coffee. He didn't know if he should accept the invite, but he slowly made his way to the open door.

He introduced himself as Hollis Twitchell and claimed that he had come in peace and just wanted to meet us. He knew that we had no use for the park or the rangers. Hollis seemed to be authentic, and after he stopped shaking, I felt bad about putting the fear in him. He openly told me that they had a one-inch thick paper file about me. I couldn't understand how anyone could write that much stuff about a nice fellow like me. Hollis was genuine, but had little say about park matters. He knew that we had been there for a long time, and that we lived a lifestyle similar to him and his village. Before he left, he commented on the great job that we had done with our cabinets and furniture. We had used five-gallon Blazo cans to make the cabinet door hinges and all of the baking pans. The furniture was made with small spruce poles and caribou hide. Anyhow, after coffee and home-made oatmeal cookies, he left in peace.

Our trapping season ended near the first of March because the furbearers start losing their prime about then. We loaded the furs into our yellow PA-12 plane and pointed our nose toward Homer.

One day when Truk was five years old, we came home from a day trip to Kenai and he was gone. Someone had unscrewed the carabiner on his chain and stolen him. We saw the tracks of the vehicle and of the scoundrel that took him, but never found him. A few years later a good friend of ours said that he saw Truk over by McCarthy. He even looked at the tag that we had put on his collar and saw TRUK scratched on the tag. Too much time had passed, so we didn't drive the 500 miles to try to get him back. I hope that the person that stole him realized that Truk was a prize and that he was the only dog in the country that wouldn't poop on the dock at the Homer Harbor.

Chapter 15

Out of Business

To successfully compete, a fisherman must be constantly upgrading. During the early 80s, it seemed that speed was imperative. Without speed, other boats would beat you to a big herring set or to a salmon set that could make your season. Our boat, the *Winter Wind*, was keeping us in the game. Along with speed, I had incorporated the best electronics, which included the best radar, the best fish-finder, and the best radios. If you were competitive, you had all of the latest gadgets, and I definitely was. Boats that I fished in the 60s served their purpose, but now we spent a great part of our time living on the boat, so we had designed some comfort into the *Winter Wind*, particularly into the galley area. We could lower the table and use the seat backs as fillers to convert it to a twin bunk, enabling us to sleep up there when on anchor or at a mooring. Being able to sit up at night and observe our surroundings was so handy. It also allowed me to see the radar, which showed our distance from land or other boats. We even had a head (restroom) with a shower. The boat was nearly as nice as our home, and we loved it.

One morning we departed the Kasilof River and headed southwesterly into five-foot cresting seas, which required me to keep the windshield wipers on. An hour later, daylight was breaking and the sky was mostly cloudy. It was a slightly rougher than an average Cook Inlet day, but not too bad. The salmon season was more than halfway over, and we'd had a decent season to date. I was in no hurry, so I traveled slowly so we wouldn't pound. When it was time to set our net, I located a small riptide that didn't have any logs or big sticks in it and made my first set crosswise to the rip. Both Winnie and I went inside where we could watch the cork-line from the windows, which allowed great viewing. We weren't seeing any fish hitting the net, but were savoring a cup of fresh brewed coffee and the warmth of the cook stove. If we'd seen fish hit the net, I would have put a tow on the net to keep it crosswise to the current, but it appeared that there was little or nothing, so I let it flag. To flag means that the wind would swing our bow in the opposite direction of the wind, not a bad thing when you are fishing in a rip, because the salmon often stay in the rips.

With no fish aboard, the boat should have been light in the water. Because of the wind and waves, it didn't dawn on me that she wasn't bouncing up and down as lively as she should have. Since we weren't catching much, I decided to reel the net in. There weren't other boats close by, so I didn't have to be concerned about tangling with someone else's net. When we got the net in, I told Winnie that something wasn't right. The boat seemed sluggish. I opened the hatch to the engine room and couldn't believe my eyes. There was water down there—lots of it. Within seconds the engines quit. The water was coming in fast, but I had no idea from where.

I told Winnie to get our survival suits out and to put her suit on as quickly as she could. I instructed her to untie the inflatable raft. The radio was still working, so I put a mayday out to anyone on channel 16 of the vhf. I gave our boat name and our approximate position, and said that we were taking on water. Then I dashed outside and put my survival suit on, and we put the raft in the water on the lee side of the boat. We made sure that our zippers were zipped all the way, and I threw the small oars into the raft. I glanced to the north and saw a tug and barge coming our way. I figured that he had heard our mayday and was coming to help us. As he bore down on us, I waved frantically. The tug was close and surely could see that we were the boat in distress. He didn't appear to be slowing down, but it looked like he was turning to avoid hitting us. I yelled for Winnie to jump into the raft. The tug barely missed our bow, but the barge that he was towing was some distance behind and looked to be heading right for us. I slid into the raft with the bowline in my hand and pushed us away from the low-riding *Winter Wind*. Winnie had thought to put the oars in the holders, so I rowed backwards as fast as I could. I think I'd gone only twenty feet or so when the barge hit the *Winter Wind*. The force of the 200-foot barge sank our beautiful boat on contact. I kept rowing backwards as the barge slipped past our raft.

I was in shock, and Winnie was crying uncontrollably. I tried to console her, but I had to turn the bow of the raft into the waves so they wouldn't splash any more water into the raft. The wind had gone down some, but we had taken on six inches of water while I rowed backwards. Winnie tried to get rid of some of it with her hands while I kept the bow into the wind.

Several fishing boats soon came to our rescue and snatched us out of the water. We surely were thankful for Bill Sullivan, Rich and Sonja Corazza, and the schoolteacher on the *Wits End*, who raced to help us when we were in dire need. Rich and Sonja are really exciting and adventurous, and are very successful fisher-people. We are so grateful for these fellow fishermen and others that came to our aid.

Perhaps the skipper of the tug didn't realize that we were the boat in distress and that's why he didn't take evasive action sooner. I realize that it takes some time to turn a barge on a long tow. The sad event is still like a slow-motion nightmare. I was thinking that the tug was coming to save us, but instead it sank our wonderful boat. For sure, we thank God for sparing us, because we were seconds from being run over too.

How do fishermen manage without a boat? As best they can. I've mentioned the old saying, "You can't catch fish if you don't put your net in the water." Well, Jesus told Simon Peter the same words and they filled two boats, but I didn't have a boat to fish with.

Most of us have times in our lives when the paths we travel are free and clear and other times when our paths are cluttered with obstacles. These instances usually come about unexpectedly and require some serious thought as to what direction to turn. We felt that the loss of our boat was equivalent to the loss of a good friend, but even as we grieved, we needed to put our heads together and think hard about our direction in life. I had been commercial fishing almost all of my adult life but it appeared that I needed to think about other options. It was extremely difficult to consider any other occupations because of the deep love and attraction that I had for the sea and fishing.

A few times in the past I had thought that I would love to try my hand at mining. The main parallel that mining has with fishing is the concept of the "mother lode." Whether on land or sea, looking for the mother lode can be downright exciting. If I had had enough money, I wouldn't have hesitated to buy another boat and continue fishing. Maybe I wasn't frugal enough to have put enough money away, or maybe it was the fault of the government system that forces you to reinvest in your business. When you reinvest, you don't have to give so much to Uncle, but it doesn't do much for you if you lose your investment. I don't mean to be sniveling, just telling it like it is.

We had actually dabbled briefly in placer gold mining with a suction dredge. Now we had time to pursue the glitter of gold on a larger scale. A couple of years prior, we had been to the Bonanza and Eldorado creeks of the Klondike area. I had learned how to acquire claims that were available through the Canadian Bureau of Mines, so now I located an area up the Little Eldorado that hadn't been mined since shortly after the '98 gold rush and even then only by shafts, and I staked several claims and filed the necessary paperwork.

After hunting season that year, I went to an auction and bought a small dozer and had it trucked over to our claims. I spent the next few months designing and welding together a fifteen-foot sluice box and gathering everything that I thought we would need for a mining camp. I had a couple of friends that were miners, and they had given me enough information to give me a start.

We didn't have enough money to buy a larger truck, so we loaded everything in our half-ton pick-up and a flatbed trailer. The trip took us over the rugged Taylor Highway. The Canadian border is at the highest point, which is cold and windy. The dusty gravel road winds downhill for seventy miles, and there is where the mighty Yukon River must be crossed. A ferry makes a trip every hour, so in no time at all we were in the quaint old town of Dawson. I love the place. Most of the original buildings still remain intact and occupied. There are a couple of sternwheeler boats on the shoreline, and the streets are lined with old stores and bars. Diamond Tooth Gertie's still lures locals and tourists just as it did more than one hundred years ago. The place is laid back, and the people are friendly. Robert Service's cabin still exists up near the last street in town. There is even a shower house that has holes carved in the walls so you can see what kind of soap your neighbor is using.

Because it hadn't rained, we were able to drive across the Eldorado and proceed to our claims. How nice! We arrived at our new home and hadn't broken anything. Another nice thing was that our "cat" (the John Deere dozer) was parked right where I had instructed the trucker to put it. It started right up and I dozed a level spot for our wall tents. I put the small wood stoves in place along with our cots and quickly erected tables out of the lumber and plywood I'd brought for the purpose. Winnie promptly unpacked the dishes, pots and pans, and food. I took my chainsaw and found a couple of dead spruce trees to cut into firewood. We were both happy as clams at high tide.

After we got settled in and had everything comfy, we drove up the river to meet some of our mining neighbors. We visited three active operations, and at each one the people were so nice and friendly. They all told us that if we needed any help with anything they would be offended if we didn't call on them.

An older Anchorage couple that owned one of the placer operations warned us not to do anything that would alert the customs people. They had brought a Winnebago to their claims to live in, but the customs officer told them they couldn't use it for their business. They didn't want Americans to bring things into the country that they could have bought in Canada. We would most certainly heed the warning.

I spent the next couple of days laying out a planned mining operation, including settling ponds. Then I mounted my nice cat and moved dirt. I was as happy as an Eskimo with a new bidarka (skin boat). I was moving dirt like a real miner, stripping the overburden. That means that I was relocating the dirt from above the hard pan where the gold settles. I wouldn't be doing any sluicing for some time to come, but that was all right. I loved knocking down the small trees and pushing huge mounds of sweet-smelling earth.

One night the rain pelted our tent until early morning. I built a fire in the wood stove to take the chill off and to heat some water for coffee. After breakfast, I put my knee boots on and slogged off to the cat. Everything had turned to mud, but I had dirt to push.

Lesson one: Don't push mud! Yes, I got stuck big time. I spent the next two days digging and cutting logs to put under the tracks. The cat just sank deeper. Nuts, darn, shucks! I was really mad at myself. I hated the thought of asking one of the busy neighbors to pull me out, because they surely would think that I was dumber than dumb. Nothing I did improved the situation, so I put my tail between my legs and meekly asked my neighbor if it would be possible for him to pull my cat out. Later that evening I heard a terrible loud roar coming up our trail. It was our neighbor on his D-9 cat, which is as big as they get. It was twenty times bigger than my puny machine. It took him all of two seconds to push my itsy bitsy cat out of the muck. He would have been offended if I'd offered to pay him, so later in the fall we took him some blueberry pies.

It was amazing to see the gold that some of the neighbors were harvesting from their sluice boxes. Some of them had gold filling the riffles for eight feet or more. One miner proudly showed us two galvanized tubs full of gold. That was truly the mother lode! I had no idea that anyone could be so successful.

The miner with the tubs of gold had his new bride with him and they were super lovey-dovey. Two years later we visited him, and he said that she'd left him and taken most of the gold. He was spending most of his time easing the pain with alcohol. His equipment was all rusty from non-use, and the place was a mess. I refer to the story as "The Younger Creek Millionaire and Her Ex."

When the ground dried, I pushed more overburden, but was more careful not to get stuck. I felt good about the progress I was making. In the meantime, Winnie stayed happily busy preparing for her parents. She had made arrangements several months earlier for them to visit us in Homer, but now they would have to come to our camp and rough it in a tent. When the time came, Winnie drove all the way to Anchorage to pick them up. In the meantime, I put up a large dome tent for them and equipped it with cots and anything I could think of to make their stay pleasant. They had never been anyplace but the hot, humid Philippines, so I wondered how they would acclimate to such a drastic change. I suggested that we cancel their visit, but there was no way to contact them.

Soon after their arrival, the sweet customs guy paid us an unwelcome visit. After asking many questions and checking their papers, he informed us that neither of them could do any type of work on our claims. If they did, they would go to jail! The guy was a total jerk, but he was the one with the big stick.

Both Maximiano and Macaria were hardworking farmers and the parents of ten kids, so it was tough for them to understand that they couldn't do anything. After a few days Max was showing signs of discontent, and I couldn't blame him. If I had been in his shoes I would have gone bonkers. Winnie and I talked it over and decided that we were going to have to send them back and hope that we could have them again when we were in Homer. I gave them some money so they could build a store in the Philippines. I felt so bad for Winnie. She had to drive them all the way back to Anchorage and say goodbye to them. We could have had a great time with them if it hadn't been for the customs guy's power trip.

Then came the rain! I don't remember how many days it rained, but it was too mucky to work the cat. Everything was saturated and the rivers swelled to muddy torrents. We were in the tent, whiling away our time by playing cribbage while waiting for the rain to subside, when a voice spoke out: "Anybody home?"

Two words is all it took for me to recognize the voice. It was Mr. NotSoNice. I put my raincoat and hat on and went outside. I wasn't about to invite that miserable so-and-so into our tent. I took my good old time digging up the paperwork for the cat, which he demanded to see. The rain dripped down his face as he announced that the paperwork was not stamped by the Canadian border people.

"Well," I said, "That's not my fault; I guess your people screwed up."

He looked me square in the eyeballs and said that I had four days to get the paperwork in order or he would shut us down and charge us ten percent of the value of the cat. I tried to reason with him, but he was on a mission. NotSoNice didn't appear to be amused. As a matter of fact, he added that he didn't even want us to use our pick-up truck to get a nut and bolt at the hardware store. His reason was that we didn't buy the truck in Canada.

I now had a problem that would not be easy to solve. I would have to go seventy miles to the border and have them stamp and sign the stupid paper. The problem was amplified by the raging Eldorado Creek. The same creek whose one foot of clear, slow-moving water we normally drove across now was five feet deep and burnt-brown in color. My options were zero, squat, nada. I had to go; otherwise our little mining operation would be done for.

The rain persisted, but I had no time to wait. The next day I had to get my buns up to the border. Winnie made a lunch for me as I loaded a handyman jack and a shovel for emergency. When I approached the creek, I was taken aback by the size of it. It was a full-fledged river, and it was mad! I got upstream as far as I could and angled slightly downstream for the crossing. Water was splashing over my windshield as I pushed the gas pedal almost to the floor. I smiled to myself when she started climbing out the other side.

I had just barely gotten out of the water when she quit. Pooh! I opened the hood and saw that everything was steaming. Maybe if I let her be for a while, the heat would evaporate the water by the spark plugs and all. I just closed the hood and sat in the cab and watched the steam. I waited ten or fifteen minutes and gave her a try. Darned if she didn't start. Yeah! Now I had to drive through town and get a ferry ride across the Yukon, then motor seventy miles up the muddiest road ever. Several times I considered turning around, but my mission overruled my caution. It took most of the day to travel the seventy miles, but I made it. I stuck the paperwork under my coat to keep it out of the rain as I scampered to the border building. When I told the man and woman on duty that the papers for my dozer weren't stamped or signed, they said that they'd known that when the trucker came through with it, but that the border guy that looked at the papers wasn't on duty now. I asked if one of them would sign the paper, since they'd been there when the trucker hauled my cat across their border.

"Sorry, we can't do that," they quickly answered. They also informed me that the guy that forgot to sign the paper wouldn't be on duty for another week. Again, I tried to reason with them, and again it was to no avail. They offered me no options. Perhaps I was paranoid, but it seemed that all the customs and border people had instructions to get rid of the Americans. Maybe there was another explanation, but I sure didn't have a clue what it was.

This was another one of those times when I had no choice but to put my tail between my legs and bite the bullet. I turned around and fought my way back through the mud to the swollen Yukon River. It was late when I got there, so I had to sleep in the truck till morning because the ferry didn't run at night. The rain finally stopped during the wee hours. It sure was nice not to hear it pelting on the roof.

Even though the sky was showing scant openings in the clouds, my mind was still troubled with the persistent problem of the cat paperwork. When I drove off the ferry and into town, I dreaded the visit to the customs office.

I tried to be positive as I smiled at the receptionist. She directed me to the office where a different officer was sitting in his comfy cushioned chair.

He was a heavyset gent, who didn't make any effort to get up or to shake my extended hand. He took my paper, gave it a quick glance, and said, "That will be $2500."

Again I tried to explain why the paper hadn't been signed, et cetera, but he didn't care to discuss it with me. I had to go to the local bank, get a certified check, and take it back to him. I stomped out of there and didn't bother closing the door as I exited. My face probably matched the lipstick that the receptionist was wearing.

When I got to the Eldorado, it was still having a fit, so the procedure was the same as when I crossed the day before. Winnie was happy to see me coming up the hill to our camp, and was sympathetic to my story, even though no one else was.

The next day we drove up to the Alaska neighbors' place and found out that they had gotten the same treatment from the customs people. This confirmed my "let's get rid of the Americans" theory.

It was disheartening, but after pondering what to do, we both agreed to "cut and run," so to speak. All of my adult life, I've called the shots, and with the help of God, have had control of most situations. I'm quite sure that most adults that have been around the block a time or two have had occasions when they've had to come to the realization that they weren't at the helm. If we had stayed at our gold claims, the customs people would have found some other reason to shut us down.

I inquired around town for someone with a big truck and found a guy that was willing to haul our stuff to Homer. It cost plenty, but I was a bitter man. If my claims had been in Alaska, things would have been different. It was a terrible decision to leave, because we loved Dawson, the neighbors, and what we were doing. I guess there is some truth to the saying "Life's a bitch, and then you die." No doubt, I was slightly daunted by being put out of business twice within a short period of time. Fortunately, when I'm dealt a bad hand, I generally get over it quickly. Like I said before, I don't like snivelers, so I try not to be one.

When we got home, we went for daily runs, which helped cure the blues. Ever since I started running in 1969, I'd noticed that none of my problems surfaced while running. All I think about is running. My eyes, nose, and ears take in the surroundings. I realize that I'm in harmony with nature, so I've made running my escape from all things that are ailing me.

The beach below our place is one of the most wonderful places to pound the sand. The smell of the sea and the kelp is so luscious that you wonder why perfume isn't made to duplicate it. Kachemak Bay shows off shades of blue and green, and across the emerald water the majestic Kenai mountain range looms, punctuated by vast glaciers that dazzle you with their size and beauty. When I mention the sea, I can't help thinking about the endless variety of colors that she displays: black, white, grey, and all the shades of green and blue, all vivid in my mind. Black is never good, because it means that nasty water lies ahead. White is no better because white caps generally cause uncomfortable conditions. Grey is a sign of glacial runoff or shallow water. Green and blue are the colors that make people ooh and ah, and both come in innumerable shades.

We were building another house, so we used the precious time to make it livable. Carpentry is another thing that gives us great satisfaction. Perhaps if we were doing it for a living, it wouldn't have had the same effect, but building our own house was so rewarding. Swinging a hammer all day gave pleasure, but it also antagonized my carpal tunnel problem. Just like when I was picking fish, I would wake at night and have to swing my arms to temporarily stop the unrelenting pain. It was a small price to pay, because we were able to incorporate some detailed custom woodwork. I had gotten a fair amount of diamond willow during the prior year, so I made the banister and rail going up to the loft out of the willow. When we were finishing the kitchen, we designed scenes to be etched on the glass panes of the cabinets. All of them depicted our lifestyles. There were hunting, fishing, and even a mining scene.

Although the house was quite small, it felt homey, and with a forest surrounding three sides, the place seemed magical. Moose used their main trail by the house daily, and we frequently saw rabbits and spruce grouse in the woods.

During most of the years that I fished, I had vowed that if I didn't have to spend all my time killing fish I would spend more time training for running mountain races. I had no excuses now, so I drove to the mountains at least twice a week and ran up and down as fast as I could. I did lots of lower body weightlifting and speed work when I was at home. It all paid off on the Fourth of July when the Mount Marathon race took place. Each year for years afterward, I won gold or silver medals in my age group. An added benefit was that it was a perfect way to get in shape for hunting.

With fall approaching, I knew that it was time to make a decision about Twin Lakes. I might hate myself later, but after all that the park service had put me through, I decided to sell my Twin Lakes property and move on. It was another time when I shed tears for the land that I was giving up. Like my homestead, I had a fondness for it that came from the work that our family put into the cabins and from the fantastic times that we shared in the wilderness. It didn't take long to sell the place, because the guy that bought it realized the value of it and I was ready to get the "monkey off my back." Yes, I've kicked my backside a few times since, but at the time it seemed like the right thing to do.

I've noticed that I'm not alone when it comes to making decisions that I live to regret. I refer to it as the "180 syndrome." For example, some people, even some with a high I.Q., make a decision to vote for a particular candidate for president. Soon afterward they can't understand how they could have been so stupid to vote for the dumb dick! Then there are the people that think they have chosen the perfect person to be their mate. Down the road, they realize that they would have been better off choosing anyone else—blindfolded. Yes, they too take a 180-degree turn from their well-thought-out decision. I don't know if there is anyone out there that hasn't regretted a decision. If there is, I hope he will find me and give me instructions about how to do it right.

Sometime after I bade the Twin Lakes property goodbye, Ron, an old friend of mine, came by and asked if I'd like to go to the west side of the Alaska Range and hunt caribou. Of course I agreed because I love hunting and it would take my mind off my problems. Ron's plane was a Cessna 180, which is big enough to carry both of us and two caribou. We lucked out with the weather. When we got airborne that morning, the sun was shining and there was no wind. We crossed Cook Inlet with plenty of altitude and continued over the mountains. Once we passed the last of the range, we began scanning the tundra for "boo." There was a rumor that the herd was quite a distance to the west, so we flew another 75 miles, but didn't see any critters. We were getting to the point where we had to head southeast toward Iliamna so we could refuel. It was also time to find a place to land and empty our bladders. A couple of years before, we had landed on a gravel area that was to the west of Iliamna, so we decided to land there to "drain the pickle." We were almost there when the plane started to vibrate. We looked at each other, wondering what the problem was. The vibration was getting worse by the minute. Ron throttled back and lined up for an approach to the gravel landing spot. Just as we touched down, it felt like the engine was going to make a nasty departure. The thought of having to take a leak was quickly replaced with the question of whether we would make it before the engine came apart. Ron shut the switch off before we came to a stop, and it was none too soon. Upon inspection we found that something inside the engine had come apart. Had the problem occurred any earlier, we would have had to make a crash landing. No doubt, we were two lucky guys, because for the previous two and a half hours the terrain had been ragged with almost no place to land. It was another bit of luck that we were able to contact an air taxi at Iliamna to pick us up. This was another one of those times when you just have to be thankful for life, because there will be other hunting opportunities in the future.

Chapter 16

The Wonderful Gift of Children

Parents want the best for their children. If we're lucky, we'll live long enough to see our kids turn into adults. There will be no more diapers to change or messes to clean up, and we won't have to try to explain what's going on when they open the bedroom door because they heard loud sounds coming from in there and thought something bad was happening to Mommy. And no longer will they be teenagers that think they know everything, presumptuous enough to suggest that we're clueless and unknowledgeable about the do's and don'ts of life.

We'd like to think that we're sending them out into the world armed with all that it takes to be good survivors and good contributors to society. Presumably we taught them right from wrong. Perhaps we encouraged empathy for their fellowman so that they might help others in need, and maybe we took them to church to instigate a belief in God so that they might have something to fall back on during tough times. And of course to thank the Old Man for all the good that is bestowed upon them.

When they do something bad, it's not our fault. Must be a throwback to some ancestor on the other side of the family. When they do something good, well, that's obviously because of our superior genetic endowment or the sterling upbringing we've given them. Nothing is more satisfying than seeing our children displaying our best traits or developing an interest or a talent that we claim as our own.

My oldest daughter, Cheryl, apparently enjoyed the commercial fishing that I introduced her to, because she came to me one day and asked what

I thought of salmon set-net fishing at False Pass. She had heard of a permit that was for sale for that area, and it sounded appealing to her. I explained that I personally liked to chase fish rather than wait for them to run into my stationary net. I also cautioned her that the Aleutian Islands were home to one of the largest concentrations of brown bears in the world. The area that she was talking about is one of the wildest, most remote places on the planet. It could properly be referred to as "a thousand miles from nowhere." And, I vividly remember telling her with extreme conviction that "the wind is born there"!

After pondering the idea for a few days, I told Cheryl that I admired her spunk, but if she meant to follow it through, she would need a very strong, competent guy to help her, and I knew just the guy. Charlie Ess had helped Dean Osmar at his Clam Gulch set-net sites the year before. If she could talk Charlie into leaving Dean, she would have a good helper. I had met Charlie only one time, but he impressed me no end. Behind his long scraggily hair and beard was a muscular, fast-moving, competent Alaska man. Even though he had only been in Alaska a few years, he possessed the same make-up that I had when I came to the great land. We were made for Alaska, and it was made for us. Charlie also figured that he had a better chance of making more money than he did with Dean. Dean didn't pay the crew much but he taught them well. If you fished one season with Dean, you would leave with a wealth of knowledge.

I wasn't there when Cheryl met Charlie, but I have no doubt that he was immediately set back by her beauty. They hadn't even discussed the percentage that she would pay him before he eagerly accepted the job. They had qualities that complemented each other; for example, when they were gathering camping and fishing supplies, each of them would think of items that the other hadn't. After gathering everything on their list of things that would make such a venture successful, they arranged for a tender to transport them and all their supplies, including two skiffs, to the ever-so-remote False Pass.

These two hearty young adults were embarking not only on a new career, but also on an adventure. I'm sure that neither of them could have visualized what nature had in store for them. Their camp was basically a wall tent over a flimsy frame, not what you would call a good structure to keep bears out. They had given a little thought to griz; they took a twenty-pound dog with them. As it turned out, the dog was the best thing that they took to False Pass. That little guy could smell or hear a bear a mile away. Day and night the big browns would visit, and the dog would warn Charlie and Cheryl. Usually they could run the bears off by shooting Charlie's 44 magnum near the critter. When the tide went out at night, the net would be partially dry and the bears would come for a free evening snack. Again, the dog would let them know that *Ursus Horribilis* was stealing their precious catch. A couple of times, Charlie had to defend Cheryl and himself against an overly aggressive bear.

Bears weren't their only problem. Nasty sea lions would make huge holes in the nets while attempting to get the luscious red salmon. Occasionally, a whale would cruise through the net and leave a hole the size of a tank. That is when their net-mending skills came in handy. With the continual net mending, and being on bear watch, there was little time to relax.

The worst thing that they had to contend with wasn't the animals; it was the hellacious winds that are common in that neck of the sea. I would have said "neck of the woods," but there are only a couple of leaning dwarf trees in that part of the country. Winds of fifty to seventy knots are common, and occasionally 100-knot winds would play havoc with this hearty couple. They were able to keep their tent from blowing away by putting guy-lines on it every couple of feet. Even then, the tent would tear and they would have to sew it back together. A couple of times a seiner towed back one of their skiffs that had blown away.

The local people at the small village of False Pass dubbed them the Beauty and the Beast. I don't know why, but they did. It didn't matter because Cheryl and Charlie had a good sense of humor and came up with some names for some of the village people that were really hilarious.

After the first season together, they got married. They became our favorite hunting partners. It was several years later that they made a couple of kids, Lindsey and Clarence, our wonderful grandkids.

Suzie, my second-eldest daughter, didn't care about life on the sea, but she was the most high-spirited of the five children. She got married at a young age, as did I, and before you could bat an eye, Winnie and I were grandparents five times over. Suzie loved dogs, so she raised and sold Saint Bernard's.

Then I'm really not sure what went wrong, but Suzie seemed to veer off in a different direction. It's easy to get lured into the wrong crowd, and I think that is what happened to my vibrant daughter Suzie. I am having the hardest time writing this, but one night a few years ago, I was awakened by a phone call. Suzie was dead. I cried all night. I went outside and screamed and cried. I couldn't accept the thought that my beautiful, full-of-life daughter was gone. Not only was I feeling sad, but I also felt guilty for neglecting to help her more than I did. There was nothing I could do to change the past. I'm so sorry, Suzie.

Then there is number three, Laurie. Like the older sisters, she is beautiful. With bright blue eyes and blond hair, and a personality to match, she turns heads wherever she goes. Alaskan kids have a tendency to "go south" when they get out of high school. They want to see what is going on in the warmer Southern 48. Many of them return when they find that the differences are not what they had hoped for. Not Laurie. She didn't like the cold, so she and her husband Mike, settled in Texas. They have a lovely daughter named Wren, who is Laurie's best buddy.

Cindy Lynn is number four and, you might remember, the first 59er born in Alaska. She loves adventure, and when she was barely old enough to walk, she would wander down to our homestead lake (Reflection Lake) and pick up a stick and pretend to be catching fish. When she got old enough, she loved to go into the bush and trap and hunt. Like me, she has lots of wild hairs, and when she was in young adulthood, she traveled from one end of the U.S. to the other. Cindy is married to Steve, who is a great, understanding guy. Their daughter, Seeri, is as beautiful as her mom. She's shy, but her bright blue eyes catch the attention of all the guys.

My only boy, Eric, was destined to be an electronics whiz. When he was barely knee high, he had wires going all over his bedroom, and I was constantly cautioning him about "death by electrocution." He had bare wires stuck in every outlet. Sure enough, after high school, he headed to the capital of electronics, Seattle, and enrolled in an electronics school. He soon became a genius in the wireless world. He has the physical traits of a Wills, but he got his smarts from a different department.

When we went to Seattle for Eric's wedding, we had a fun experience at the local zoo. There were about twenty family members that toured the zoo together. We had taken in most of the animals when we happened upon the gorillas. The front of the enclosure had thick glass that separated the sightseers from the apes. There was one exceptionally large gorilla sitting next to the glass, so we all gathered close by to get a good look at him. When the furry critter saw the big gathering, he lifted his butt off the rock that he was sitting on and turned toward us with what looked like a smile on his leathery face. He reached under his crotch and pooped a big green gob into his hand. Then he promptly shoved it into his mouth and ATE IT!

Tears rolled down our cheeks as we laughed hysterically. When the ape saw us laughing, he did a repeat! He must have enjoyed the show, because he laughed too. For the rest of the day we kept breaking out in giggles when we thought of the "recycling ape," and to this day, the subject comes up and always brings on gales of laughter.

Eric soon realized that he had met his match in his wife, Kathy. She is sharp and full of fire. Their boy, Blake, is an extension of Eric's rib. The kid hasn't reached his eleventh birthday, and he thinks that he is on the planet for one reason: electronics. I'm betting that if we could look into his dreams, we'd see everything electronic. He's bad though. When I visit them, he beats me in every game we play. He obviously has insufficient respect for his elders.

Blake's little sister is much too sweet and beautiful. She's too petite to fight with Blake, so she has mastered the art of manipulation. Before her fifth birthday, she knew how to use reverse psychology. I wonder where she learned that. Actually, they are both a ton of fun to be around.

Eric has his own business in wireless applications, and really enjoys the challenges of his job.

That leaves my number six child, whom I'll put off telling about until a little later on.

When you are driving south on the Sterling Highway and come to the hill that overlooks Homer, you can understand why the old-timers settled on the north shore of Kachemak Bay. The land has a gentle south slope that invites the rays of sun to warm the soil. The warmth of the bay also helps to keep the bench from extreme cold temperatures. It is a fertile place to grow just about anything. The early settlers had no problem growing potatoes and other root crops. Through the years, a little experimenting and imagination not only produced vegetables, but many different kinds of fruit. Today, there are several people that successfully grow orchards of apples, cherries, and other fruits that have been adapted to the climate.

When I first came to Homer I couldn't help chuckling about one of the crops that some people were growing. I had never seen "weed" being grown before, but it looked like conditions were perfect for it. Eight-foot trees were common. Such agricultural practices were unknown to me, but were apparently common in these parts at that time. I had a lot to learn! I never was into smoking cigarettes or weed. I did try it twice but didn't care for it. I think that I was afraid I might lose control and be like my dad and brother. I was the same way with alcohol. I will drink a beer or a glass of wine, but that's enough.

One of the most prolific and cherished crops is the red raspberry. The berries flourish on this lower slope. They do almost as well as "pushki" (cow parsnip) and nettles. The berries are as big as any you've laid eyes on and as sweet as any you've tasted. The patch that I planted produces so much that we put many gallons in the freezer, and I make wine with the rest.

Poopdeck and I moved to the Homer area near the same time, and it so happened that we both became "bug juice" producers. Bug juice was Poopdeck's term for Alaskan homemade wine. It was unheard of to go to Poopdeck's without going down to his root cellar to check out all of his bug juice. One time when we were in the cellar sipping a little, Poopdeck handed me a gallon jug of some pretty raunchy-looking juice. There was a considerable amount of sediment in the bottom. I cautiously tipped it up and just about gagged on it. It tasted like pure vinegar. When Poopdeck saw me pucker, he said in a matter of fact way, "Grandpa says don't knock it till you try it three times." Later he admitted that some of his bug juice turned to vinegar.

We often exchanged recipes and knowledge of things that could be used to make wine. I didn't try to make dandelion wine until I tasted Poopdeck's. It was one of his best wines, but he always told me that it wasn't worth making because it took three to five years before it was worth drinking. One year the yellow flowers popped up everywhere, so I just had to pick blossoms and start a batch. Six months later I was under my house and decided to sip a little. Darn if it wasn't the best in the west. Ah yes, Dionysus, the Greek god of wine.

I've since made bug juice from almost everything including rhubarb, fireweed, bananas, coconut, peach, apple, pineapple, rose and fireweed blossoms, and other secret stuff. As I write, I have three batches that are happily bubbling. The most active is one of my favorites, a combination of raspberries and bananas. The other two are blueberry-raisin and blueberry-coconut. After each batch finishes the fermentation process, I bottle it and put it in the crawl space under the house. That is my wine cellar. You're not supposed to drink the wine until it goes through the aging process, which is from one to two years. I have to admit that most of it gets sipped a little prematurely.

Winemaking is not an easy hobby. It actually takes a fair amount of work and lots of trial and error to consistently make a good quality wine. On the average, the berry wines require three gallons of berries, and if you don't put all the right ingredients in the recipe, you can end up with vinegar or worse. We don't drink much, but it's a fun hobby, and it makes good gifts. Also, I notice that our friends come to visit more often.

A handful of us that had known Poopdeck for a long while gathered one night when he was dying. He had said many times that he was going to dance with every woman in Homer on his hundredth birthday. He came close to making it, but the ladies will have to dream about what it would have been like to dance with him at 100. Kenny Moore, who is another long time friend of Poopdeck's, came out of the bedroom where he was trying to make some conversation with the old guy and asked me if I would go in there and keep Poopdeck company. I talked for ten or fifteen minutes but got no response. Just about the time that I wondered if he had passed on, he sprung straight up and blurted out, "I got to pee again!"

I can't say that I enjoyed watching him struggle through his last few hours, but that is the way he wanted it. I still have a couple of gallons of his bug juice under the house.

Ever since I was a kid, I've planted a garden. Whoever my dad was, he must have been a farmer, because nobody else in the generation before me stuck their fingers in the soil. It probably came from my great grandfather that homesteaded in Michigan. I'm thankful for the gift because there has always been a satisfaction that comes with a harvest. I still grow the best banana potatoes and purple potatoes. They are both appetite pleasers.

When Winnie and I were first thinking of marriage, I felt that it was important to tell her what my life was like as a mariner, and one other important matter: already having five children, I didn't care to participate in the production of any more babies. I had gotten a vasectomy to make sure that I wouldn't be scattering more seeds. Even though the subject came up several times after that, I was strong and would not relent.

Oh sure, Jerre, you are a soft pushover and you know it.

Off to Seattle we went, and I found myself in the office of one of the best surgeons, listening to him explain that the success rate of a reversal was 85%. I guess it sounded reasonable, because I had him put the thing back together. A few weeks later we made our first trip to Mexico, and I was back to my old tricks again. Winnie was pregnacated. Wow, that didn't take long! We didn't find out for sure that she was pregnant until a couple of months later when we were at Kona, Hawaii. An old, weathered Kahuna woman diagnosed the pregnancy. I had never seen Winnie glow with such happiness. We were both thrilled.

I fairly well knew the procedure. Winnie would have to cut back on some of the types of work that were in her normal routine, and we would alter her diet slightly. We hadn't given much thought to a check-up until one day when we had a rugby game. Dr. Dan, who played on our rugby team (the guy that had his ruptured spleen taken out), noticed that Winnie was pregnant. He offered to check her to see if the pregnancy was going along okay. I had been doing some reading about water births, and I was convinced that there were many benefits to it. The French did lots of them, and claimed that it was totally safe and that it was a more natural way for a woman to give birth than on a table in a hospital. They also claimed that the child would be stronger. It really appealed to me. When I told Dr. Dan about it, he confirmed everything that I had read. He added that if I needed any help, he was just a phone call away.

While we were visiting Dr. Dan, I mentioned that it would be nice if something could be done about my arms going numb at night when I was fishing or pounding nails.

He said, "Oh, you have carpal tunnel syndrome."

I had never heard of such a thing. I told him that I had been swinging my arms at night for more than twenty years but didn't have a clue that there was a name for my condition. Dan told me that a simple operation could cure it. I couldn't believe that I had suffered for so long, thinking that it was just something that went with the territory. It wasn't long after that that I got both wrists operated on, and ever since my arms have been fine. Like they say, "Better late than never."

I designed a tank with glass sides so that we could film the birth. I sloped the back so that Winnie would be in a comfortable position. Kat Stiers, who had helped several women in the area with their birthing, also offered to help.

At the time we were starting another new house, the one that I had been dreaming of for a long time. It was to be a log house done with a Swedish cope design, which employs round logs that have a concave groove cut in the bottom of each log to allow the logs to stack firmly on top of each other. We had already poured the footings and put the floor joists down. We were nailing the flooring on when Winnie let out a cry of pain. She was due at any time, so I hadn't let her do any heavy work. Within a couple of minutes, her water broke, so I knew it was time to get her home and make preparations. We gathered our tools, jumped in the car, and off we went.

I filled the tank with body-temperature water while keeping track of how many minutes apart Winnie's pains were. I set up our movie camera and kept checking the water temperature. If it cooled down a few degrees, I would take a potful out, and replace it with a pot of hot water. I called Cat when the contractions got closer together. Although Cat was a midwife, I wanted to play that part. If she thought I wasn't doing something right, then she could set me straight. She agreed to be the photographer. The labor took quite a while, but finally it was clear that the birth was about to happen. I got in the tub and coached Winnie to give a hard push. She did just that, and out shot our little daughter just like a torpedo! I did just like the book said: brought her up slowly out of the water and placed her on Winnie's breasts. She started breathing as soon as she got out of the water.

It was a perfect event, and we had a perfect daughter. She had dark brown hair like her mom, and she was nice and clean from the water. Yep, there were ten toes, and the same number of fingers. Cat had turned the camera off for a while so it wouldn't run out of film. Unfortunately she forgot to start it again when the birth was taking place, so we have film of the labor but not the birth. It was no big deal, but it would have been nice to have it to show to people that might contemplate a water birth.

We had no more than put a diaper on our new little girl when she let loose some terrible black stuff. Cat looked at me and said that it was a perfect time for me to bond with my new baby, so I should change the diaper. I had escaped doing it for my other kids, but now Cat was making it sound like it was some kind of a great honor. Damn, I would rather gut out a rogue elephant any day, but I did it. Yuk!

I had given lots of thought to a name, and it was a good thing that it was a girl, because the boy's name that I had thought of wasn't nearly as impressive as the one I came up with for a girl. Because she was a water baby, she was destined to have a name that had to do with H2O. No, that isn't her name. It's Nahanni Deshka Iwalani Yentna Wills. Both Winnie and I loved the name Nahanni, which is a river in Northwest Territories in Canada. The word "nahanni" means mystical powers. Deshka and Yentna are major salmon streams that flow into the Susitna River in upper Cook Inlet. Iwalani means, "heavenly bird of the sea" in Hawaiian. You are right if you think that I didn't give my other five kids such long names. Well, I figured that this would be my last shot, and I didn't want to miss my last shot, because I might run out of bullets someday. She loves her name, and I made a song about it.

The song came about shortly after I nailed a big griz bear. I had taken the hide out on the lawn so I could flesh it. Nahanni was just a little twerp at the time, so we thought she might like to feel the bear's fur. The skull was lying on the hide, and the tongue was hanging out one side. We sat Nahanni on the hide and went to get a camera. I returned to see our little daughter chewing on the tongue! It must have tasted good, because she smiled when she looked up at me. I didn't taste it to see if it was yummy, but I did take it away from her and take a couple of pictures. It was then that I thought out the words to a song. It goes like this:

"Nahanni and Paw went hunting one day.
Nahanni said to Paw, "I've something to say.
If you kill a bear, I get to eat his tongue,
Because it will help me to be a mean son of a gun."

Nahanni is in her late-twenties now, but we still have fun singing the song together. A few years ago, when she was thousands of miles away at college, she bought a teddy bear that had a device inside that allowed her to record her voice. When I got it on my birthday, I squeezed the stomach

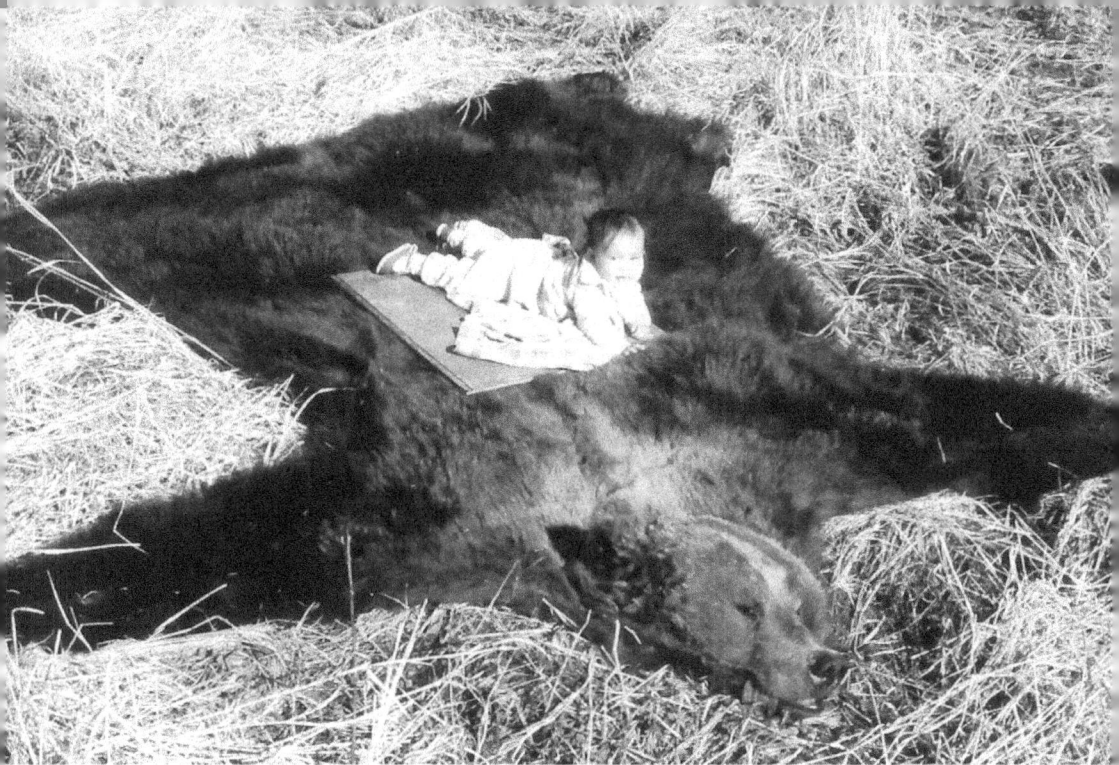

Nahanni chewing on a bear tongue

and it sang the bear-tongue song. I guess I don't have to tell you that it brought happy tears to my eyes. Our little girl was not little any more, and she was my last child to leave the nest.

When I was contemplating the reversal of the vasectomy, I visualized the potential changes it could produce. There was no doubt that it could change some positives to negatives, but it could also make Winnie's life more complete and fulfill the female need to give birth. I also felt that at that time of my life I had more time to spend with a child. Perhaps with my experiences, whether they were achievements or failures, I had more to offer now than I did when I raised my other five kids.

Nahanni was only 6½ pounds when she was born, but she was healthy and strong. At three weeks, we took her to the pool at the school, and she was like a fish. When we put her underwater, she did like all animals and held her breath. She even dog paddled.

One of those negatives that I thought about when I was considering a vasectomy was about to present itself. Late in the winter, Nahanni made a strong attempt to show us that she was going to rule the household. It's amazing how a baby that is less than six months old figures out that they can get whatever they want by crying. Our nights were becoming more and more sleepless because of her desire to suck up some nice warm milk. Of course I had gone through the act many times before, so I was wise to the trickery. If the kid doesn't have a fever or wet diapers, there is probably nothing wrong. I had a tough time convincing the new mother though. No matter what time of night, Winnie would spring out of bed when Nahanni began her crying act. I took my turns, but when I finally concluded that we were being taken advantage of, I knew that I had to take a stand.

After a week of trying to make Winnie realize that we were being scammed by a 22-inch terrorist, I could see that I was losing ground. I had to change my tactics. I told Winnie that I had never disallowed anything that she had wanted in the past, but that now I would hold her down if I had to. "Let her cry," I demanded.

The terrorist changed her tactics too. She cried louder and longer. I began wondering if there really was something wrong with our precious little gem of a daughter. No! I would not give in. Sure enough, I was right: after two nights of perpetual crying, peace descended on our household. I won. My method proved effective, and now we all slept at night.

One thing that I didn't realize at the time was that Nahanni's circadian rhythm was different from ours. Winnie and I were natural morning people and Nahanni was a night person. My mom was the same way. She would stay awake until two or three in the morning, and then sleep till noon or later.

Nahanni was born in September, so we had all winter to think about how her presence would alter our fishing lifestyle. We had no intentions of trapping, because we had too much to do on the new log house. I had lucked out and got Carl Jones to help with the construction. Carl is a master log builder and has built many top quality homes in the area. It's a real art to make a good scribe-fit Swedish cope, and Carl was the Picasso of log building. It not only takes a good eye, but it requires lots of patience. I hadn't acquired the patience part, but Carl taught me. My homestead house and the cabins that I had built were "skunk-bear" style. "Skunk bear" is slang for "wolverine." Like the wolverine, precision is not in my make-up. Rustic fits me much better. Although Carl was the boss, he never acted like one. I learned much more from him than I could have from any ten crafts-men. After working with him, I became more patient with others and a better instructor or coach. Carl definitely did most of the work, but together we produced a custom A-1 home.

When building a home, most rural Alaskans do the finish work as time and money allow. For some, their homes never get finished. I would never think of getting a loan to finish our new house. Fortunately, a lot of the finish work in a log house doesn't require supplies from the hardware store. I used smaller logs to construct the staircase, and I made several tables from various types of wood, such as driftwood and burls. The finish work was much more time-consuming than it was costly.

I had always wanted to incorporate some rockwork into the house and surroundings, because I feel that rocks complement log work. Shaping a house out of logs is a long, laborious process, but rockwork takes much longer. First of all, you have to acquire an eye for gathering rocks. Some people are natural artists, but most have to go through a trial and error system that doesn't allow impatience. Most of the rocks that we accumulated came from various beaches, which meant that we had to have the proper equipment to retrieve them.

If you were built like the Hulk, you could use brute strength to gather some good-sized rocks. Even though I'm in okay shape, I'm no Hulk, so I decided quickly that I needed some equipment to move the ones that were more than 100 pounds. A four-wheeler and a five-foot pry bar was a good start. A "come-along," which is like a hand winch, makes rock retrieving easier, but having knowledge of the use of a fulcrum was priceless. When I was homesteading, I had met a Finn named Wilho Kuopala. He had a rosy-cheeked smile, and was slight in stature, but because he lived by himself, he learned how to do everything and anything with no help. Bill (he liked to be called that rather than Wilho) possessed more knowledge on the use of a fulcrum for leverage than anyone I have ever run across. He would laugh when I asked him how he built with big timbers, or how he managed to stack huge logs. After he had his little laugh, he would show me how he used "leverage."

Logs of various sizes also are a help when moving rocks that are four hundred pounds or more. Using my biggest pry bar, I would lift one end of a rock and place a log under it to be used as a roller. Once I got the rock winched a bit, I would keep placing more rollers under it. Then it was a simple matter to get it on the tilt bed of my trailer.

I've done extensive rockwork around our place, but it has taken several years and a strong back. Winnie has a better eye for location and placement of rocks, so between the two of us, we have done a nice variety of rockwork. We've made several rock gardens with petrified wood. They make a nice accent around the lawn. Winnie is a 115-pound lightweight, but I constantly have to restrain her from lifting too much. I'm always afraid that she is going to hurt herself.

Sometimes when I'm out on the Homer Spit trying to catch a salmon, there are kids throwing rocks in the water—not a good thing when I'm trying my darnedest to bring home a tasty fresh salmon. I started referring to the little rock throwers as "RR's," which is short for "rock re-locators." We have two friends, Debbie and Ben, who joined us in "rocking," so together we came up with the phrase, professional rock re-locators, or PRR's, to name our pastime. Winnie and I had been re-locating rocks for some time before Debbie and Ben got hooked on rocking. We have flower gardens that are made exclusively with petrified rocks. The log walls of our house have rocks set in the bottom four feet. We have a rock fire pit, and around the pit are tables and chairs that are all made with large rocks. It's been nice having another couple to go rocking with, because some of the rocks are 500 pounds or more. Debbie and Ben have great imaginations, which have given rise to some awesome rock stairs and paths at their place. Well, enough about kids with rocks.

During the course of the winter, we decided against buying another boat and getting back into commercial fishing. Our new daughter was a tad too small to deal with on a boat, so I would have to come up with another project in order to keep a sound mind.

I had always wanted a shop, and I thought there was a possibility of building my own boat if I had a shop big enough to do it in. I sat down and carefully designed a multi-purpose shop that would be big enough to build a 46-foot boat. I also incorporated a woodshop room, a reloading room, and a greenhouse into the plan. I figured that "if I was going to New York, I wasn't getting off at Chicago," so I decided to put radiant heat in the cement floor. When the building was complete, I made a law: NO ALASKAN CAN BUILD A HOUSE UNLESS HE BUILDS A SHOP FIRST! After fifty years of freezing my hands working outside and busting my knuckles against frozen nuts and bolts, I now realized how pleasant a shop can make life.

Due to a variety of circumstances, we never built a 46-foot boat in our shop, but it has served many other functions. I painted the floor with some special epoxy floor covering that required three coats. I enjoy playing basketball, so I carefully painted the necessary lines to make an official court. When I did this, I had no idea how much use it would get. During Nahanni's school years, there were countless hours spent on that court. I also put up a trapeze and added ping-pong, foosball, darts, and various weightlifting devices.

The three specialty rooms get just as much use. Every spring I plant tomatoes, cucumbers, and other veggies in the greenhouse. I catch rainwater off the roof for watering the plants. The woodshop room has a never-ending list of projects going. Hopefully when I croak, someone else will finish some of the projects that I didn't complete. I'm really good at not finishing stuff, but that doesn't make Jerre a bad boy. I'm just making sure that the next generations have something to do.

Believe it or not, I have finished a few projects in my time. I've found that the best way to get something done is to consider a matter as a contract. For example, if I decide that I want to be a better runner, then I select some races and enter them ahead of time. By doing that, I have set a goal and I will not procrastinate. If I don't commit to some races, it's a good bet that I will skip training sessions. I'm past seventy, so I've had time to figure out what it takes to make me press on.

Chapter 17

Back to Sea

One day, as I was going down the ramp at the Homer Harbor, I ran into Jim Cobb. He was wearing a big, white gauze bandage on his head. When I asked him what the other guy looked like, he laughed and admitted that the other guy hadn't suffered any head trauma. As a matter of fact, the guy didn't get so much as a scratch. Apparently Jim had a go-around with the guy and his buddy before. This time, when they spotted Jim coming up the ramp as they were going down, one of the guys was carrying a pipe wrench and Jim was carrying nothing. One blow from the pipe wrench ended the fight—if you want to call it that—just as quickly as it started.

Jim, whom I've known for a long time, was blessed with Yupik and Irish blood or some great combination that produced a wild man. He has been fun to have in my life, because he laughs a lot and has zero moss growing under his feet. When Jim was a little turd, he worked alongside his dad on the old steel boat called the *Hex*. They also owned the *Wilson*, a larger wood boat that was built in 1918. Jim's dad was one of the earlier crab fishermen, and before Jim was knee high to a parka squirrel, he had to bait the crab pots. Jim became a great fisherman and still defines the term "wild hair."

It requires more time to be successful at some things than others. Starting a new family is one of the things that takes considerable time, especially if it is to be done right. I was thoroughly enjoying life with a young, beautiful bride and a vibrant and also beautiful daughter, but there was a feeling inside me that persistently tugged at my inner being. The tugging was at a peak during the summer months when the salmon were running. I felt as if I were losing contact with a lot of my fishing buddies because I had nothing to offer to conversations, nor could I claim any pretense of being a fisherman. My heart was telling me that I was a fisherman, but I surely didn't have my net in the water.

My love affair with Alaska had lots to do with the sea, and I realized that an affair isn't always stimulated by everything nice and wonderful. The wide variety of sea conditions, the smell of the salt spray on your face, and of course the near-death experiences all have their allure, and the sea has a sly way of hiding what is beneath the surface.

Spike Hoyt, a friend of mine, died while crossing Whale Passage near Kodiak. His skiff was swallowed by some angry water. I knew Spike's dad, Roy, from my homesteading days. I went to Roy and asked him if he would consider selling me Spike's boat and permit. We reached an agreement and shook hands on it. I was back in business! The boat was an older fiberglass 32-footer named the *Snug 7*. Perhaps it wasn't exactly what I would have preferred, but it didn't matter at the time. Fishing was more than a passion; it was what I was meant to do. Besides, man cannot live on love alone. We were in need of some income, and fishing usually produced a few bucks.

There are two things that a fisherman dreams of pertaining to business: large quantities of fish, and high prices. The odds are against both things happening at the same time, but that year, in the mid eighties, we lucked out. Red salmon kept coming and coming. The major rivers reached their optimum escapement, so Fish and Game gave us lots of extra fishing time. For some uncanny reason, several cash buyers came into the inlet and drove the price up. For several weeks, we fished sixteen to twenty hours a day, every day. There was not much sleep to be had, but it didn't matter—we could sleep in the winter. Each morning I cast off and left the river without waking Winnie. When I got to where I thought the fish would be, I would wake her and we would catch another 600 to 1000 reds. It wasn't like striking the mother lode, but it was the next best thing. Seasons like that one helped make up for the years that we didn't catch enough to pay for fuel.

Sometimes we brought a babysitter with us to watch over Nahanni, but because she was a night person, she didn't wake up until noon or so. She almost never cried, and she seemed to enjoy the rocking motion of the boat. Yep, we had a natural born fisherman aboard.

We were high-liners again. It was as though we hadn't taken a break from fishing. I was so thankful that I had gotten back to my mariner world, and—call it accident or destiny or the will of God—the timing couldn't have been better. Through my long career as a fisherman, I've witnessed many hearty souls trying to become fishermen only to be forced to give it up, their attempt thwarted by a bad season or two. They might have been the best of fishermen if they had had the fortune of good seasons when they started. We have little control over many extrinsic factors that might make our choices, in hindsight, seem good or bad. Hence the saying, "Timing is everything."

The following spring I decided to build a 24-foot skiff. People had been speculating that Fish and Game might open a small area close to the mouth of the Kenai River if the predicted record run came true. The skiff might prove to be the only way to get in the shallow water and make some good catches. We laid up the hull with fiberglass. It required many layers of mat and mat roving, and it was a nasty job. At the end of each day, we smelled like resin and itched terribly. Even though we wore protective clothing, it was miserable. If I burped, it smelled like resin. The finished product made it worthwhile though. The hull was wide and deep enough to accommodate lots of red salmon. She was shallow draft, which would allow us to get into ten inches of water. We named her *Hungry Eyes*. When it came time to use her, she performed just as we had expected. We loaded her several times with those bright, silvery sockeyes, and as a plus we netted forty kings. *Hungry Eyes* had lived up to her name.

On Nahanni's second birthday we went to Kodiak Island to hunt deer with my oldest daughter, Cheryl, and her husband, Charlie. I fashioned a backpack to carry Nahanni so that she wouldn't have to walk through the rough terrain and so she could look forward. There are two things that Kodiak has plenty of: rain and bears. To protect Nahanni from the rain, I cut three holes in a black plastic garbage bag. She wouldn't win the Little Miss Kodiak contest, but she was warm and dry.

Early on the first morning of our hunt, Winnie shot a nice buck. Rain was dripping from our noses and chins as we slogged through the wet grass to the dead deer. Nahanni, who was riding in comfort on my back, took one look at the blood coming from the side of the deer and exclaimed, "Deer hurt!"

Cheryl and Charlie weren't far away, so they came to help. They weren't the only ones that heard the shot. An oversized brown bear was less than 100 yards away and was headed right for us. All of us joined together in hollering at the bear, which was enough to make it change its mind about a free lunch. So often such tactics don't work. The bears on Kodiak have learned that when they hear a gunshot, they can intimidate the hunter and steal the deer. Except for a few people lucky enough to draw a permit, killing a brown bear is illegal on Kodiak. The bears seem to have figured that out. Not only do hunters lose their hard-earned venison, but I'd venture a guess that in many cases the hunter instantly ages a few years and acquires a few grey hairs.

During the fall months, Kodiak deer become obese, and their meat is the most delicious of the Alaskan herbivores, with the exception of Dall sheep. If you're lucky enough to see a bear coming for the proverbial free lunch, there's a good chance that you can change his mind if you shoot near him, or if there is more than one person, then lots of yelling might help. There are masses of books that will give you all kinds of advice regarding bear confrontations, but when it gets down to the nitty-gritty, be prepared to protect yourself. It might be cool to survive a bear mauling and be able to show people your scars where a bear bit holes in your hide or tore half of your scalp off, but it's definitely cooler to show them pictures of the bear that you had to shoot that had closed to a distance of ten feet or less.

Cheryl, Charlie, and Charlie's brother Matt once survived an unprovoked attack by a big brown bear. They were going uphill to get into deer country when the bear came tearing down on them. Charlie is always prepared for just such a situation. He always carries his 44 magnum in his hand when on Kodiak, and it was a good thing that he did on that day. He wouldn't have had time to get a handgun out of its holster. He knocked the bear down with his first shot, but the bear got up and its adrenalin gave it a second wind. Cheryl and Matt unloaded on Ursus, and it finally went limp only six feet away.

Another trip to the rock (Kodiak) that is worth sharing is the time that the four of us were flying with a local air taxi in a Beaver. The Beaver is one of the most coveted planes for hauling good-sized loads and for getting around Alaska's bush. Cheryl had drawn a permit for a mountain goat at Crown Mountain, which is a ways south of Kodiak town. We were about

100 feet above the ground and near the top of the mountain when the engine suddenly quit. There was no sputtering or warning, just abrupt silence. Being a longtime pilot myself, I hollered at the pilot to turn ninety degrees to the right, because there was a draw that led to the ocean that we might make if he turned immediately. The plane was on floats, and that was the only water in sight. He ignored me, and instead fumbled with something near the floor on his left side. The ground was coming up quickly. We were less than fifty feet from crashing. Mr. Pilot miraculously switched fuel tanks (which he had forgotten to do earlier) and pushed the start button. Luckily for all five of us, the Beaver came to life just an instant before we would have gone to meet our maker. The floats barely missed a conglomeration of rocks, and we all breathed again. After that fun event, we decided to forego the goat hunt and stay in the lower elevations to hunt deer.

Two years later, I was able to get Cheryl to commit to another deer hunt. Charlie and Winnie weren't able to get away, but we were in need of some meat. When Cheryl and I got to Kodiak, we hired a different air taxi to shuttle us to a bay that was not too far away. The hunt was short and sweet. Cheryl blasted four deer on the first day, and I took two more on the second day. That evening we saw the pilot come in to pick up some other hunters. We weren't due to leave for another day or two, but we had our meat, so I scurried down to the beach and told the pilot that we were ready leave if he had time to come back and pick us up. He said that it would be no problem, so we raced to break camp and pack the meat to the beach. By the time we got everything to the beach, the wind was snorting, and as the day-light faded to dusk, the whitecaps were growing. It was nearly totally dark when we heard the drone of the plane. It bounced a couple of times when touching down, but Jack, the pilot, was able to taxi to shore without flipping over. Jack had been flying around Kodiak for many years and knew what he was doing. We loaded the plane as fast as we could, and Jack poured the coal to her. We bounced off one wave and then another. I didn't like the sound of it, and I'm sure that I was puckering a bit. When we finally got airborne, the small plane bounced around like a toy. The wind was really turbulent and strong. Several times during the short trip our heads almost hit the ceiling. We were hanging on to the metal tubing, and we kept cinching our seatbelts down. The wind was somewhat blocked where we landed, so we didn't bounce terribly on landing. Other than the city lights of town, it was pitch dark. We secured the aircraft with extra lines and loaded our gear and meat into Jack's van.

Without hesitation, Jack insisted that we stay in his basement. That surely was gracious of him, because we didn't have much money for a motel; plus we had several hundred pounds of deer meat, so I don't believe that we would have been welcome at a motel. When Jack opened the door to his house, the door almost got away from him. He hung on while we darted in with our sleeping bags. Jack introduced us to his wife, and she was as gracious as he was. After a warm hug, she insisted that we join them for some homemade soup.

When we retired to the basement, it was obvious that the wind had increased. You could hear it making all kinds of noises as it tried to come in through the windows and doors. I knew that I wouldn't be able to sleep through all the noise. I honestly didn't think that the wind could blow any harder, but was I wrong! Cheryl kept asking me if I was sleeping, and I assured her that I was not. We had to raise our voices to hear each other over the horrendous sounds that the wind was creating.

We were lucky and thankful that we had such wonderful hosts to stay with during such trying times. For three days, the wind seldom blew less than 100 miles per hour. The airport was shut down, and the windows were blown out of the airport tower. Nobody could venture out of their homes because the wind would have blown them into the next county.

The wind was the subject of most of the stories the four of us shared during the three days we were pinned down. Cheryl had seen her share of hundred-mile-an-hour blasts while fishing at False Pass. Jack had a great way of making his stories sound like fun adventures, so time went by as pleasantly as possible under the circumstances, and on the fourth day it was finally still. Jack had given us some wet lock boxes to put our meat in, and the meat was frozen solid, which was perfect. Our trip home was pleasant and uneventful. Thank God for that.

During the past ten years or so, I've done much of my hunting by myself. There are several reasons that I do the solo hunts. Most of the people that I used to hunt with have jobs and can't take time off. It's difficult finding a compatible partner that has similar hunting and camping skills, and my tolerance levels have lessened, so I just hunt by myself. Not many critters have ended up in my freezer, because I've gotten too fussy when it comes to what to shoot and what not to shoot. I'm sure that most of my friends think I'm getting like Elmer Fudd and the wabbit. He has many opportunities but never gets the wabbit. Likewise, there have been many times that I could have shot a ram that was barely a full curl or a caribou that would have scored mid-way in Boone and Crockett but chose to hold out for something larger. Consequently, too many times the wabbit has gone unscathed.

I haven't given up the chase though, and maybe someday I'll come home with a DOUBLE CELESTIAL HERCOMITE!

Chapter 18

Winter at Jerre Lake

The leaves had fallen from the trees, and the brisk breezes of autumn were rapidly turning to the chill winds of winter. It would soon be time to go to our new trapping cabin. I had sold my PA-12 plane, so we hired Wild Bill of Sterling to fly us to Jerre Lake. The lake is located about 50 miles west of Twin Lakes. When it was time to go, Bill called us and said that he wouldn't have much time to get us over there, because he was leaving for Hawaii as soon as he dropped us off. It was one of the coldest days of winter when we loaded all of our foodstuff and supplies in Bill's plane. Our thermometer at Homer hovered at zero, and I knew that it would be much colder at our trapping cabin in the interior.

Winnie and I wore our bulky parkas and otter fur mittens. Our three-year-old daughter, Nahanni, wore her fur-trimmed snowsuit. We were adequately dressed for sub-zero temperatures. I knew that I would have to work fast and get the stove and stovepipe hooked up as soon as we got to the cabin. I had cut lots of firewood when we were building it, so there would be no problem starting a fire and getting the cabin warm in short order.

When Bill's plane plopped down on Jerre Lake, the skis glided to a stop in ten inches of new soft snow. The thermometer on the outside of his side window read -42˚. Bill said that we would have to hurry and unload because he was running late. His prop-wash covered us and our pile of supplies with snow dust. It seemed to get awfully lonely as soon as the drone of his engine was quieted by the vast countryside.

Winnie and I strapped our snowshoes on and, with me carrying Nahanni on my shoulders, trudged through two feet of powder snow. It was only sixty yards to the cabin, nestled in the tall spruce trees. I caught a glimpse of something sticking out of the snow just a short ways from the lake, but didn't think anything about it until we got to the cabin. The stove and stovepipe and all the supplies that the air taxi pilot was supposed to have left in the cabin were not there. It was as though someone had hit me between the eyes with a big rock. Without a stove, our chances of survival were next to none. At 40° below zero, everything freezes rapidly. Even with all of our winter clothing, we would have to build a fire outside and keep it going until someone chanced by. But with the temperatures so far in the minus column, there was no way that any small planes would be seen. I put Nahanni on the upper bunk and covered her with sleeping bags. Then I remembered the thing sticking out of the snow down by the lake. I donned my snowshoes, grabbed our only shovel, and headed out there. Sure enough, that damned pilot was too lazy to take the supplies to the cabin as agreed. Now it was all snowed under and the insulation, along with everything else, had gotten all wet. Most of the stuff was frozen to the ground, which made it difficult to retrieve. Most important and my foremost concern were the stove and chimney pipe. They had weeds frozen to them, which had to be scraped off, but I rushed back to the cabin and was able to set the stove up and run the pipe through the roof. All of this took time. Nahanni was crying. Winnie was keeping her little face from getting frostbitten, but the poor little fart had reason to cry. When I started the fire in the stove, it smoked up the place because of the bits of weeds still on it, but it wasn't long before the vegetation burned off and we could shut the door. Soon the cabin was cozy.

A lazy pilot that didn't think about the consequences had put our survival seriously at risk. In Alaska a man's word is good as gold, but I guess that the pilot didn't know that.

The next morning the sun woke me, so I rolled out of bed, stoked the fire, and started coffee. The little outside thermometer showed -25°. It felt warm compared to the night before. I spent the day retrieving the rest of the snowed-under supplies and salvaging what I could. The dry goods were no longer dry. Navy beans don't fare well when soggy and covered with mouse droppings. Twenty-five pounds of beans and the same amount of rice were shrew food. Rabbit and ptarmigan meat would have to replace the loss.

After making our home on Jerre Lake as comfortable as possible, I chopped a hole in the ice so we would have a water supply. It would be easier to pack five-gallon cans of water than to melt snow. Winnie was busy getting the sourdough ready for use. It was the main ingredient for making bread, hotcakes, and an occasional chocolate cake.

Next on the agenda was to build an igloo so that if our cabin burned, we would have a survival shelter. I used a machete to cut blocks of solid snow and form fit them. Winnie and Nahanni brought softer snow to pack between the joints. I poured water on the joints and, with the sub-zero temperatures, the water froze and made a tough little igloo. We made it big enough for the three of us to lie down in, with some room to spare. Nahanni thought it was the greatest fun. The finished product was functional and looked authentic. We stayed in it for a few hours to make sure that it provided adequate warmth and ventilation.

Now we could settle down to the business of trapping. Trapping on snowshoes requires lots of trail breaking. After the initial trail has been made, it firms up and can be walked on without snowshoes. I did most of the trail breaking by myself. I made a short three-mile loop that Winnie could work. I designed it for martin sets only, because she could set the smaller #1 traps.

One sunny, calm day when the thermometer climbed all the way up to +10°, we went together to check one of the trap-lines. The trail was solid, which allowed us to go without snowshoes. So, here we were, a complete family strolling along on a warm, sunny, quiet day. The only noise to be heard for miles was the crunchy, squeaky sound of our footsteps. Then, out of the blue, our three-year-old Nahanni piped out, "Pa, you sure are handsome." It sounded so touchingly sincere that I stopped and almost cried. I thanked her and gave her a big hug. Nothing could have made the day any better.

We hadn't seen anybody for more than two months when a Super Cub landed on our lake one afternoon. Clark and Cheryl Whitney were old-time friends of ours, and they trapped every winter thirty miles to the west of us. They totally enjoyed their solitude, and always did well at trapping. Actually I think Clark took Cheryl over there so he wouldn't have to watch all the guys goggling at her.

Clark said that they were on their way back to Soldotna to get some supplies. He asked us if there was anything we would like them to get for us. For some reason, Jell-O came to mind, and some evaporated milk. We used the latter to make our most coveted treat, snow ice cream, and we were down to our last can. I couldn't imagine that they would go out of their way to bring such frivolous items, but a few days later they brought us what we asked for, plus some other goodies.

The remainder of the season wasn't much different from past years except that we caught lots of martin. The fur of martin is almost as luxurious and soft as sea otter fur. They almost never have any fat, so they're easy to skin.

When it came time to leave, our igloo was still in perfect shape, so if we had needed it, it would have helped us greatly. When Clark had gone to town, he called Wild Bill and reminded him about the date to pick us up, and he came on the day we had agreed upon. I can't begin to express how much it is appreciated when a plane picks you up when it is supposed to. Waiting for a plane can be worse than going fishing and catching nothing.

Leaving our winter home brought sadness to our hearts. The solitude and purity of that world would be replaced with the helter-skelter and clutter of a world full of phones and paperwork. Even though Homer is a small town, it seems overwhelming when returning from three or four months in the wilderness. On the other hand, we would get to see old friends and show off the big fur catch. We had stories that were worth telling, but none of that could top the super time that we spent on the trapline together.

The next day found us knocking on Sylvia Thompson's door. We had to knock hard because, at 100 years of age, Sylvia was hard of hearing. She greeted us with a hug and a warm smile. While she made tea for us, she informed us that the cribbage board was in its usual place on the table. Even though we couldn't beat her very often, it was worth playing just to see her smile and hear her wonderful laughter when she counted a big hand. The wisdom that this grand lady shared with us was something to pay attention to. She talked about a friend of hers that was "only" 85, who was always complaining about her aches and pains. Sylvia told her to learn how to deal with her pain and reminded her to "use it or lose it."

Me, Winnie, and Nahanni at our survival igloo.

For the most part, Homer is a wonderful place to live. It is the end of the road, and where the sea begins. It is home to hundreds of mariners, and it has more artists per capita than most places. The scenery can't be matched, and it is on the edge of total wilderness.

Homer is where pop singer Jewel was taught by her mom and dad to sound like a warbler. Her dad, Atz, is a good friend, as are most of the Kilcher family. All of them learned to sing while growing up on their homestead.

Published authors abound in Homer. There are so many good authors that I wouldn't dare name them for fear that I might forget to mention someone. I believe that the reason there are so many writers is the endless adventure that lies at their feet. The water, the mountains, the animals, and the people produce a myriad of things to write about and share with others.

All of us need heroes in our lives, and Homer is an easy place to find some of the best. Libby Riddles immediately comes to mind. She is a dog musher with no fear. Her Iditarod win was a triumph of pure guts. While several other top notch teams were hunkered down and waiting out a terrible storm that blew so hard that visibility was zero, Libby hooked up her dogs and let her lead dog take her to victory. She is a superhero in anybody's mind, and so are her dogs.

Of course Homer doesn't have a patent on heroes. Fine role models can be found in other places as well. Bethany Hamilton, for instance, is another genuinely tough young lady. She was surfing in Hawaii when a shark bit her arm off. As soon as she recovered, she was right back catching waves again whenever the surf was up.

Aron Ralston wouldn't accept death when he got between a rock and a hard place. Most people can't imagine cutting their own arm off in order to survive, but that's exactly what he did. He doesn't whine about the loss. He just lets people know how thankful he is for life.

Most of Homer's Coast Guard people are unsung heroes. When they are called upon to leave port to save someone's life, the weather is usually too miserable for anybody else to consider going out in the stormy waters.

Although I mentioned several heroes, one that stands out like a single stout tree in a meadow is Frank Libal. Frank is big in stature and big in heart. He spent most of his life coaching young athletes. Now Frank does battle with cancer, but he doesn't snivel about it. Between chemo treatments he goes hunting and fishing with his sons and buddies, and has an uncanny ability to come home with "the beef." I made an ancient Hawaiian hook from ivory for Frank to wear because he never stops providing. He is a true warrior. His wife, Donna, is a solid rock as well as a genuine gem.

All of the people mentioned above are not only heroes, but also deserve the distinction of being the best of the "hybrids." If you don't have any heroes, get some!

The moose are talking today. Not vocally, but with body language. February was extremely mild, and now March appears to have something in store for us. There are nine moose in a neighbor's field. The only reason moose would gather like that is that they sense a change in weather. Two that are hanging out at our house are moving unusually fast and for no apparent reason. I've observed moose going through these abnormal gyrations before. BATTEN DOWN THE HATCHES! We are about to get some blustery weather.

Sure enough, Kushtaka has been storing up some heavy-duty weather, which he proceeds to unleash with glee right after my daughter Cheryl and her family arrive for a visit. Their timing couldn't have been better. They have been here for a few short hours when the blizzard starts. It rages on for two days and nights. The drifts stack up and nearly cover the cars. Winnie needs to go to work when it is at its worst. I don't think it's possible, but Charlie says that he will chain up all four wheels of his four-wheel drive pick-up. We can barely get the front door open to get outside. Not only is the snow packed hard against it, but the wind is terribly strong. There are white-out conditions with visibility cut to twenty or thirty feet. It doesn't faze Charlie. He digs each tire out and then puts on the chains. Winnie nearly blows away trying to get into the truck. It takes us more than a half hour to go four miles plunging into the drifts, but we get her to work. Then, three hours later, they cancel work and send everyone home. Winnie gets a cab to take her to the end of our country road where we pick her up and plunge through more six-foot drifts. Charlie smiles and says, "Fun stuff!"

Chapter 19

Black Death—Ship Happens

"WE'VE FETCHED UP HARD AGROUND." Those were the repugnant words that Joe Hazelwood, the captain of the *Exxon Valdez*, muttered out of his toxic mouth when his vessel struck Bligh Reef. It was March 24, 1989, when word of the catastrophe spread around the world.

Prior to that moment, commercial fishermen had enjoyed their occupation and worked hard to make a dollar. Natives and whites had subsisted from clams and other seafood. Hunters had hunted ducks in the fall. Eleven million gallons of black crude oil ended it all. After polluting Prince William Sound, the Black Death was carried on the currents to Cook Inlet, Kodiak, and the sea beyond.

I personally witnessed the devastation that it caused all around the southern end of the Kenai Peninsula. Within a couple of weeks of the scourge, I began helping to transport clean-up crews with my 24-foot skiff. We located oiled beaches and tried to clean them. The stench from the crude and the dead birds and animals wasn't easy to get used to. There were so many dead seabirds and seals and sea otters that it brought tears to all of us. Most of the beaches had six to ten inches of thick, black crude. At first glance, some beaches looked untouched, but lying under a thin layer of sand was the same nasty oil.

Daily we saw birds and sea mammals covered with oil and struggling to survive. We would call the rescue team and give them the location of the sighting, and they would pick up the bird or animal. At first, the survival rate was dismal, but after some trial and error, the crew was able to save some of the critters.

I did a short stint at the bird recovery building, and I can tell you that there is nothing easy about cleaning the icky stuff from a bird that thinks you're trying to kill it. The loons were especially hard to work on. Their beaks are four inches long and as sharp as a needle. I didn't work on any mammals, but that must have been a bigger challenge because of their teeth, claws, and strength.

Nobody had a plan for removing the oil from the beaches and rocks. We started shoveling the slimy stuff into heavy-duty garbage bags and were making some progress, but after a couple of days, they told us to stop and stand by. They didn't give us any reason for stopping, but it appeared that no one wanted to accept the responsibility of calling the shots. It was a sure thing that Exxon didn't, and the Coast Guard didn't have the expertise or the tools to work with, so who would take charge of the operation?

A few crab boats were hired, but after they filled their holds with crude, nobody seemed to know what to do with it. Essentially, there was no plan. The crews tinkered around for months, but when the cleanup came to a final halt, there was still oil everywhere. The initial destruction of the spill was staggering, to say the least, but it was a small part of the devastation that followed—for the next twenty years!

The phrase "Zero Tolerance" determined when and whether any of the commercial fisheries would open. Because of those two words, we could not fish salmon at all in Cook Inlet. There was oil in all the riptides, so we had to forgo the entire season. Most of the set-netters that fished the beach were able to fish during the majority of the season, and they had an excellent season. It was so frustrating for the drift fleet. We waited day after day, month after month, hoping they would announce an opening. We lost the whole season, and it would have been one of the best ever.

The Prince William Sound fishermen had a similar experience. Not only were they unable to harvest salmon, but they lost the herring season as well. Perpetually the herring had returned to the sound, and the early spring season ordinarily gave the fishermen a shot in the arm after the long, hard winter, but not that year. The herring never came back.

The year following the spill, prices for fish dropped like an anchor. Worldwide, people balked at eating Alaska seafood because they were

The *Bronze Maiden*

afraid that it might be contaminated. Then the domino effect set in. Prices of boats and permits plunged. Potential new fishermen opted not to buy into Alaska's fisheries. If all the above sounds sad, read on. The years that followed caused more decline in boats, permits, and fish. Fishermen that had been proud of their occupation and had worked so hard to provide for their families were losing everything. I'm not just talking about their business; the strain took its toll in more disastrous ways. Many fishermen, especially from Cordova, Valdez, and Tatitlik, lost their homes and were forced to relocate. Some couldn't bear the losses and took their lives.

It must have been so difficult for them to stand at the harbor and look down on the boats with tons of moss and seaweed growing on the unused hulls. When they got brave enough to go on board their vessels, the smell of mold in the cabins and fo'c'sles and the rust that had covered the engines were still more reminders that "black death" had killed their livelihood.

There had been little attempt to reimburse the fishermen for their losses, so it became apparent that a lawsuit would have to be the tool for justice.

Our judicial system is designed to make guilty parties pay for their wrongdoing—right?

All of the fishermen, natives, and processors that had losses due to the spill joined the litigation. A lot of hard work went into gathering and presenting the proper paperwork. Most fishermen accumulated boxes full of paperwork as the years passed by. The first decision was from an Anchorage judge and jury. They awarded the plaintiffs five billion dollars. Everybody except Exxon thought that the award was just. Exxon used their mighty stick to appeal, and appeal, and appeal. They made a total mockery of our judicial system. I'm not suggesting that they paid judges or used any illegal methods to cause the case to drag on for more than twenty years after the spill and to end with a pittance of the original award, but something caused the judges to side with them. The Supreme Court gave us a pitifully small ten percent of the original award. Not only were most Alaskans appalled by the decision, but people from all corners of the States that knew the facts of the case were disgusted with the final decision.

After going the distance with the record twenty-year case and observing other "giant corporation" cases, I realize that it is indeed rare that "the people" are able to beat big-money corporations. For that reason, I contend that any time a big corporation comes to town and wants to "do their thing," we say NO before they can even get their feet in the door, because you won't stop them once they get their grubby feet inside. I won't "beat my drum" any more on the subject.

Chapter 20

Move On

A catastrophe doesn't always cause a change in lifestyle, especially in the case of the hybrids or "wild hairs" of the planet, but we were about to experience some extreme changes. When we were trapping and our little daughter posed at the entrance of our igloo, we had no idea that we would not return to the trap line.

Before the oil spill, I already had the wheels in motion to have a new boat built. After the spill, I realized that it would be more difficult to make a living commercial fishing, but the new boat was already in the making.

Jim and Marilyn Roberts had built many quality fishing boats, so it was a wise choice when I signed the contract for them to build a custom 37-foot gillnetter/long-liner for me. These folks were so accommodating and loving that it was a joy to do business with them. Not once did they hesitate about making any alterations or additions. If I told them that I would like the cabinets rounded where they were exposed, they complied. Not only did they agree to everything that I proposed, but they often had suggestions that I hadn't thought of.

I chose to power the boat with a 425-horsepower diesel Cat engine. The boat had everything that our house had, including a shower. Winnie and I both thought that the hull should be burgundy with white trim. I had given considerable thought to a name. She would be the *Bronze Maiden*. When the beautiful vessel was complete, Winnie christened her appropriately with a bottle of champagne.

I bought a trailer to put the boat on, and shipped it up to Alaska. I was too busy preparing for the upcoming halibut season to run the boat up myself. The halibut and salmon seasons that followed were nothing to crow about, but we made our payments. Fish prices dropped as we had expected, but to make up for it, we worked harder than ever.

Nahanni was barely more than five years old, but she had no problem entertaining herself while we were picking salmon. I hung a big, bright red buoy from the boom, and she would swing on it out over the water, laughing the whole time. On calm, sunny days, she would swing out as far as she could, let go, and plunge into the icy Cook Inlet water. It scared us at first, but she refused help getting aboard, insisting on climbing up the side of the boat by herself.

The *Bronze Maiden* was the most trouble-free boat that I had ever fished. We kept her clean and polished because we were proud to have such a beautiful, sleek boat. When the season ended, we put her high and dry, and she was as clean and shiny as when we got her.

Again, the summer was stolen by commercial fishing. Although I loved it, there was little time for anything else. Alaska summers are shorter than those of the other 49 states, so when fall arrives there isn't much time to dillydally. Picking berries, making jellies and jam, catching halibut, canning salmon, and hunting are traditional means to fill the freezer and pantry for the approaching winter. Some things could be postponed or put off, but not the above-mentioned.

We decided to leave Nahanni with friends and team up with Cheryl and Charlie on a trip to the Illiamna Lake area. At the time, it was a quality hunt that was affordable. We would fly on a commercial flight from Anchorage to Illiamna, then hire an air taxi to fly us a short distance to a lake. Experience had taught us that there is a period of time that the caribou gather up and begin their migration. Like I mentioned before, if you go too late, the "boo" might already be in rut. Caribou bulls are NOT fit for consumption when they are rutting. The meat stinks badly when you are butchering the critter, but it's even stronger when it's cooking. Anyhow, caribou meat is very good when taken at the proper time.

After hunting for several days, the girls had gotten nice bulls, and Charlie stuck one with an arrow, but the horns on his bull were quite small and terribly ugly. One horn was somewhat deformed and stuck out in a weird direction. We ribbed Charlie forever about "Mr. Ugly."

I was holding out for a high-scoring bull, and I'd yet to see any. On the day that the pilot was to pick us up, Cheryl spotted several bulls that were 300 yards away from camp. She pleaded for me to shoot one. They were moving along at a fast pace. I plopped down on the tundra and shot the largest one. As it turned out, it was big, and the rear tips of the main beam almost touched each other. We just finished packing the meat to the lakeshore when we heard the plane coming.

Besides having a ton of fun and harvesting our year's supply of meat, we found that all four of us would lose ten pounds on those ten-day hunts. Most days found us walking many miles, and of course packing big loads of meat required thousands of calories.

When the late fall raindrops turned to white flakes, it was a reminder that it was time to think about gathering stuff for trapping. "Stuff" is a good word for the conglomerate of things I needed to gather. Fall weather was lingering longer than usual, which was nice for the people that waited too long to ready for winter, but we were anxious for the lakes to freeze so we could get the trapping season under way. January was nearly at its end, and our pile of stuff still sat in a heap in our shop. Winter didn't want to happen. Perhaps it was time to go to plan B.

A couple of years prior, I'd made a short trip to Hawaii and bought a piece of real estate in Kona. Property was cheap then, and I had it in my mind that I could build a house on it and spend some of the winter there when the cold and the dark got us longing for sunshine. It seemed bizarre that unseasonably warm Alaska weather would claim the honor of sending us to Kona instead of to Jerre Lake.

Changed plans meant that we had to make a new pile of stuff. Parkas were out; bikinis were in. Carpenter tools would replace traps, and shorts would take the place of long underwear. There were no apprehensions on my part. I was excited, and had no problem making the transition. For me, it was just another one of my wild-hair, hybrid ideas. What would life be without wild hairs? Winnie liked the idea because she wouldn't have to worry about her nose and cheeks getting frostbitten. Nahanni was too young to comprehend what we were about to do.

The contrasts make Hawaii especially alluring to Alaskans. First-timers probably have formed some ideas about these islands from movies and books, but nothing prepares you for that moment when you step off the plane and are overwhelmed with the tropical warmth, fragrances, and the pleasant easy-going manner of the local people. The longer you're there, the more you appreciate the culture and traditions. I had to give considerable thought to some of the differences. For example, when I built a house in Alaska, I didn't have to get permission from any government agency. I just drew up some simple plans and started pounding nails. In Hawaii there are hoops to jump through, and the hoops are slow motion only.

When we settled at Kona, I had it in my mind that we would build immediately or sooner. We drove around a few subdivisions to see if we could find a house that looked appealing to us. To fit both our budget and our desires, it would have to be simple but nice looking. As soon as we laid eyes on one particular house, we knew that it was the one we wanted to duplicate. The most pleasant couple greeted us when we knocked at the door. Stan and Mary Sacks were thrilled when we told them that we admired their home so much that we hoped to build one like it. Within five minutes we were the best of friends. Stan excused himself and came back shortly with a set of his house plans, which he insisted that we take. He had done most of the work on their house, and it was as professional as it gets. He'd designed the roof to extend over the lanai (porch), which kept the midday sun from beating in. Another feature was a hallway that went through the center of the house, which created a natural breeze that kept the place nice and cool.

I was like a kid with a new toy when we left with "plans in my hands." Little did I know that I was about to run into the first of the governmental "hoops." When I approached an excavating company to have my lot leveled, Henry, the guy that owned the dozer, asked me if I had gotten the permit to do it. Permit? Not only did I have to get a permit, but I also had to get a water hook-up for the closest fire hydrant so that I could keep the dust down while the dozer was working. Most of the ground in Kona is solid lava, so the big D-9 Cat had a ripper on the back of the machine to break the lava before he could break it to smaller pieces with his tracks.

Of course, every construction phase for which a permit was required had to be approved before we could proceed to the next phase, and they came to inspect the project when they felt like it. Some of the local people referred to it as "Polynesian paralysis." At first it was frustrating, but I learned that I was on their playing field, so I would have to play by their rules.

Before we went to the Planning Commission to get the plans approved, we learned that we were in a subdivision that had covenants that had to be complied with. Our plan didn't meet the minimum square footage, so I made an addendum and altered the plan. When I presented the blueprints to the commission, the woman shouted that I couldn't change a plan by myself. I gave her time to get it off her chest and then I calmly asked her if her nametag was correct. I told her that she had the most beautiful name that I had ever seen. I might have mentioned that her name complemented her looks, but I can't remember for sure. Whatever I said had a mellowing effect, and she took the blueprints to the supervisor, and they both agreed that the change was okay. The plans were approved.

The building process taught me the value of patience and how to be courteous and flattering. Everything from stem to stern required a permit and approval. We hired a carpenter to help. He had just finished building a house in the subdivision, so he knew the required procedures. Tom Mahony was fun to work with. He claimed to have "an eye for detail," and he even sang while he worked. The only problem with Tom was that he was a surfer. Surfers are a breed of their own. When the surf was up, Tom didn't show for work. For that matter, none of the surfers in Kona showed up reliably for anything except the surf. Kids didn't go to school, and adults didn't go to work. They didn't tell you that they were going surfing; they just didn't show. It was easy to figure out. If you heard the waves crashing on the rocks in the morning, you knew that they wouldn't be pounding nails.

We bought an inflatable raft and filled it with water so Nahanni could play in it while we worked. She enjoyed bringing us nails and an occasional tool. It made her feel like she was helping, and we loved her attitude. The sun quickly turned her pale Alaskan skin to a beautiful brown-bronze color like her mom.

I was thoroughly enjoying working in shorts and flip-flops. The only time I wore a shirt was when we went someplace. Another great thing was that I never had to endure one minute of carpal tunnel syndrome. and that was before I had my wrists operated on. The climate seemed to prevent it. My arms never went to sleep.

The house was designed to be built on a slope, and that fit our landscape perfectly. It allowed for a carport under the front part of the house. I decided to cover the posts with rockwork. Lava rock puts a Hawaiian touch to a home. I had seen two guys doing some rockwork on a new house nearby, so I asked them to give me a bid on the three posts on the front of the carport. They were a father-son team who seemed to take pride in their work. A constant wisp of smoke from thin, black cigars filled the still air as they pondered where to put the next lava rock. When the younger man, Billy Keepo, found that I was a hunter, we became instant buddies. He hunted pigs and sheep every chance he got.

He was so intrigued with hunting in Alaska that we spent most of our lunch breaks "talking story." One story that I told took place not in Alaska, but several years prior on the island of Maui where we'd spent a few of the winter months doing a small commercial fishing operation. For the most part, we bottom fished. It was all done by hand, so we got plenty of exercise pulling long lines from depths of sixty fathoms or more. A day breeze was an everyday occurrence. It produced two- to four-foot waves. One day while bouncing up and down in the choppy sea, I saw something black sticking out of the water fifty yards or so away. Neither Winnie nor I knew what it was. It was long and jutted toward the sky. As it got closer, I realized that it was a whale flipper. For some reason, this humpback whale was on its side, slowly cruising our way. "Oh, yes!" I shouted to Winnie. "We can get some close-up pictures of it if it keeps coming our way." We had two long lines on the bottom, and the engine was off, so I got the camera out of the bow compartment. No sooner had I gotten the camera than the flipper submerged and the whale seemingly went away. I had the telephoto lens, which would have allowed me to take a great picture at twenty yards or so.

Something caught my eye next to the long lines. The whale was under our boat! Its flippers were touching the long lines and its back was nearly touching the bottom of the boat. Panicking, Winnie straddled the bottom with her feet and clung to the sides for dear life. I tried to calm her by telling her that whales are harmless. I had no more than gotten the words out of my mouth when the whale bumped the boat hard enough to almost lift us out of the water. I was no longer Mr. Calm. I had heard of a couple of instances where whales had destroyed boats, but I had assumed that the boats had been harassing the whales. Suddenly our boat seemed just about as adequate as an eight foot dingy.

I didn't dare start the engine for fear that it would anger the whale. We just held on for dear life. Yes, I was straddling the boat too. It seemed that hours went by with the whale in the same position, but it was probably more like five minutes. Finally, it went deep and disappeared from sight. Immediately we began pulling the lines up as fast as our arms could retrieve them. We had been pulling for about thirty seconds when out of nowhere the whale hit our transom and knocked us both down. For some strange reason it had decided to tell us in no uncertain terms that it didn't want us in this part of the ocean.

I responded by starting the engine as quickly as possible, and our eighteen-foot boat screamed out of there with the lines dragging behind. That whale could have destroyed our puny boat easily, but I guess it was just warning us to boogaloo. We didn't see a calf, but maybe it was getting ready to give birth. Whatever the reason, it didn't choose what I would call a subtle way of telling us to go away.

Amid all the storytelling, I took mental notes when I watched Billy and his father mortar and set rocks. I had some visions of things that I would like to build with rocks in the future. During the next couple of years, Winnie and I would search the lava fields for rocks to do a variety of projects. I built rock walls, an enclosure for a mailbox, and a fountain with a waterfall and pond.

When we finished the house that first winter, I contracted a boat builder in Waimea to construct a small fiberglass boat for me. I knew that it was mandatory that I get on the water or I might turn into a moldy Twinkie. I wouldn't need the boat until the following winter, so the builder would have plenty of time to build it.

We celebrated when I finished painting and putting the final touches on our new "coffee shack." It turned out better than either of us had imagined. I had two different stained-glass artists do windows, which were awesome. The one at the peak of the front of the house was of several shearwaters skimming the water in search of food, and the one next to the door was of reef fish. I had also done some Koa wood trim that really gave a custom look to our modest house.

Building our Kona house was a fantastic experience and gave us a great feeling of accomplishment, but it was nothing compared to what I learned about Hawaiian culture. I really feel compelled to tell you about hula dancing. It's not just a dance; it is total love being gathered into the heart. If you have the opportunity to see a Hawaiian woman dancing a slow hula, you will know what I am trying to describe. It is not only the most graceful of all dances, but it will cause you to shed "happy tears" because of the intense love that is depicted. Every time I see the hula, I feel that there is no better way to express the universe of love.

Spring was coming on when we returned to Homer. It was then that I realized that we had made a serious change in our winter lifestyle. I knew that we would return to Kona when the snow started to fly the following winter. There would be landscaping to be done, and maybe I could help thin out the marlin population. With these thoughts in mind, I decided to clean up the pile of trapping stuff that was taking up valuable space in my shop. It never crossed my mind at the time, but we haven't set a trap since. I replaced the trapping experience with marlin fishing.

When the boat that was built for us had been completed and was ready to fish, we asked the local Lutheran minister to perform the Hawaiian tradition of blessing her prior to launching. He was happy to accommodate. I named her *Nahanni* and took her over to the church parking lot where she got blessed properly. Even though the boat was small, we had Winnie christen it with another bottle of champagne. Yes, another bottle of champagne went down the drain.

A guy that we knew quite well, Gary Eoff, made marlin lures. I traded some Alaskan ivory items for several lures. He didn't mind sharing his knowledge of which were the best catchers, and he was quick to tell me that if I wanted to catch some ahi (yellow-finned tuna), I needed his best lure, the one that was called the Ahi Pussy. How could I argue with that?

The first few days of fishing were trial and error (mostly error), but then one day I must have been holding my mouth right, because one of my eighty wide reels started screaming! The line was zinging out at high speed. I had set the drag so that I could barely pull the 130-pound test line. When the blue marlin that was on the other end flew out of the water, I felt the hair on the back of my neck stand up. I had mentally rehearsed the procedure many times, so I immediately hit the throttle to set the hook. Then I had to crank the other two lines in so that the fish didn't make a giant tangle.

I took the pole that had the fish on and put it in the gimble that I had installed on my fish box. So far, so good.

The fish didn't appreciate a hook in its jaw, and it showed it by jumping ten feet out of the water and pulling more line out. It showed off for fifteen minutes before I was able to gain any line. After a while I gained more line than the seemingly maddened marlin did. I'm not sure how much time had elapsed, but I guessed that I had been cranking for 45 minutes or so when I saw the outline of its body and the leader, which was nearing the rod tip. It suddenly dawned on me that I desperately needed four arms. Ever so carefully I put the rod into the holder and reached for the flying gaff and my gloves. The fish seemed content to tread water, so I began hand-lining the eighteen-foot leader. I would pull a couple of feet and crank the slack onto the reel. When I got the fish within two feet of the surface, I sank the tip of the gaff deep into the blue-green skin, just behind the gills.

You guessed it: that's when all hell broke loose! I held onto the half-inch nylon line that was attached to the J-shaped gaff, and immediately I became aware of the power of a 250-pound angry marlin. I didn't dare take a wrap on the line for fear of joining the beast for a deep swim. Suddenly I realized that we were in a battle of wills. The fish knew that I was to be reckoned with and that it was a fight to the death. I knew I had to do everything possible to land my first marlin, so I wasn't about to let loose. The battle and the thrashing got worse when I got the critter close to the surface. My hands and arms were taking a terrible beating, but there was no way that I was going to give up. The 250-pounder had the same thoughts, and now he tugged and twisted like an 800-pounder! I was drenched with sweat and all the water that the wild fish had splashed on me.

Finally I could feel the power of the fish ease a bit. Then it stopped pulling long enough for me to tie off the gaff line. Yikes, the fish came alive again and gave another burst of the tug of war. But then it all stopped. I was battered and bloody, but I had won my first marlin. Triumphantly I grabbed the rough bill with both hands and with all my remaining strength pulled the stout adversary aboard the *Nahanni*. I sat down on the helm seat and admired the beauty of the fish while I downed a quart of water. The tail protruded two feet beyond the transom. That kind of made me proud.

Through the next few years I learned how to handle the big fish more easily and without getting maimed. I caught lots of marlin, most without any help. None of them gave me less excitement than the first one. They all made the hair on my body stand at attention, and it was always the most fun workout that can be imagined. I had always envisioned landing a grander, a marlin that weighs a thousand pounds or more, but that dream didn't come to pass. Sadly, I have to admit that I am not the Old Man of the Sea.

Life in general is a lot like fishing, and the future is similar to the sea. It can be rough or smooth, and nobody knows what lies beneath the surface. Our lives are constantly altered by the unforeseen. We are little specks in a big universe controlled by God. As a young fellow, I might have thought that I knew myself quite well, but the older I get, the more I realize that I am constantly learning more about me. I used to think that I would never excel at anything, that I would be mediocre at best. Then I became a fisherman and excelled at it. If fishing were a classroom, I would have earned my first "A." I've made some attempts to make cabinets or do other finish carpentry that requires precise workmanship, but I've never got more than a "C." I did, however, learn that I could make rustic tables, staircases, and such, and even win the blue ribbon at the State Fair with my rustic abilities.

When I took up flying, I not only passed the test with an "A," but my bush flying would have earned me an "A" also. I can plumb and wire a house, but both sometimes baffle me, so I spend too much time scratching my head and looking at diagrams: "B-" on that. There have been a couple of subjects that I flunked and got the big "F," but I'm still learning about me, so maybe there is still hope. "Mediocre" isn't such a bad word after all, so I'll be content with that.

Hope is one of the most appreciated words as we go through life. Once in a while I have to remind myself of a study that was done on hope. Researchers put three rats in a small tank of water and three others in an identical tank. All six rats treaded water. The researchers took the first three out of the water for a few seconds and then put them back in. Within a short time, the three that didn't get rescued for that brief period drowned. The ones that had the short reprieve lasted much longer *because they had hope.*

Hope is a wonderful thing. Just a glimmer of it can really help. Keep treading water, folks.

A new restriction was implemented for the drift fleet in Cook Inlet. Whoever came up with the idea must have had a vendetta against commercial fishermen, because it had the 666 mark all over it. With the new restriction, the fleet could fish only a 1½- mile-wide area on the east side of the inlet. You can imagine the difference from prior years when we fished the whole inlet, which is thirty miles across and twice as long. After the new restriction was implemented, the whole fleet, which consisted of 600 boats, would compete in the narrow strip referred to as "the corridor." This restriction came with a bundle of problems for the fishermen. The set nets come out 1½ miles from the beach, and we had to stay 600 feet out from them. Also, we were forced to buy sophisticated electronics to make sure that we didn't get more than three miles from the contour of the landmass— not an easy task when you are constantly being pushed or pulled by the strong currents that the big Cook Inlet tides produce. Adding to the fun was the constant patrolling by the Fish and Game boats. They worked diligently to catch us a few yards across the line so they could refer to us as culprits and write us a citation. Honest fishermen that misjudged the current would accidently be pulled across the line and get cited.

At the time, I was fishing with a group of eight other fishermen. All of us had radios that only those in our group could tune in to. We shared information about how good or poor the fishing was and anything else that would help to improve each other's catch. We also made a habit of spreading the word as to the location of the Fish and Game boat. If it cruised by, we would get on the mike and say, "The man is going by."

One day most of the fleet was crammed into a small area north of Kenai. The red salmon were bunched up and attempting to make their way to the river through the maze of nets. A couple of us were trying to find a place to set our nets without going over the line. The water was choppy, but you could see fish in the waves. The boats were tight. It was total mayhem. One of the group members came on the radio and told Bobby and me to set our nets outside of him because he was loading up. I replied that I would be over the line if I set there. Then Bobby came on and said that if I had any hair on my balls, I would do it. Quite a number of times I had heard guys refer to the size of one's testicles or the amount of hair that covered the two eggs, but I never understood how any of that made you a better fisherman, or better at anything, for that matter.

I quickly responded, telling Bobby that he surely was better qualified so for him to go ahead and set his net there. He cranked the whole net out, and the fish hit his cork line as it was flying off the reel. I got excited and found a small open spot and was able to put half of my net out. Then one of the guys came on the radio and hollered that the "man" was coming. Yikes, I hadn't even had time to check my position to see if I was the least bit over the line. I immediately sprang into the stern and started reeling in the net as fast as I could. I just wound the fish on the reel and didn't take time to pick them. I could see Bobby doing the same, but he had all of his 150 fathoms to bring in. I was just bringing in the last few feet of net when I saw the Fish and Game boat coming full bore. It was like a fast forward movie. Bobby didn't have a chance. I glanced over and noticed that the officer was handing Bobby a piece of paper. I sneaked off and took refuge behind the city of boats. So much for big balls, because mine shrunk that day.

Often, because of the tight quarters, neighboring boats would set close to another boat's net. We referred to it as being "corked off." Getting corked off often caused shouting, fist waving, and other nasty gestures such as fingers pointing to the sky. You might have a good set going, but when you got corked off, you were forced to pick up your net, because you weren't going to catch another fish.

On one such occasion, we had just finished setting our net and the salmon started hitting immediately. Another boat that was looking for a place to make a set came by, and when he saw the fish hitting our net, he took the liberty of setting ten feet from my net and did it cork for cork. When he completed the set, his boat was close enough to spit on. Now get this: the name of his boat was *So Su Me*. The guy turned his back to me so he wouldn't have to deal with a confrontation, but he was so close that he heard every word I screamed at him. I told him to pick up his net, but he didn't flinch. Winnie was madder than a hatter too and was doing her share to make him understand that he had committed an uncalled-for, irresponsible act. My yelling and fist shaking were to no avail. He barely glanced at me.

I jumped down from the flying bridge, ran to the cockpit, and started picking the net up as fast as it would come in. I didn't even pick the fish out of it; I just wound them on the reel. Then I bounded up onto the bridge again and gave her full throttle. The smoke belched from the exhaust stack as I blasted to the end of the *So Su Me* net. I reset my net within five feet of his. When I finished, I was within smiling distance of Mr. Not So Happy.

Another time, I was fishing a low water set that put me within 600 feet of the set-netters. I was on deck keeping a close eye on things because when the tide started to flood, I would have to bring my net in. Otherwise, I could lose it to a submerged rock. There weren't any other gill-net boats in the area when I made the set, so I was startled when I heard someone hollering obscenities like he was trying to set a four-letter-word record. The guy was in a set-net skiff. He had one hand on the tiller and the other one waving a big knife. When he got close to my broadside, he was in a rage and said that he was going to cut my net in half! My instincts sent me hurtling down into the fo'c'sle where I snatched up my 30.06. When I got back on deck, the beach leech had my net in his hand. I got his attention and racked one in the chamber. When he saw my rifle pointed in his direction, he politely put my net back in the water and made a quick exit without even saying good afternoon. I would never have shot the fellow, but I might have put a well-placed bullet hole in his skiff. Ah yes, those were the days, my friend ....

Perhaps you're thinking there must have been lots of fishermen that were the recipients of a bullet hole or two, but in the half century that I've participated in the Inlet fishery, I can't say that I've ever heard of a mariner wondering where that new orifice in his body came from.

The corridor was responsible for thousands of instances like the one I just described. I'm sure that the *So Su Me* wouldn't have corked me off if it hadn't been for the corridor. Nor would good honest fishermen have had to donate money because of a citation written by an overzealous officer attempting to show his authority. The stress placed on us fishermen could have been avoided if a bit of common sense had been used when they needed to restrict fishing.

When I began fishing in the early 60s, there were no other user groups to deal with. Sport fishing was almost nonexistent. Also, there was no such thing as dip netting. Now, fifty years later, sport fishing swings the big stick and dip netters scoop up hundreds of thousands of red salmon in the Kasilof and Kenai rivers. Because of the newer user groups, the commercial fishermen have more and more closures when escapement goals are short. It became terribly frustrating not to be allowed to fish when the other user groups were gobbling up hoards of salmon in the major rivers. Frustration and anger became common amongst commercial fishermen, and I was no exception. My love affair with fishing was waning. I tried to do my part in the political fight, but majority rules in most cases, and the sports fishermen outnumber commercial fishermen many times over. The number of commercial salmon fishermen can't be increased because we are regulated by the "limited entry program." It's easy to understand why dip netting became so popular in such a short time. The average family of four can take 55 red salmon, and they usually have no problem getting their limit or more. During the peak of the salmon run, the dip netting is equal to a wolf pack in a feeding frenzy.

Rather than risk the chance of scowl wrinkles on my forehead, I quit commercial fishing shortly after the year 2000. I had enjoyed most of forty five or more years of being at sea and working diligently in the attempt to figure out where the fish would be on any given day. The Old Man (God) gave me that niche in life, which I loved and appreciated.

The law is the law, and I must abide by it; I just don't always agree with the way that they are introduced. There's no doubt that we humans would ravage the planet, whether on land or sea, if it weren't for the law. Kachemak Bay is a good example of that. There used to be an abundance of shrimp and three species of crab. With little effort a person could catch all of the King, Tanner, and Dungeness crab that he needed. Now, due to overfishing, there is no open season for any of the crab or shrimp. We are supposed to be the smartest members of the animal kingdom, and yet I can't help thinking that most of us flunk when it comes to preserving the resources we depend on. Almost all of the sea mammals and fish have been depleted because of our selfish ways.

Nahanni and her friends were bouncing off the walls. Puberty is an exciting time for the kids, but it can make parents old quick. We actually lucked out because Nahanni was an "A" student, sang in the choir, and was a great track and cross-country runner. I don't have a clue how a kid can do so much. When I was her age, I would have been lucky to get a "C-" in just one of those three endeavors.

Winnie and I had some expertise in running, so we helped with the coaching. For several years we tried to bring the best out of the kids.

Sometimes it seemed that it was in vain, but once in a while there would be a glimmer of hope and it would all be worth the effort. There were a handful of the runners that had some self-motivation. I would invite them to do some extra workouts after the regular coaching. They were the kids that would excel and go to state, and some set records. Those kids are adults now and have gone into the world knowing how to compete, and feel good about themselves.

Just the other night we were out dancing and a guy came up to me and asked if I remembered him. He said, "I'm Travis Kaufman. Do you remember me?"

"Of course I remember you. You were one of the hardest-working runners that Homer had on the track team," I replied.

He was truly happy to see me, and we shook hands for the longest time. I knew that Travis had gone into the service and was deployed to Iraq, but I didn't know he had returned. He never stopped smiling while he told me that I was the reason he excelled and survived in Iraq. He also added that he was the fastest two-mile runner in their squad and that it was because of the coaching that I gave him. I wanted to cry happy tears, but I managed to keep a smile on my face. Knowing that I helped in a small way was the best reward that I could ever receive.

A couple of years prior, another runner teammate gave me the same kind of compliment, and in the same manner. Aaron Ulmer not only set a school record in the 400-meter run, but also excelled in swimming. When he went out into the world, he became a successful businessman. Both of those fellows have wonderful, supportive parents, the kind that it takes to help mold a young person into a gift to the planet.

Nahanni excelled at cross-country, track, and mountain running. She made her parents proud. We tried to stress to the running kids that they should always respect their competition and make friends along the way.

Chapter 21

Wild Hairs and
Mountain Animals

It seems that the hairs on my body are indicative of my personality. If I didn't trim the hairs in my nose and on my eyebrows, I'd either be tripping on them or braiding the little fellers. Just recently I came out of the shower and my wife reached for the right side of my chest and said that she was going to pluck a seven-inch hair that seemed to have grown there overnight. I talked her out of it by suggesting that we should see how long it would get. It was no longer than the one on my lower back. Maybe one of them will make The Guinness Book.

Mostly by choice and not by chance, I've done plenty of stuff that is what you might expect of a wild-haired, hybrid type of person. I recognized the trait early in life and tried not to let it be a negative issue. My wild-hair ways are probably responsible for much of the adventure in my life.

My children wouldn't be quick to admit it, but all of them are the recipients of the wild-hair genes. Sorry, it couldn't be helped. It was in the hands of someone much bigger than I am. Actually I shouldn't be apologizing, because the wild-hair factor imparts strength and produces some super exciting times.

I have noticed that most of the people I hang out with are shaped by the same cookie cutter. We have lots in common. For the most part, we enjoy being around each other, and besides, it's a bit difficult sharing stories with those that didn't get wild-hair genes. So many rural Alaskans are more adventurous than your average two-legged creature of the earth. I don't mean to imply that no city dwellers are ever the recipients of wild hairs. It's just that whereas we prefer to live a country life, some of us have had to squat in the city because of the need for a job. I know several people in Anchorage that definitely qualify as the wildest of wild-hairs. But percentage-wise, there are more of the hairy critters in the country than in the city. I really can't say that I would make a pimple on a good wild-hair's butt, though I'm quite sure that most people that fit the category of wild-hair don't consider themselves anything of the kind.

I just made a quick dash to my shop for a drill bit and another thingy that I need for a project. I barely made it between rainsqualls, which made me appreciate the comfort of our modest log cabin. Last year at this time, I was pinned down in my siwash camp on a mountain. My tarp did little to keep the cold from the nearby glacier from penetrating my bones. I was doing a solo hunt for Dall sheep, but the rain and scud never relented, so the only things that I got were COLD and WET.

Sheep and goat hunting is what originally got me hooked on the mountains, but running mountain races is what sealed the deal. Since I started that sport, I've been up and down more than 900 peaks. Most of them are only 3000 to 6000 feet, but nonetheless they are mountains. I'd always claimed that if it weren't for having to make a living at fishing, I could do better as a mountain runner; yet it took me quite a few years to realize how much effort it would require to win a gold medal. Bronze and silver weren't too hard to come by, but I would have to buckle down if I was to be the top mountain animal in my age class.

I had always been able to pump out fifty or so pushups and 100 or more sit-ups, but now it was time to get serious. I had put my spurs away (quit fishing), so I took advantage of the spare time to train. Getting serious about working hard at what qualifies as play sounds a bit on the weird side, but there are weirder things to do. I pushed myself to do whatever it took to get my core in shape. When I turned seventy, I could do 600 sit-ups without stopping. I ran the mountains in the snow from March until the end of May when most of the snow has melted. I tried to make sure to do at least two mountains a week and would have done more except that I had a long drive to get to the mountains. I incorporated more hill sprints, lunges, lots of leg weight lifting, and some biking. When most of the snow gave way to the spring sun, I would camp at the bottom of a mountain and run it twice a day. I realized that I needed to get rid of every ounce of baby fat, so I also worked hard on improving my diet. All of the effort paid off, because I finally set an age record and took the gold. It's obviously easier to take gold in an older age category than in the younger classes, but it was every bit as satisfying. I even managed to win the Alaska Mountain Running Grand Prix in my age group.

An anonymous person sent my name to *Masters Athlete* magazine for the Geezer Jock of the Year competition. My oldest daughter called me one day and told me that I won. I couldn't believe it. I was the national 70 to 79 Geezer Jock of the Year! Soon after winning the title, I got a letter of appreciation from our governor, Sarah Palin. Satisfaction with one's effort and accomplishment is the best reward at any age. I've been lucky and thankful for an obedient body.

Records are meant to be broken, and sure enough, three years after I set the record on Mount Marathon, Fred Moore shattered my record. Fred and I started running the race together in 1970 and have been mountain buddies ever since. Perhaps if I live to be 120, I might beat him.

I've tried my best to pass on that special feeling to others by getting friends and relatives into mountain running. Almost always when they start, they think it's crazy, and then they get so thoroughly hooked that they can't stop. It's good clean fun, and if a person prepares their body properly, it holds up and is injury-free. The best part of Alaska mountain running is that you become a part of a super family of athletes. It's rare to detect any signs of anyone thinking himself superior. No one is on an ego trip.

This spring I had a humbling experience, which brought to mind the saying "If you're going to play, you've got to pay." I woke one morning to excruciating pain in my right leg. It started in my hip, then moved to the front of my upper leg, and then, within 36 hours, my shin felt like someone was pushing a dull knife against it. My wonderful body, which had served me so well for so long, didn't want to be obedient any more. Sciatica was the diagnosis. It appears that the spaces between some of my vertebrae are

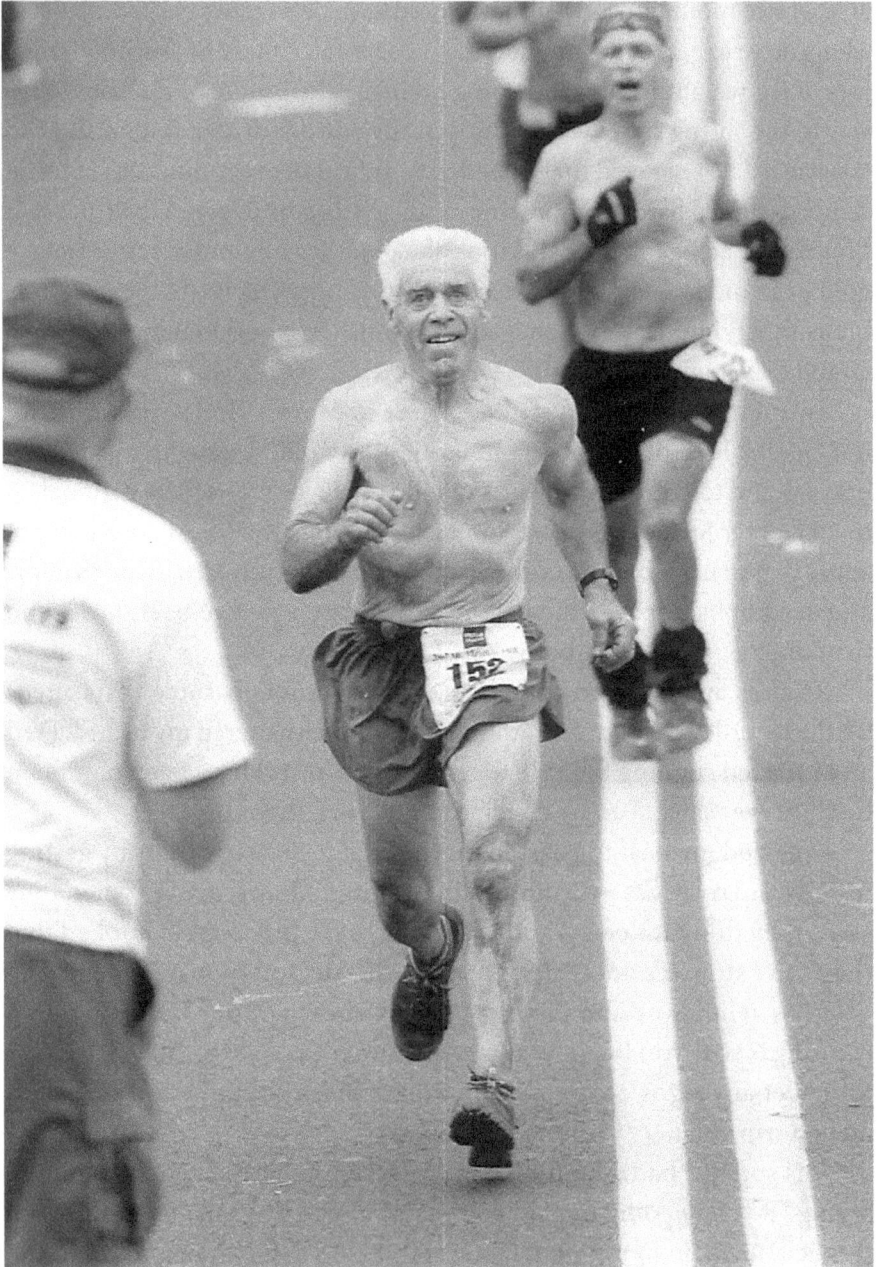

Near the finish line of Mount Marathon
"Run with a smile and your feet will never touch the ground."

narrowing, allowing the bones to touch, and I believe that my piriformis muscles are pinching the nerves at the tailbone. Long needles in two of my vertebrae and some exercises made it better, but now I'm careful about lifting heavy objects, and I've slacked off the mountain-work a bit. Also I guess that I will take more trips when packing moose meat out, and with less weight.

You may be thinking that it's contrary to be tooting my horn in one paragraph and complaining about my leg problem in the next. I tell myself that age has nothing to do with it. Even though I'm in my 70s, I still think that I can get back in shape and run like a 28-year-old. I just need to pace myself and gradually work up to competition shape. During most of my adult life, I carried heavy objects, not only rocks, but logs, heavy packs of moose meat, cement, et cetera. I always thought it was better to pack one large load than two medium-sized ones, but now I'm probably paying for it. Also, the piriformis muscle has to be strengthened to the maximum in preparation for the mountains. Maybe I should plead guilty of doing too many workouts too close together.

One time I was blasting full bore down a mountain and an onlooker yelled at me, "You are a mountain animal!"

Hearing that, I blasted down the mountain even faster with reckless abandon. I felt invincible as I plunged down the gulch. I've never had a better compliment. Mountain goats and snow leopards have the reputation of being some of the toughest, most agile animals on the planet, so perhaps I was being compared to these animals. (In my dreams.)

For a couple of years I had recurring dreams of running down Mount Marathon and my feet never touched the ground. Then a few years ago, someone took a picture of me when I was almost to the finish line, and both of my feet were off the ground! Since then I tell others to smile when they're running and their feet will never touch the ground. I now address other mountain runners as "mountain animals."

After spending most of my adult life on the sea, I've been left with a great void now that I'm not commercial fishing any more. I do go out and chase fish for personal use, but I don't expect that anything will come along to replace my love for commercial fishing and the wild sea that made it so exhilarating. Even so, the mountain running definitely helps to fill the empty spot.

I'm a light sleeper. I'm guessing that it's because of the numerous times I've been on anchor watch, plus the encounters I've had with bears. The '64 earthquake might have something to do with it too. I think it would be nearly impossible to sneak up on me while I'm sleeping because I wake to the slightest noise or disturbance. I've tried my darnedest to sleep on boats or big planes, but it just doesn't happen. I'm quite sure that sleeping lightly is not the best thing for one's health, but I have no control of it and I don't dwell on it. (Like I've told my deckhands through the years, we can sleep when we die.)

A number of years ago, I got out my tools and some fiberglass and decked *Hungry Eyes* and built a nice cabin on her stern. It's nice and comfy with the heater and all. I do have the desire to go out on deck and get a little salt spray in my face now and then. It makes me feel like I'm still joined with the marvelous sea. I must confess, though, that it takes less salt spray to make me feel in touch with the sea than it used to. When it drizzles down the front opening in my rain gear for an hour or so and my teeth start chattering, I have to say "uncle" and retreat to the comfy cabin.

Incorporating comfort into a boat doesn't necessarily make me a twinkie, although there are some mariners that would scowl at the mere thought of comfort. For me, it allows more time at sea without the need to snivel. Plus, I can entice family members and others to share the experience with me. The boat doesn't sit idle like a rich man's sailboat. We use her plenty. She's the perfect tool for harvesting seafood or for going across Kachemak Bay to pick berries, hike trails, or visit friends.

Hungry Eyes is only 24 feet long, but she's quite beamy. She's nearly ten feet wide, so we have plenty of room for six people to fish without being elbow to elbow. I have a nice big aluminum davit and a hydraulic pot puller, which make it easy to pull crab pots, if there were a season. Nothing is "Mickey Mouse" on her. The rail, the cleats, anchor, hatch covers, and everything else are big and strong. I've witnessed small cleats rip off rinky-dink boats and cheap anchors bend with a little stress. There are sealed compartments that would keep the boat afloat during the worst conditions. I have made sure that all my safety equipment is in tip-top condition and up to date.

Hungry Eyes isn't the prettiest boat in the fleet, but she purrs like a panther in heat, and I love her. You might say that she is a poor man's yacht.

If she could talk, she would whisper sweetness in my ears because I treat her like a gentleman would treat a woman.

This summer we put *Hungry Eyes* to use many times, and again she performed like a lady. We caught lots of red salmon, halibut, and Tanner crab. Crab have come back in good enough numbers for Fish and Game to declare a personal use opening. Our freezers are filled to capacity with seafood, and there is not a canning jar that is empty. My shoulder still hurts from cranking fish in. It's not so bad having a bothersome shoulder when it was caused from catching fish.

Late this fall I went out twice and harvested my limit of winter kings. They are not only fun to catch, but the 20- to 25-pound fish are the best-tasting finfish that cruise Alaska waters.

Oops!

Winnie, from all the way in the kitchen, accuses me of farting. I assure her that it wasn't me. "It was Mr. Scruffy!"

That big bear stands there with the most innocent look on his face, but he is as capable of passing gas as anyone.

I recently started a batch of raspberry-banana wine, and this morning I took the pulp (must) out of it. I took it outside and threw it under a spruce tree near the banya. Shortly afterward, two bad boys (magpies) came along and began pecking away at the strongly fermented pile. Five minutes later something caught my eye out by my woodshed. The bad boys were trying to get into the shed through a two-inch crack. The first one made a crash landing against the wall, then proceeded to hop up slowly to the crack and, with great effort, finally made it through the crack. He then fluttered around and fell out the entrance and into the snow. His drunken buddy tried to repeat the feat, but after hitting the wall three times, he gave up. He barely made it to a nearby log and just sat there like a Fourth Avenue drunk.

Darn drunks distracted me from my writing.

Last fall I went sheep hunting. More often than not I hunt by myself, and that's what I did on this hunt. I drove to a place that was surrounded by mountains and donned my 45-pound pack along with my .243 Sako rifle. I had nobody else to accommodate, so I took only a small tarp for shelter. None of the sheep hunts that I've gone on have been easy, so it was important to keep my pack as light as possible. A four-pound tent might be the straw that broke the camel's back. A tarp would suffice.

I had checked the long-term weather forecast. It was not favorable, but not going was out of the question. As in commercial fishing, you must go when the time is right, because neither the fish nor the sheep are likely to wait for you to come along whenever the weather is perfect. Sheep season lasts for only a short time, so I had to make the attempt.

Two long, steady days of climbing got me to sheep country—the glaciers. Both days were sunny and calm, which made me want to sing. Of course I would never make a peep for fear of alerting my quarry. When I started sidestepping up the first glacier, I noticed that my shadow had disappeared along with the warmth of the sun. Also, the blue hues of the glacier had turned the same color as the sky. A gray cloud cover was coming down to greet me.

One minute I was feeling totally alive and happy, knowing that I was still "mountain strong"; the next minute I was on the middle of a glacier and I couldn't see more than fifty feet. Of course I was asking myself what the odds were of bumping into a sheep in the thick of the clouds. Getting lost or falling into a crevasse had much better odds.

A couple of days in the grayness of the fog were not fun. The meteorologist was 100% correct. I would have to abort. Darn. I had worked so hard and was so hopeful about harvesting a big ram. I would have to settle for the knowledge that I still had what it takes to do a mountain hunt, but at the time that seemed of little significance. When I got back to my car, I was disheartened, but I was stronger because I made the attempt. It was a good decision to come down, because the next three days were carbon copies of the preceding two days. I've been reminded that that's the reason it's called hunting.

Whenever I sheep hunt, I can't seem to shake the thoughts of a hunt that I did years ago. I hired a pilot from Palmer to fly me to the Wrangell Mountains. I had him land me on a short strip that I had knowledge of. He didn't impress me when he landed his Super Cub, because he nearly went off the end of the 400-foot strip. I told him to pick me up in seven days, and he wrote it on his map.

The days were unseasonably hot. It was so hot that I hunted naked during the midday hours. I was getting a nice tan but no sheep. I was seeing some full-curl rams, but none that were bigger than several that I already had on my walls. The night before I was to be picked up, I made sure that I was back to the strip. I thought sure that the weather would turn sour, but I awoke the next morning to another bluebird day. I broke camp and packed all of my gear. Then I waited and waited. Every once in a while I thought I heard the faint sound of a plane. My ears were playing tricks on me. There was no plane. Waiting for a plane to pick you up can be miserable even if you have the greatest of patience. You have to stay put because your ride could show at any time. You can't wander off and hunt or go sightseeing.

When dusk fell on the mountains, I began thinking that maybe the pilot had an accident. He is the only one that knows my whereabouts. Best not to dwell on that thought, but I couldn't help noticing that there was not a cloud in the sky. I was getting low on food, so I ate a small candy bar for supper. I had a hard time going to sleep because I hadn't done anything to wear me out.

The next morning greeted me with another perfect weather day, which I was thankful for. Again I waited as patiently as was possible for me. It was a replay of the day before. Now I was more concerned that the pilot had had an accident. He was either dead or in a hospital and unable to talk. I was beginning to feel bad for his family. Again I took my sleeping bag out of my pack. I munched slowly on my last wafer of pilot bread. Fortunately there was a small pond close by, so I washed the dry pilot bread down with water. I started singing; "Teeter totter, bread and water…" Eventually I went off to la la land.

I couldn't believe it, but on the third day of waiting, the weather was still cooperating. The sun had barely broken over the mountain to the east before it had dried the dew off my sleeping bag. I didn't have anything for breakfast, but it didn't bother me much. There were no sheep close by or I would have considered shooting one to stave off starvation.

Late that afternoon I definitely heard a plane. I started cramming my sleeping bag into the pack, but while I was cramming, the drone faded. It wasn't my ride, and it didn't come close enough for me to try to wave it down. I picked up my rifle and tried to find a parka squirrel to shoot. Not one of those little guys got curious enough to come out of its hole. I didn't dare get too far away from the strip, so hunting was limited. There were other times that I had gone without food for two or three days and it was no big deal, so I wasn't overly concerned—yet.

A growling stomach does have a way of making the brain go into survival mode. Soon I would have to try to walk out. It was a long way, and at some point I would have to cross the raging Nazina River. Three sunny days of waiting had passed, so I figured that the pilot must be dead. If no plane came by noon the next day, I would begin the trek out of there.

The next morning while rummaging through every pocket in my pack, I was jubilant to find a power bar. I ate half of it, savoring it as though it were chocolate cake. I carefully wrapped the remaining half and put it in my shirt pocket. Then I proceeded with the task of re-packing. I put my small survival mirror in a handy pocket with my compass. Everything needed to be in its proper place for the long walk out.

For the hundredth time, I thought I heard a plane. I can tell the sound of a Super Cub from that of other planes. This sounded like a Cub and, sure enough, low on the horizon was a white and red Cub coming right for me. I honestly had a hard time believing that it could be my ride, but I recognized it as it got closer. It touched down and taxied to where I was standing. The pilot got out, and the first thing that he said was "Looks like you didn't get a sheep."

I asked him what the problem was that kept him from coming to get me. In a nonchalant manor, he announced that there was no problem. When I reminded him that he was four days overdue, he replied, "Hey, I've got good paying customers that I have to tend to."

Now I was beginning to fume, but I managed to keep my calm as I locked my seatbelt on and closed the door. Not a word was spoken on the flight back. By the time we landed by my car, I was so mad that I felt my face getting red, and it wasn't from the sun. I yanked my pack and rifle out of his plane and threw them in my car. Then he came over and told me that I owed him $300. I told him that he is the one that owed me for having to go through a four-day ordeal. Then I really got mad and told him never to leave anyone out like that again and to vamoose before I beat him to a bloody pulp.

As he slouched back to his plane, he shrugged and said, "Whatever."

Fortunately there aren't many pilots like that guy. I often wonder what planet a person like that comes from. Since then, I've realized that such happenings should serve as reminders that life is not perfect. Shrug it off and smile about all the good stuff.

We have a prolific weed that grows here that reminds me of Alaska in general. The locals call it "pushki," but most people know it as cow parsnip. During our short summers, it grows eight to nine feet. Then it shows off by producing a huge white flower that is as beautiful as Victoria Secret's top model. But in a blink it can cause serious discomfort and pain like a rapid change of weather can make for an ugly trip in a small plane or a stormy sea that was flat calm just an hour before, can trap a mariner in its clutches. If you get the pushki juice on your skin on a sunny day, you will experience a terrible burn. Alaska is so pushki.

Alaska produces endless adventure. Just a few days ago we had another experience of a lifetime. A young couple, buddies of ours, asked us if we would accompany them while they paddle boarded. There had been several humpback whales in the bay recently, and they wanted to get close to them. I agreed to run the boat, and Winnie and I would do a photo and video shoot of it.

We had gone only a short distance when we came upon the first huge sea animals. The bay was flat calm, and the shoreline was punctuated with the yellow and gold that are part of autumn's beauty. Debbie was a bit apprehensive as she put her board in the water and mounted it. She had paddled just a few strokes when two behemoths surfaced next to her. I think she suddenly felt a bit insecure, because she turned and quickly paddled back toward the boat. Then Ben paddled out with her, and they soon found themselves a few scant yards away from the surfacing whales.

Meanwhile, I could see whales spouting and breaching as far as I could see. There must have been 100 of them. I've never seen so many in one spot. There must have been an unusual amount of krill or other food for them in the bay.

No matter what direction the adventurous couple paddled, they were surrounded by whales. Winnie and I were busy photographers! I worked hard to capture the event on video and on two still cameras. At times we held our breath when the boarders found themselves within six feet of the monster-sized creatures. Two times whales headed for the boat and glided under us. But none of the whales tried to upend us like the one in Maui.

After two hours of nonstop encounters, we loaded the boards and headed for the harbor. All of us were on a high from the event. I'm sure that Ben and Debbie will cherish the experience forever.

There are days that I feel like the Alaska flag that I've always displayed. I'm a bit tattered and weathered, but so fortunate that Alaska has been my home all of my adult life.

It's a bit nippy on the shores of Kachemak Bay this morn. Mid-December can get a tad on the cold side, and at 10:20 a.m. the sun made a meager attempt to warm the land with its distant rays. Mr. Scruffy and I are in agreement that the sun won't make it on the first try. Sure enough, as the ball of orange travels its slow course to starboard, it seemingly collides with a taller mountain than the one it peeked over at first. We'll have to wait fifteen minutes for it to emerge again, and then it'll stay on the horizon just long enough for us "south slopers" to wander around outside without the use of a head lamp. We have to move quickly if we want to get a few outside chores finished before the fiery sphere dives into the westerly sky for another nineteen to twenty hours of darkness.

There isn't enough snow to warrant the use of snowshoes, but I'll strap on the old leather bindings of my Tubbs trail snowshoes and get some exercise jogging around the borders of my domain. My lungs anticipate the exhilaration of each breath of fresh Alaskan air. After a few short minutes I unzip my coat. The 10° temperature seems like fifty. When I'm finished, I feel like I added a day to my life. Today is my birthday, and while I was jogging, I got a whiff of coffee beans roasting. The small coffee shop is a mile away, but the light breeze has brought the pleasant aroma as a gift to me.

I glance over to the neighbors' place 100 yards to the southeast. It is lifeless and desolate. They were good neighbors, but having come from California a few years ago, they longed to see their children and grandchildren more often.

Wayne would walk his dog, Clyde, daily, and when the big black canine saw me outside, he would disobey Wayne's command to stay and race to my place to greet me. Wayne was a photographer who spent a good deal of time going to various places in Alaska, seeking the extraordinary and capturing it with his super digital camera. He and I always had good conversations. Kelly, Wayne's wife, grew more and more restless with the desire to be closer to the relatives, so they elected to move back to the south 48.

When Wayne came to say goodbye, I hid my sorrow behind a fake smile. We shared a firm "man's" handshake, and as our hands parted, he turned and, with sadness in his eyes, said, "I will tell people that I met a real Alaskan!"

I don't know if he knew it at the time, but other than being called a mountain animal, that was one of the nicest compliments I've ever received.

Come with me Mistress Alaska. Take my hand. Let's run off for one more adventure. On a mountain top where we can be by ourselves and breathe the fresh, crisp air that only you can provide. And to gaze into the vast beauty that you are made of. Or we can venture out on one of your wild and exciting seas. The salt spray in our faces will be the finest of perfume, and we will laugh as we ride the white cresting waves. I've grown to know your soul and your spirit that I still long for. And you Alaska know that I will succumb to the touch of your gentle northern breeze, and like the many times before, escape with you.